"Religious trauma isn't a ~~fad~~—it's a painful reality for an ever-increasing number of Christians. Tiffany does a beautiful job of helping readers understand what it is and where to begin their healing journey."

—ANGELA J. HERRINGTON
author of *Deconstructing Your Faith without Losing Yourself*

"This book will be a source of peace for anyone who experiences spiritual anxiety. Brooks adroitly describes common sources of spiritual anxiety, examines biblical texts used in support of spiritually abusive tactics, and offers healthier, life-giving interpretations of Scripture. Readers who feel ghosted by God or church will feel seen and heard by this book."

—CHARLES KISER
coauthor of *Trauma-Informed Evangelism: Cultivating Communities of Wounded Healers*

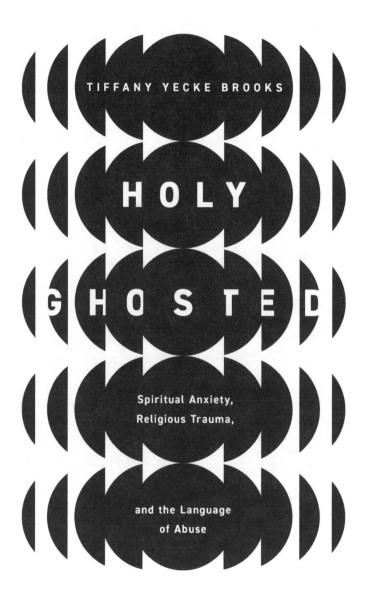

TIFFANY YECKE BROOKS

HOLY GHOSTED

Spiritual Anxiety,
Religious Trauma,

and the Language
of Abuse

WILLIAM B. EERDMANS PUBLISHING COMPANY
GRAND RAPIDS, MICHIGAN

Wm. B. Eerdmans Publishing Co.
4035 Park East Court SE, Grand Rapids, Michigan 49546
www.eerdmans.com

Book design by Lydia Hall

Printed in the United States of America

30 29 28 27 26 25 24   1 2 3 4 5 6 7

ISBN 978-0-8028-8280-6

Library of Congress Cataloging-in-Publication Data

A catalog record for this book is available from the Library of
Congress.

Unless otherwise noted, Scripture quotations are taken from the
New Revised Standard Version, Updated Edition.

To the worriers, the hand-wringers, the wet blankets,
the "nervous Nellies," the perfectionists, and the pleasers—
To those who have hated themselves for questioning, doubting, or raging—
To those who have believed they could not trust their own mind or gut—
To those with a tender conscience whose own heart is broken at the
thought of breaking God's heart—

This book is for you.

*Some people feel guilty about their anxieties and regard them as
    a defect of faith.*
I don't agree at all. They are afflictions, not sins.
*Like all afflictions, they are, if we can so take them, our share in
    the Passion of Christ.*

—C. S. Lewis, *Letters to Malcolm: Chiefly on Prayer*

But though I have wept and fasted, wept and prayed,
*Though I have seen my head (grown slightly bald) brought in upon
    a platter,*
I am no prophet—and here's no great matter;
I have seen the moment of my greatness flicker,
And I have seen the eternal Footman hold my coat, and snicker,
And in short, I was afraid. . . .

But as if a magic lantern threw the nerves in patterns on a screen:
Would it have been worth while
If one, settling a pillow or throwing off a shawl,
And turning toward the window, should say:
"That is not it at all,
That is not what I meant, at all."

—T. S. Eliot, "The Love Song of J. Alfred Prufrock"

CONTENTS

Introduction: Poisonous Piety   1

1. Kool-Aid Man Jesus and Other Phobias   7

2. The Mind and Christ   27

3. Involuntary Internalized Legalism   45

4. Discipline—Control through Fear   65

5. Dogma—Control through Indoctrination   95

6. Decoration—Control through Praise   128

7. Denial—Control through Rejection   152

8. Degradation—Control through Shame   176

9. Diminishment—Control through Dehumanizing   210

10. Domination—Control through Power Imbalance   237

Conclusion: Preach, Write, Act   265

Discussion Questions   275

Acknowledgments   283

CONTENTS

Notes   286

Index of Scripture and
Other Early Christian Writings   293

Introduction

POISONOUS PIETY

In 1917, with the United States having recently joined World War I, twenty-year-old Amelia "Mollie" Maggia, of Orange, New Jersey, started a new job painting self-luminous watch dials to be used by soldiers preparing to ship out for Europe.

She felt fortunate to get the position. The pay was fair, and since it contributed directly to the American war effort, it was considered patriotic work, which carried special significance for her parents, who had emigrated to America from Italy. Two of Mollie's sisters joined her at the factory, as did a number of other local young women.

The convenience of a self-luminous watch quickly caught on, and demand for these devices grew even more following the war. Mollie stayed on at the factory for several more years, as did hundreds of other women at factories in Connecticut, Illinois, and elsewhere as competitors vied for a piece of the market. The dial painters were encouraged to use their mouths to moisten the tip of the brush and manipulate the bristles to a fine point by rolling it on their lips in order to keep their painting as neat as possible—a practice called "pointing." Employees who questioned the safety of this practice were assured that the luminous paint carried no risks even though they often left the factories at the end of their shifts so coated in the radiant yellow-green pigment that they were nicknamed the "ghost girls."[1] Some young women even used it as a kind of novelty makeup, painting more on their teeth or face to appear as if they were glowing when they went out in the evenings.

But then, on September 12, 1922, Mollie Maggia died at the age of twenty-five. For the past year, she had been complaining of pain in her jaw, which led to the removal of several teeth but no improvement in her condition; in fact, the pain, swelling, and abscesses spread throughout her body. After a diagnosis of rheumatoid arthritis failed to respond to an aspirin regimen, doctors concluded that the young woman must have syphilis. By the time she passed, the tissues in her mouth had disintegrated so completely that it was possible to remove pieces of her crumbling jaw by hand.

Soon, stories of more young women suffering a similar fate hit the news. Within five years, more than fifty women died of the same cause, and countless more were seriously sickened. Speculations regarding their conditions and their character were rampant, but further investigation found a single commonality between every victim: they were all dial painters who worked with the strange new glowing pigment. What the young women had not known while they were employed in those factories was that they were rapidly poisoning themselves. The chemical that gave the paint its unique luminosity was radium—the element discovered barely twenty years earlier by Marie Curie and that ultimately contributed to her premature death due to its extreme toxicity to the human body.

The factory owners, however, *were* aware of the risks that radium posed to their workers. One chemist who analyzed the paint noted: "Radium has a very violent action on the skin and it is my belief that the serious condition of the jaw has been caused by the influence of radium. I would suggest that every operator be warned . . . of the dangers of getting this material on the skin or into the system, especially into the mouth."[2] But the companies kept this knowledge from their employees, instead encouraging the women to continue using their lips as the fastest way to "point" their brushes. The more dials a worker painted, the more she was paid, praised, and promoted—and the faster she poisoned herself. The very substance celebrated for saving lives in trenches and ushering in an age of comfort and convenience for the dapper man-about-town was slowly killing the women who consumed it believing it was their patriotic duty and honor to do so.

From 1917 to 1928, hundreds of young women were exposed to radium in toxic doses as a result of their work as dial painters. When some of these so-called "ghost girls" or "radium girls" in Illinois approached their employers about a lawsuit brought by a few of their counterparts in New Jersey, they were told that the East Coast workers were suffering from viral infections (possibly sexually transmitted) that had nothing to do with exposure to radium. It took years of court battles before the victims saw justice. Economic pressures and political influence were placed on the judges in an attempt to sway rulings in favor of the large corporations, and several more women passed away before the companies were finally deemed culpable and required to pay for the medical care of their workers.

Even now, more than a century after the first victims died, when Geiger counters (devices that measure radioactivity) are passed over the grave sites of the radium girls, they will register higher-than-normal levels attesting to the chronic toxicity to which those young women were exposed.

Spiritual anxiety is a condition that afflicts countless believers who find themselves working exhaustively for Christ, for the mission, for the kingdom, for eternity—but who struggle to feel peace, acceptance, or assurance in their relationship with God or within the church itself. They are wracked with guilt that they aren't doing enough or don't believe enough or aren't good enough to merit divine favor. They may question their worthiness to approach God or doubt their own salvation. They may second-guess every decision, questioning whether their motives are pure or their inherent sinful nature is keeping them from making the "right choice." Because they've been taught that "the flesh" can't be trusted, they have often learned to suppress their common sense and ignore their intuition, viewing them not as gifts from God to keep them safe but as tools manipulated by Satan in order to lead them astray.

People seeking God in such environments are prime candidates for spiritual abuse and religious trauma. Those who speak up are cut down or cast out; those who stay silent are further victimized by systems designed to keep a predetermined power structure in place. The ones who leave are accused of immorality while the ones who remain are exposed to toxic environments that may harm them irreparably.

Certainly *not all churches are guilty of abuse*; there are many wonderful communities of Christians that, imperfect as they may be, are committed to loving, serving, listening, welcoming, and growing. Nor is spiritual anxiety limited to believers in authoritarian or toxic religious environments. But for those who have been exposed to such poison—whether in the past or as part of an ongoing situation—healing brings a desire to understand more fully the tactics used, the conditions under which they can thrive, and their broader impact on the well-being of those involved.

Like Mollie Maggia and the other ghost girls, those who speak openly about their pain may be discounted, shamed, or even have their character disparaged with a spiritual diagnosis of ignorance, weak faith, lack of commitment, or secret sin.

Conversely, those who stay quiet and carry on are often applauded as glowing examples of what God-filled, kingdom-oriented lives ought to look like. So they do what they must to keep going—lie about who they are or what they believe, suppress their qualms in order to toe the party line, deny who the Holy Spirit is calling them to be, gaslight to themselves about their own doubts, worry even more about eternal damnation, or ignore the sound of their own intuition crying out that *something is wrong here.*

The very behavior their toxic faith community encourages is eating away at their emotional well-being. But because they have been taught to believe that *this* is the path most pleasing to God, they paint themselves with the language and practices of their abusers and step out into the world radiating not with the Holy Spirit but with the poison that is killing them from the inside out.

1

KOOL-AID MAN JESUS
AND OTHER PHOBIAS

"Ghosting" is a common term for the sudden ending of a relationship with no explanation or communication. There was a
connection, and then there just . . . wasn't anymore. Presence
was simply withdrawn with no further engagement. The ghosted
party may feel confused, hurt, or abandoned. Was it something
they said or did? Was there some offense they weren't aware
they'd committed, or something they should have done but
didn't? Did the other person suddenly realize they could do better—that the ghosted person just wasn't good enough? Or was
it all just an illusion, a bond that was always one-sided, with
one party deeply invested and the other largely indifferent or
perpetually displeased?

The hardest part of ghosting is the lack of resolution to the
swirling questions that only seem to grow with time. There is no
way to win: if you reach out more to spark engagement, maybe
you're irritating the other person, which will only drive them further away. If you give them distance, they may simply leave you
behind. Sometimes, they might circle back briefly, which makes
you believe everything is okay after all—only to break your heart

all over again when the cycle repeats. Or maybe they offer an angry outburst, dredging up every mistake you ever made but never offering closure before disappearing again. Maybe you even try to connect with their friends, only to feel alienated and shunned. In the end, it doesn't matter whether you reach out in the desperate hope of being reunited or just for some basic understanding of what went wrong, the ghosting party will leave you feeling hurt, confused, betrayed, and desperate for something you cannot have.

This is how many people with spiritual anxiety feel about their relationship with God. The Holy Spirit, it seems, has "ghosted" them by inexplicably cutting off communication, withdrawing a sense of presence or comfort from their personal lives, or suddenly seeming absent from the body of Christ and the definition of "Christian." The spiritually anxious person had a connection with God at some point in their life, but it now feels distant, disrupted, or severed. Or maybe they have always viewed their faith with a sense of trepidation, wondering what "peace that passes understanding"—that magical, mystical state that church people love to talk about—might possibly be like. They know how faith is "supposed" to look—what it seems to be for everyone else—but their reality hasn't played out that way, and they can't seem to figure out why their experience of God seems so different from that of the people around them. Maybe they can't wrap their head around why everyone else seems to believe in a God so vastly unlike Christ. Or maybe their fear of God makes eternal judgment seem like an ever-looming, ever-threatening hammer about to fall. It's as if God were both insurmountably distant and much too close for comfort.

It's as if God were both insurmountably distant and much too close for comfort.

Whatever the case, these individuals have learned that it isn't safe for them to speak honestly about their concerns. The worries that keep them up at night or make them cry when they are alone are brushed off as spiritual immaturity or condemned as signs of religious rebellion or weak faith and lack of trust in God. Conversely, these scruples might be celebrated as signs of the believer's great virtue, even though they are actually a form of emotional torture for the person living with them. Sometimes, a person is actually on very close terms with Jesus but struggles to interact with Christians because life in the church leaves them feeling nervous, judged, and under a microscope. Whatever the case, the end result is almost always the same: frustration, burnout, or shame. Shame that they can't rely on God more to see them through the questions. Shame that they can't just "trust and obey." Shame that they are living a lie no one else can see. Shame that they don't fit the mold. Shame that they aren't a better Christian. . . .

Spiritual anxiety is nothing new.

Moses, having been raised in a culture that enslaved and dehumanized his people, may have struggled with spiritual anxiety, given his repeated insistence on his unworthiness in response to God's call in Exodus 2. Jeremiah, the so-called weeping prophet, laments his calling in the twentieth chapter of the book that bears his name and condemns abusive and corrupt religious leaders in the twenty-third chapter. For all his bluster elsewhere, Peter (who grew up in the very religious atmosphere Jesus sought to make less controlling and legalistic) seems to have wrestled with feeling unworthy of Christ's attention; consider his response to Jesus in Luke 5:8, "Go away from me, Lord, for I am a sinful man!" Similarly, the centurion of Luke 7 berated himself as completely unworthy of Jesus's care. Beyond the familiar Bible characters, some of the early Christian hermits—the so-called desert fathers and mothers of the third and fourth centuries—wrote about repeatedly witnessing demons trying to yank their souls hellward. Medieval ascetics went to extreme measures to deny themselves basic needs and violently punish their own bodies through self-flagellation in an effort to beat back the sinful nature that constantly threatened to tarnish their souls. Martin Luther experienced a condition he called *Anfechtungen* (literally, "challenges")—the deep despair he felt contending with frequent spiritual attacks that left him feeling alienated from the divine. In 1666, John Bunyan described not being able to feel relief from Satan's attacks unless he was preaching. In the twentieth century, Mother Teresa wrote extensively in her journals about her soul-fears and her experience of crushing silence from God.

These great figures of the faith can all be understood through a lens of spiritual anxiety when considering how they wrestled with feelings of fear, unworthiness, alienation, condemnation, or distance from God. In other words, spiritual anxiety isn't some trendy new complaint against twenty-first-century, Western Christianity concocted by people who hate the church and want to see it destroyed. The difference is that now we finally recognize it as a detrimental condition that can be harmful to a person's mental and spiritual health rather than as a sign of spiritual rebellion to be driven out of the church or as divine devotion to be celebrated and emulated.

Before we can examine the causes of spiritual anxiety, however, let us first take a moment to explore what it is, what it can look like, and how those apprehensions might present themselves in our spiritual and day-to-day lives. Spiritual anxiety is marked by:

- obsessive fears of angering God through intentional or unintentional sin
- deep doubts of one's own worthiness or of God's attention, care, or love
- constant feelings of failure at living a moral, Christ-centered life
- faith responses shaped by or rooted in unhealthy thought patterns
- persistent concern about being rejected by or losing community and identity, or

- incessant stress about feeling out of step with or alienated from one's faith tradition or religious body.

Though they may wane and wax depending on which other emotions or stressors are making demands of us at any given time, these feelings are almost always present with the spiritually anxious person in some way. Even when relatively calm, this kind of anxiety is sort of like a smartphone app that runs constantly in the background, monitoring, filtering, and occasionally sending out alerts for the sake of our soul.

Those alerts (flare-ups, pings, notifications, warnings, eruptions, outbreaks) can take on a variety of forms. For some people, they may appear in just a few predictable ways that are relatively easy to recognize or even anticipate when triggered. For others, the symptoms might be less predictable, running the gamut of reactions and "tells," which may include (but are in no way limited to):

- unwelcome, intrusive religious thoughts
- excessive worry about eternity or damnation
- pervasive doubt about one's own salvation
- fearfulness or terror of God
- perfectionism
- aggressive evangelism
- extreme legalism or scriptural literalism
- fixation on piety or "rightness"
- compulsive praying
- obsession with sins of omission (good things you could have done but didn't)
- persistent negative self-talk
- compulsive actions, rituals, or superstitions
- extreme indecisiveness
- fear of standing out or speaking honestly
- feelings of alienation from other believers

- deep-seated fear of rejection
- persistent second-guessing of one's own motives
- strong risk aversion.

The response to such anxieties can range from depression, despair, withdrawal from community, spiritual burnout, or feelings of spiritual immobility to almost manic action like reciting prayers or performing rituals with a vigor that borders on superstition—frantic fasting, excessive giving, overly zealous worshipping, practicing extreme self-discipline or "mortification of the flesh," fanatical evangelizing—anything to get a response, generate a reaction, or spur some kind of divine movement. Desperate people resort to desperate measures.

Some people struggling with spiritual anxiety may not exhibit any obvious outward signs at all—at least not any that are obvious to the casual observer. People often manage to hide their spiritual anxiety very well, so their outward behavior may not always accurately reflect their inner experience.

Of course, some people inherently have a deeply tender conscience or are just born worriers. They embody stress at a higher level than most and tend to see things through a more naturally anxious lens. They may even identify as one of the more high-strung Enneagram types (*Where are my fellow 3s?*) who tend to have a little extra nervous energy when they aren't operating at the healthiest level.[1] When these traits are present in a person's religious impulses or faith responses, however, the result can be devastating to their spiritual well-being. Even among people who are just more naturally anxious, it is important to remember that many of these fastidious characteristics may actually be trauma responses because spiritual anxiety itself is a trauma response.

Trauma responses happen when the brain determines that something about its environment feels dangerous or threatening and adapts accordingly. These responses may be physical—as in the fight-flight-freeze-or-fawn reaction—or they might be psycho-logical, influencing the way a person processes information or emotions. When someone is exposed to the same kind of intense stress over an extended pe-riod of time, their brain's adaptation to these conditions becomes a normalized part of the way that individual perceives and interacts with

Spiritual anxiety itself is a trauma response

the world. In other words, the brain learns which thoughts and behaviors generate a sense of safety, stability, or control and turns to them as means of protection or soothing. Eventually, these adaptations, which were only supposed to be temporary responses until the threat passed, may be converted into long-term behaviors even if they aren't sustainable in any kind of healthy manner over extended periods of time. Typical trauma responses include things like replaying difficult moments in your head, second-guessing yourself, struggling to trust people, and shouldering a tremendous amount of guilt.

That sounds an awful lot like spiritual anxiety, doesn't it?

Dwelling on your soul's deepest fears may not bolster a sense of stability, but at least it feels like doing *something*—being proac-tive or expending energy on behalf of a problem. The same is true for obsessively questioning your motives or punishing yourself for sin so that God doesn't have to. Maybe you keep your opinions tucked away inside your head so no one can accuse you of being a dissenter. Maybe you leave church halfway through the service so that toxic beliefs don't contaminate the sacred ones you hold dear. Maybe you avoid church altogether, despite longing for a faith community, because if you reject the people there first, they can't reject you. It all creates an illusion of control that, in itself, may be temporarily soothing.

The thing is, spiritual anxiety doesn't happen in a vacuum. People don't fear rejection for noncompliance unless they be-lieve rejection or condemnation is a possibility. Children are not born with an inherent fear of eternal damnation. No one wakes up one morning suddenly afraid of God condemning their soul to an infinite hell unless they have been taught that

1. there is a God,
2. that God has authority to pass judgment on human souls,
3. they have a soul,
4. they have the power to win God's approval or rejection with that soul,
5. those who do not win God's favor are discarded on an eternal level.

In other words, spiritual anxiety is a learned behavior rather than an inherent one.

In other words, it is the result of cultural conditioning aimed at invoking feelings of fear, invalidation, rejection, shame, dehumanization, or powerlessness.

In other words, it is not your fault. It is not a lack of faith. It is not a moral failing. It is not a sign of weakness. It is not a reflection of your worthiness. It is something you were taught—both directly and indirectly—by the environment in which you were raised and its attitudes toward faith, power dynamics, theology, and the heavenly realm.

Like anything else, spiritual anxiety varies in form and severity depending on the individual. Many people with spiritual anxiety also have mental health challenges (such as depression or generalized anxiety disorder) or neurodivergence (such as autism,[2] ADD/ADHD, obsessive-compulsive disorder, giftedness). But many others don't. Spiritual anxiety may be *enhanced* when coupled with a clinically recognized condition, but it is situational rather than chronic—that is, it is initiated by one's environment rather than one's biology. Fear of losing community or identity outside of the church, overwhelming worries about godliness, unwelcome and

> *Spiritual anxiety is a learned behavior rather than an inherent one*

intrusive religious thoughts, persistent uncertainty about salvation, and even incessant negative self-talk are not spontaneously generated without cause—something in the person's surroundings, culture, or background has set the stage for such obsessive concerns or doubts. Again, these thoughts may be exacerbated by other conditions, but spiritual anxiety originates in a person's external conditions, *not* their neurological wiring.

A person can have clinical depression and spiritual anxiety at the same time. Or ADHD and spiritual anxiety. Or OCD and spiritual anxiety. The conditions may influence one another—someone's depression is made worse by their spiritual anxiety, for example, or their neurodivergence may make certain aspects of spiritual anxiety more of a challenge—but the factors that spark spiritual anxiety are external; they have been taught, modeled, and reinforced. No one is born into the world with a

Spiritual anxiety originates in a person's external conditions, not *their neurological wiring*

fully developed theology of divine discipline or fear of rejection by their religious body. Those beliefs and feelings are formed by *experiences* that may be made better or worse by any number of factors, including culture, environment, neurodivergence, natural disposition, or mental health challenges. But the experiences have to come first because spiritual anxiety is a learned behavior, and learned behaviors must be, well, *learned.*

This book is not a memoir, but please indulge me as I share a bit of my own experience.

In the mid-1990s, my identity as a varsity cheerleading co-captain, international science fair finalist, class officer, honor student, and model "good church girl" was the visible side of my all-American teenage years. Internally, however, every day was a constant wrestling match with my brain and my soul. Sure,

I had some quirks, but I could live with that. Quirkiness can have a certain charm to it, after all. What I couldn't live with—what was keeping me in a constant state of panic and desperation—were the obsessive thoughts that swirled constantly in my brain, screaming that I was always only a breath away from sin, a second away from the end of the world, and a moment away from the final judgment that would inevitably sentence me to an eternity in hell because of that one sinful thought that just stained my soul.

Why? Well, to be honest, I wasn't exactly sure. I rarely watched MTV, I carried a laminated copy of my signed "True Love Waits" pledge card in my wallet, and I certainly would have "just said no" if any drugs were ever offered to me. (*Relax, Mom and Dad—they weren't.*) I spoke openly about my beliefs to anyone who would listen. I stringently avoided the three S's (smoking, swearing, and sex) and the two D's (drugs and drinking). I was reluctant even to say the word "beer" because even if it wasn't a true "bad word" it was still a word that *represented* something bad. But, even so, the fear of God's wrath haunted me. I had been taught that the only way to please God was to take the Bible seriously—more seriously than anything else in my life. And so I did.

The psalmist writes that "I shall set no wicked thing before my eyes" (Psalm 101:3), and Paul admonishes believers to "pray without ceasing" (1 Thessalonians 5:17), so in an effort to be the best Christian I could, that was what I did. Sitting in the movie theater with my friends, whenever anything flashed on the screen that might be considered even vaguely objectionable, I would pray for forgiveness. If I thought about a boy I had a crush on, I worried about "how far" I might allow that chaste little fantasy to go, lest my lecherous hormones pull me away from Jesus as the bull's eye at the center of my life. At Friday night football games, in between peppy chants and cheers, I would pray while smiling broadly and waving my pom-poms: "*God, please forgive me for any sin I might have committed since my last prayer so that if the world ends in this instant, I can go to heaven. In Jesus's name I pray, amen."* My last prayer, mind you, had taken place roughly ninety seconds earlier.

L-E-T-S G-O! Let's go! Let's go!

I had been baptized at church camp at age thirteen and had participated in every vacation Bible school, either as a student or as a volunteer, from the time I was in kindergarten. I had my purity ring, my WWJD? bracelet, and my "No Jesus, Know Fear / Know Jesus, No Fear" T-shirt. My parents had keys to our church building; my dad was a deacon and the church treasurer, and my mom taught Sunday school and organized potlucks with ruthless efficiency.

Church was an important part of my life, but certainly not the only part. My congregation was small but fairly "normal," for the most part; we weren't a borderline cult by any means. My parents were fairly strict but certainly not authoritarian monsters: I was expected to keep up my grade point average, but my weekend curfew was midnight, I could listen to popular music, and I recognized that angsty teen Kevin Bacon, not uptight preacher John Lithgow, was the sympathetic character in *Footloose*. In short, there was nothing particularly sinister about my homelife or religious upbringing—just good, suburban, middle-class Christian values.

This may not sound particularly extreme, but please allow me a moment to recount just how stressful growing up Christian was for Gen Xers and early Millennials. We successfully navigated the "satanic panic" of the 1970s and 1980s, when we were warned against rock music with subliminal messages, hidden occult symbols in common household brand trademarks, and devil-worshipping cults supposedly sacrificing livestock and opening daycares in small-town America. Then we found ourselves coming of age in the midst of the so-called rise of the Christian Right. Evangelicalism was marching steadily forward, and it was an all-or-nothing proposition. You were either wholly on the side of superpolitical Jesus or you were against him. There was no middle position.

Each month, the teen girl magazine published by a *very* prominent "family-centric" Christian organization arrived, and I pored over it, awed by the various warnings about ways that life in Roaring Nineties could yank me off the straight and narrow at any given moment. My home church was, for the most part, a warm, welcoming, and reasonable community of faith (a fact for which I will always be grateful), but even a relatively "normal" church life couldn't stave off some truly terrifying faith warnings in the broader late-twentieth century, Western Christian world.

For me, growing up outside of Washington, DC, meant that every major pop culture Christian event came through the area, filling arenas and ears with messages that railed against sinister political plots designed to lead us astray—plots like feminism and the mysterious "gay agenda" and evil college professors determined to brainwash us with lessons about communists who wanted to teach us evolution in hell. Okay, that's a *slight* exaggeration, but also the rapture could happen at any moment because *everyone knew* it had been approximately two thousand years from Adam to Noah, then two thousand years from Noah to Jesus, and now the new millennium loomed before us. (But actually that monk who had established the BC-AD system back in the sixth century had been off a few years because he based his calculations of Jesus's birth year on the wrong census so we could be in the two thousandth year *right now* and not even know it. So, really, it could happen at any time. . . .)

And, of course, there was Purity Culture. It seemed like nearly every teen-oriented evangelical book and publication out there focused on how hostile "the world" was toward people "like us" and how hypervigilant we needed to be in word, thought, deed, and wardrobe in order to keep ourselves "pure" for our future spouse and that mythical event that was promised to be the absolute pinnacle of our entire lives: The Wedding Night (capitalized, of course, because it was *that* important). If not (teen girls were warned) we would end up, at best, unwanted and discarded like trash—because what godly man could love a woman who had stolen a peek at her "Christmas present" (*weird euphemism, but okay*) ahead of Christmas morning? Was that the kind of Wedding Night we wanted—one where the surprise and anticipation of God's special gift to us had been ruined?[3]

Never one to do things halfway, I embraced almost everything pop evangelicalism was selling. In middle school, I began to concoct a long-term plan for keeping myself worthy of my future spouse, which involved staying away from any seventh-grade boy who didn't seem like "marriage material." In high school, I studied up on every political zinger I could fling and composed smugly confident op-eds I sent off to the local newspaper long before I could even vote because Jesus *definitely* had a strict party affiliation in American politics—and I knew exactly what it was. But that wasn't enough. True Christianity, we were told, meant totally selling out to Jesus. The goal was not to see how close we could get to the world without crossing the line, but how close we could stay to the center that was Christ. Anything less than 100 percent commitment was sinful.

I inherently knew my panicked thoughts about religion were irrational—fanatical, almost—but I had also been conditioned by broader evangelical culture to disregard and distrust my intuition; that was "trusting in the flesh" and a sure sign of vanity and worldliness. So if I couldn't trust myself, how in the world could I hope to fix my broken brain, let alone save my soul?

((()))

Writing this now as a fortysomething looking back at my own spiritual journey, I feel exhausted on a soul level just remembering it all. I worried I wasn't winning enough people to Jesus on the playground. I started worrying about disappointing my future spouse at the age of twelve—*twelve!*—which meant that by the time I got married in 2004, at age twenty-five, I had been carrying that anxiety for more than half of my life. I worried about avoiding even the "appearance of evil" (1 Thessalonians 5:22 KJV). And that was on top of worrying that Jesus stood poised to burst through the clouds like the Kool-Aid Man at any second, ready to judge my soul and determine my eternal fate.

Raise your hand if any of this sounds familiar.

If your hand stayed down—*congratulations!* You're probably a healthy and functional member of society. Sounds dreamy. But many of the rest of us Gen Xers and Millennials who grew up during the ascendancy of modern American evangelicalism have morphed into adults who still foster a tremendous amount of spiritual anxiety, even if we have matured past black-and-white thinking. Even if we can recognize social, political, and moral nuance. Even if we swallow our cognitive dissonance each week at church when the pastor says something problematic. Even if we have done the hard work of separating ourselves from toxic religious ideologies and the communities that promote them.

Yet whatever stress and shame *we* experienced, I can only imagine how intense it was for the generations that went before us who grew up in a time when cultural values masquerading as "the Christian worldview" often meant resisting things like civil rights or married women pursuing careers outside the home. Nor do I imagine that life right now as an earnest, God-loving, Christian kid in America has gotten any easier in the past quarter-century since I was a teenager.

The truth is, growing up is hard whenever and wherever you happen to do it. But growing up in an environment that regularly employs manipulation to ensure cultural conformity and strict obedience—all while insisting that its path is the only one out of a fiery eternity—can take a toll.

The verses that probably immediately come to mind when I mention anxiety are Jesus's famous pronouncement in the Sermon on the Mount ("And which of you by worrying can add a single hour to your span of life?"; Matthew 6:27) and Paul's exhortation to the believers in Philippi ("Do not be anxious about anything, but in everything by prayer and supplication with thanksgiving let your requests be made known to God"; Philippians 4:6). You've probably heard them so often you recited them along with me just now, but they aren't as simple as just saying, "Don't worry about it."

The Greek word *merimnaō* is the same word used in both verses to describe the emotion of heightened nervousness; it means, literally, to be drawn in different directions, pulled apart, or distracted. According to *Strong's Exhaustive Concordance of the Bible*, it can even be translated "to go to pieces." This figurative definition may be the most apt, as spiritual anxiety can feel precisely as if we are falling to pieces with worry even as we are trying desperately to live the very best life we can for our faith. While these passages in Matthew and Philippians do offer solid advice (Don't let yourself fall apart over things you can't control), we all know that simply saying "Don't be anxious" is about as effective at staving off anxiety as saying "Calm down" is in getting a person to calm down. And anyone who believes otherwise has probably never experienced the emotional torture of living in constant spiritual fear.

It's essential that I point out that I am not a psychologist. What this means is that I cannot diagnose anybody with anything. I can't speak authoritatively on behavioral disorders versus mood disorders, and I certainly can't explain the neuroscience of your brain when you wrestle with spiritual anxiety—at least not with any authority.

I am a literature professor, author, writing coach, and seminarian by training. I specialize in words. This means what I *can* do is harness the power of language to call attention to damaging behaviors and beliefs. I can describe what spiritual anxiety feels like and how it is treated in religious settings. I can help uncover new significance in old familiar passages—and old significance we were conditioned to read past, through, around, or over. I study the way humans create meaning through texts and speech and the way that rhetoric shapes how we transmit and receive messages. Simply put, my area of specialty concerns the ways ideas are communicated and how they convey significance— especially spiritual significance—in various cultural settings.

To this end, each chapter in this book incorporates passages from a number of prominent works of literature across hundreds of years to help illustrate universal themes of anxiety and to set the stage to explore how specific manifestations of anxiety may look in religious environments. I want to identify the myriad ways that spiritual anxiety can take shape by examining seven primary causes: fear, indoctrination, praise, rejection, shame, dehuman- ization, and power imbalances. If we can break down the over- arching topic into its individual components and give each one a name, we will have the vocabulary for recognizing, analyzing, and understanding what spiritual anxiety is, how it functions, and how to combat its negative impact on our faith and on our life. I'll be the first to admit that this book is imperfect and in- complete; there are many kinds of abuse that there simply isn't room to cover in detail here. Ultimately, however, these behaviors are usually rooted in some form of manipulative language, which can be difficult to spot because it *literally creates the lens through which we perceive reality and the belief system we use to make sense of life*. In order to break out of this kind of thinking, we often have to upend our entire understanding of what we were taught about the world, other people, and God. And that can definitely lead to anxiety on a soul-level.

Again, other factors such as mental health challenges or neurodivergence may undergird any or all of the sources of spiritual anxiety, but these are separate concepts—distinct from one another as well as distinct from spiritual anxiety. Some conditions require professional medical care; some modes of thinking thrive when under the guidance of people trained in specialized engagement; some don't need any intervention at all because they are simply the way someone *is* in the world, which is what makes life beautiful, rich, diverse, and wonderful. Several of the people I interviewed over the course of writing this book are considered neurodivergent or have diagnoses such as generalized anxiety disorder or depression, which colors their perception of things. But many other people are considered "neurotypical"— that is, their mind works within what behavioral science experts consider a "normal" or "typical" way of functioning. Yet everyone I spoke to understood the impact of spiritual anxiety based on their own experiences within the church, and those feelings all seem to follow the same basic pattern of causes and effects.

I am not here to write a book about mental health or neurodivergence in the church, nor am I qualified to do so, though heaven knows we need more good books on exactly those topics. My concern is with naming the issue, understanding how it happens, giving concrete vocabulary to nebulous concepts and vague impressions, and looking for ways to push back against abusive religious language and toxic misapplications of Scripture. Having a name for The Thing can be one of the first steps in overcoming it because it helps put flesh and bones on vague, haunting feelings that rattle their chains but never show their true nature. Once you define a problem, you can start the work of dismantling it. It's like the old fairy tale of Rumpelstiltskin: as long as you can't name the thing, it holds power over you. But the moment you are able to identify it rather than fear it, its grip loosens.

I speak as someone who has struggled with spiritual anxiety for much of her life. If I had had the words to express what I was experiencing, I might have recognized much earlier on that this was not the way most other people engaged with God. I simply assumed that this was what religious devotion looked like for everyone. I couldn't understand why no one else at church seemed as soul-tired as I was by the ripe old age of fifteen, but I figured that if this was how we were all relating with our faith, then I just needed to buckle down and try even harder so that I could build up my spiritual muscle. If I'd had language to better define my experience, I could have saved myself years of spiritual anguish as I struggled to understand why other people—even wonderful, devout, Spirit-filled Christians—seemed so much less stressed out about spiritual stuff than me.

I had grown up in church, loving God fiercely and absorbing every Bible lesson I could, but I was too young and too impressionable to understand that not every message I heard from the pulpit, in Sunday school, or in Christian media was healthy. The Bible, read literally, taught me to submit without questioning authority (especially male authority); this meant that challenging anything that seemed "off" was stepping outside of my God-appointed role. Meanwhile, the popular theology woven throughout mainstream evangelicalism insisted that the only thing that really mattered in this life was making it to heaven in the next, so if whatever good I managed to accomplish didn't have eternal implications, it was a waste of God's resources.

Eventually, I learned there was another factor impacting my religious experience as well. I was diagnosed with obsessive-compulsive disorder in my early twenties, which meant that my OCD sometimes affected my spiritual anxiety not in the compulsions, but in the obsessions—namely, in being obsessed with my own salvation. I learned that many of the distressing behavioral patterns and thoughts plaguing me had a name; they weren't just neuroses or an overly fastidious brain, but, more importantly, neither were they divinely inspired nudges from the Holy Spirit. I came to understand that my brain fixated on topics sometimes.

But what I still didn't have a name for was the shrapnel from the so-called culture wars that had been embedded in my soul—and this seemed to have disrupted what should have been the most natural connection in the world: the bond between created and Creator.

I continued seeking to restore that peaceful, comforting connection, and in time I came to learn that there were other people who struggled with many of these same religious fears who did *not* have OCD. So where was the dividing line between the indwelling of the Holy Spirit and whatever was going on in my brain? If my religious impulses intertwined with my OCD, then what was my soul? And, in the end, if I couldn't tell the difference, shouldn't I err on the side of caution? Wouldn't it all prove worth any inconvenience or temporary discomfort when (if) I was gathered with the saved on judgment day? Because, after all, I knew I was saved, but . . . then again, how did I *know* I knew I was saved? And how could I ever do enough, give enough, be enough for God?

My spiritual anxiety was certainly intensified by my condition, but it did not originate with it. The anxiety was already present due to a mix of well-intentioned (but ultimately misguided) messages and straight-up toxic theology designed to manipulate believers into compliance with the structures and systems that maintained the status quo—a status quo in which one specific view of Christianity reigned supreme. My atypical brain simply found a perfect match for its obsessive energies in the environmental conditions that already existed: an overarching evangelical culture that fostered a high-pressure, fear-based, shame-oriented theology promoting strict compliance and conformity to the party line ahead of anything else—even the gospel itself.

If any part of my story rings true for you as well, I hope that this book can help give you language and clarity about what your lived experience has already shown you is true. Maybe it can help you feel less alone and more empowered. Maybe (and this is my sincerest and most earnest prayer) it can help you see past the manipulation and agendas that other people and systems have forced upon you in the name of Christ and will help you find that place of belonging and comfort in God that you crave—exactly as you were created to be, exactly as you are.

2

THE MIND AND CHRIST

This topic can be unpleasant, uncomfortable, and even unnerving, but it needs to be uncovered. Spiritual anxiety is something rarely discussed above a whisper (if at all) in many churches or else loudly decried as a failure, as feebleness, or as evidence of scriptural and theological ignorance. Rarely does one find a compassionate, nuanced, and trauma-informed approach to spiritual anxiety despite its potentially lifelong impacts both for those who remain in the faith traditions that have triggered this response as well as those who leave them. But spiritual trauma is a very real and deeply profound wound to the "heart, soul, mind, and strength" of affected believers. It can negatively impact not only a person's relationship with God and the church, but also their family bonds, their intimate relationships, their ability to trust their own intuition, their connection to community, and even their sense of physical safety.

Whether pretending it doesn't exist, sweeping it under the rug, deprecating it loudly from the pulpit, or encouraging (sometimes even exploiting) the outcomes it produces, the modern church has largely failed to adequately address the matter. As a result, some people carry spiritual anxiety in their soul like an emotional dripping water torture device—a psychological torture technique where cold drops of water fall onto the victim's fore-

Spiritual trauma is a very real and deeply profound wound to the "heart, soul, mind, and strength" of affected believers

head at an unyielding but unpredictable rate. The inability to anticipate the next drop and brace for the shock of it or to rest in the unknowable period between drips can cause a rapid mental breakdown.[1] This is the same challenge that faces believers who can't control the drips of anxiety that strike their soul with worry that is unbidden, unwelcomed, and inescapable.

When they respond with increased commitment and obsessive devotion to their faith, they are celebrated as models of what all believers should strive to be. When they voice concerns about the havoc these fears are wreaking on their mental health, they are often brushed aside or shamed into silence.

"It's such a minor thing," they may be told. "I don't know why you are so obsessed with it."

"You're causing division by asking questions," they might hear. "Why can't you simply have faith like everyone else instead of challenging everything?"

"Stop making a mountain out of a molehill," someone may say. "If you had even the faith of a mustard seed, Jesus says you could move that mountain. So get more faith and the problem will take care of itself."

"First John 4:18 tells us, 'Perfect love drives out fear,'" someone else might warn. "If you still have fear, you must not have God's perfect love."

It's the all-too-common position of automatically trying to use the church to solve a problem rather than recognizing that one facet of the problem may be caused by the church itself. Sufferers are often treated either as religious deviants whose worries call the power of Jesus's resurrection into question or as ignorant, indolent, or immature. Yet when they look around, they feel surrounded by believers who wear their "blessed assurance" like a couture dress or bespoke suit—made-to-order grace that drapes perfectly across every contour and angle of the body without any gaping, bagging, or unflattering fits—and who can't seem to understand why everyone's faith doesn't fit the same way.

The problem, of course, is that perception shapes reality. When a single, specific worldview is held up as the standard or default against which all others must be compared for validity, that perspective usually comes to be the standard for what is "right" in that culture. Everyone else must either try to match it or else be "wrong." Anything that differs from the agreed-upon, centralized worldview is a deviation from the norm. Of course, in most branches of Western Christianity, this elevated, prioritized, and normalized point of view has traditionally been the White male perspective. When a White male preacher operates from the unquestioned assumption that his experiences in life and with God are simply the way of the world, it's no wonder that he has doubts about anyone whose engagement with or perception of the Divine is different. After all, the formula worked for him and for most of the people with whom he surrounds himself (who almost always share strikingly similar demographics), so why shouldn't it work for everyone the same way? Their success "proves" they are *inside* God's will, so anyone whose mileage varies using the same approach must be *outside* God's will. "Surely," this perspective argues, "whatever discomfort, concern, or issues you're experiencing in trying to find spiritual peace is simply the result of unresolved or hidden sin or a misunderstanding of what God wants from you. Otherwise, your experiences would fall in line with the biblical promises (the ones we choose to highlight, that is)."

This isn't a political statement or an attack on men or White people or any other group but on *systems* that have perpetuated and given primacy to certain perspectives at the cost of others—all in the name of God. Proponents of toxic theology can be of any demographic profile. And the emotional isolation this kind of prevailing attitude creates becomes even more difficult when the anxious individual is finally able to identify the source of their struggles and seeks to separate themselves from it, but lacks the support, tools, or even the vocabulary for how to begin the process of removing toxic beliefs and practices from their life. Though there are a variety of terms for this process, the most widely used one tends to be "deconstruction," a word that is already tremendously loaded with presuppositions, connotations, and broadly varying definitions.

When a single, specific worldview is held up as the standard or default against which all others must be compared, that perspective usually comes to be the standard for what is "right."

This is not a book about deconstruction specifically, but it is impossible to talk honestly about spiritual anxiety without recognizing that many people who are trying to find their way to a healthier relationship with faith will go through the deconstruction process, so I want to take a few minutes to explore it.

Detractors often say that deconstruction happens because people love "the world" and want to destroy the church, or that everyone who is deconstructing is in the process of rejecting religion altogether. This is what is known as a "fallacy of composition," in which a small part of something is presented as representing the whole (e.g., my neighbor, a member of a certain party, supports Politician X; therefore all members of that party support Politician X). For this reason, it is important to draw a distinction between those who are *deconstructing the faith traditions* in which they were raised and those who are *deconstructing God.* The first is questioning habits and practices around beliefs; the second is questioning whether those beliefs are valid at all. Those in the midst of deconstructing God may find some useful information in the coming pages, but this book is mostly intended for those in the first group—for those who are deconstructing their faith out of love for the church because they know that it can do better, because they take seriously the call to tend to the brokenhearted, and because they understand that God wants all believers to be emotionally healthy. Our dedication to Christ is ideally born out of nothing more or less than a desire to share the love of God with a hurting world.

And yet . . .

The very word "deconstruction" causes many traditionalists to break into cold sweats and sends radio preachers into tirades on the depravity of our current age. Some take the opposite tack and ignore it altogether as just a passing craze that will separate the wheat from the chaff, leaving the church stronger, bolder, and somehow "purer" than ever once all the deconstructionists have left.

Deconstruction is the fruit of humanity's wickedness, detractors cry. It is a harbinger of the end-times. It is the fault of slacker Gen Xers. Of self-centered Millennials. Of anything-goes Gen Zers. Of social justice warriors. Of the PC police. Of "woke prophets." Godless liberals. Spineless conservatives. Moral Relativists. Feminists. Humanists. Heathens. Bandwagoners. Backsliders.

But those who have staked their lives and eternities on the bet that Western, middle-class, male-centric, largely White Christianity will continue to hold a perpetual monopoly on God probably fail to recognize one glaring truth: Jesus was a deconstructionist.

Let's repeat that for the people in the back: *Jesus was a deconstructionist.*

He questioned the pillars of his faith, threatened the leadership of his religious body, invited in marginalized people, and sought to upend the toxic power structures in place in his culture. His entire message was centered on uprooting the current system and dismantling the abuses that had become a standard and accepted part of religious life in first-century Palestine.

This isn't an extreme interpretation of Jesus's character or ministry; you can hear a similar message from just about every pulpit on any given Sunday. Many preachers love to talk about how radical Jesus was, how unconventional his message and mission were, how different he was from what everyone expected. They tell us that following Christ means taking risks, shouldering unfair criticism, and facing scorn.

Then many of these same people look out at a world of seekers, questioners, doubters, sufferers, and they do three things: they condemn anyone who differs, they erect walls around heaven, and they fight like hell to protect the status quo.

That is not to imply, of course, that every church, religious leader, or belief system is abusive or that every person who holds traditional religious beliefs is a spiritual villain. Please hear me: not every person with strong doctrinal boundaries is cackling evilly and twirling their moustache while they tie suffering souls to celestial railroad tracks.

There are countless godly people and godly faith communities who serve their churches and their neighbors with the purest of motives. There are religious leaders who minister from a genuine desire to meet spiritual needs and foster a sincere detachment from personal power. There are people committed to living a life pleasing to God according to their faith traditions while humbly extending the grace of God to everyone.

Not every person with strong doctrinal boundaries is cackling evilly and twirling their moustache while they tie suffering souls to celestial railroad tracks

There are people who are trying to learn more, to listen more, to love better. They may hold views with which we disagree, but they are not abusers.

Nor is every case of spiritual anxiety the result of intentionally malicious religious manipulation. Sometimes spiritual anxiety comes about due to certain cultural practices or teachings that take a deeper or more problematic root in someone's life because of the way their mind works. I fully acknowledge that no one can control how anyone else will receive their words or process a message through their own mental framework. Just because someone has a negative or anxious response to a sermon does not automatically make the preacher an abuser.

But neither does it mean that the resulting emotional turmoil isn't real.

It is here that conversations about intent versus impact are helpful. Does the intention behind a person's actions outweigh the impact of those same actions? Just because you did not mean to ram the bumper of the person in front of you does not erase the fact that their car is now damaged. Just because a drunk uncle didn't intend to ruin the wedding with a tacky toast doesn't mean *They may hold views with which we disagree, but they are not abusers* the reception wasn't wildly awkward for everyone. Just because your preacher, mentor, or parent genuinely wanted to save your eternal soul does not mean that the emotional anguish you suffered from the resulting spiritual anxiety is inconsequential. The truth is, both intention *and* impact matter. We can acknowledge that many people may genuinely be well-meaning, but religious engagement that seeks to control behavior through apprehension, isolation, shame, demeaning language, or any other manipulative approach that attempts to elicit a specific response or allegiance to keep someone "within the fold" can still overstep appropriate boundaries and have a detrimental or damaging impact—no matter the intention behind it.

Spiritual abuse is the manipulation, coercion, or exploitation of individuals through religious teaching by using such techniques as fear, rejection, praise, humiliation, dehumanization, or leveraging power imbalances. It can take place within churches, denominations, sects, educational institutions, ministries, marriages, and families. *When you see the term "leaders" in the coming pages, it may refer to a pastor or other influential figure in a church structure, but it could also apply to an administrator, policymaker, parent, or other family member—anyone who has a position of authority or power within a system or unit.* As you read, feel free to substitute in whatever title is most consistent with your own experiences.

In order to help shine a light on the numerous shifting faces spiritual abuse may assume, I believe it is important to name the abuses and understand the way abusers use language to manipulate the thoughts, beliefs, emotions, and worldview of their victims. Christians should have a reasonable expectation that their spiritual leaders are filled with the Holy Spirit (or Holy Ghost, depending on your translation), and this should be evidenced by the so-called fruit of the Spirit outlined in Galatians 5:22–23: love, joy, peace, patience, kindness, goodness, faithfulness, gentleness, and self-control. It stands to reason, then, that someone prone to conflict, short-temperedness, cruelty, poor decisions, harmful actions, or an unwillingness to rein in their desire for power or their desire to manipulate people and circumstances is *not* walking in the Spirit.

((◆))

In my book *Gaslighted by God*, I observed that "many people are so dedicated to avoiding the victim mindset that they fail to recognize that they are being victimized at all." I noticed a pattern among the people I interviewed; many noted they had spent years excusing or explaining away abusive behavior of church leaders and other people with spiritual influence in their lives. Person after person remarked (both on and off the record) that they experienced an awakening when they finally realized that the treatment to which they were being subjected was a form of manipulation, bullying, or control—in short, abuse. But because their lives had been steeped in a culture where such behavior was normalized, they didn't even realize what would have likely been obvious to an outsider. It wasn't so much an issue of wondering whether it was okay to question or challenge certain teachings; it was failing to recognize that there was anything to question in the first place. As the old saying goes, a fish never asks, "What's water?"

It's easy, after all, to point out the flaws and abuses in someone else's faith tradition, like Taliban leaders stoning gay people in Afghanistan or the practice of ritual female circumcision to remove sexual pleasure for women in Uganda. But it is often much harder for us to recognize and name abusive belief systems that are part of the cultural fabric of middle-class American life—systems that lead to an increased rate of suicide attempts by LGBTQ+ teens exposed to religious "conversion therapy"[2] or to movements that equate a woman who is not a virgin with a piece of chewed up gum, subsequently hampering her ability to enjoy intimacy for life.

Spiritual anxiety is certainly not limited to Christianity, but given that the founder of our faith preached a pretty compelling lesson about removing the plank from one's own eye before looking for the speck in a neighbor's, this book is going to focus on issues within the body of Christ.

For many people, part of their faith deconstruction—their detoxifying and delousing process—involves putting their own faith under a microscope or applying the same standard of judgment against their own traditions that they have applied to others'. Deconstruction isn't a movement to erase the reality of sin in order to create a world without consequences, as many popular Christian thought leaders claim. On the contrary, deconstruction is stripping our faith of cultural preferences masquerading as gospel and holding ourselves accountable by shining a spotlight on the sin of those who harm others in the name of God. That is precisely why abusers want to silence anyone going through the process; they don't want to have to face the consequences of their own self-serving beliefs and behaviors. And as long as their followers are entrapped by spiritual anxiety, no one is likely to risk their soul in order to hold the guilty parties answerable.

Spiritual anxiety is more than deep remorse or repentance from sin. It is all-consuming or immobilizing fear over the state of one's spiritual life because of manipulative or toxic theology. Penitence is essential; using that penitence to extract absolute obedience or compliance is abuse.

But if "deconstructing" is not a word you feel comfortable using because it feels too drastic, too ell-encompassing, too final, too trendy—then don't use it. Find a word that works for you, like *rewriting, overhauling, detoxifying, reconstructing*, or *reexamining*.

> Penitence is essential; using that penitence to extract absolute obedience or compliance is abuse

The verb itself doesn't matter; the work of shedding damaging beliefs does. And if the work itself ever causes you to feel anxious or sinful, remember that Christianity was founded on a deconstruction movement as a response to toxic and damaging attitudes and ideas that sought to control behavior, accumulate earthly power, limit grace, and put up fences around God. Jesus challenged the religious authorities of his day and worked to dismantle structures of power that oppressed, enslaved, and diminished people. He spoke out against unjust practices and the abuse of religious authority. He numbered among his closest followers "zealots"—those who sought to overthrow a colonizing power. But most of all, he sought to heal.

Jesus was a healer as well as a teacher. Of the thirty-seven miracles recorded in the gospels, twenty-nine of them involve healing. His life was spent making hurting people well—and not strictly in the physical sense. In the Beatitudes, he spoke to people who experienced anxiety and depression; he offered kindness to women in unhealthy or unstable relationships; he showed compassion to people in the midst of mental or emotional crises; he interacted with people society overlooked. Jesus addressed the emotional needs of people, and he spoke out emphatically against those who did not. In fact, Jesus's primary message against the religious leaders of his time was aimed at their harsh treatment of others and their love of personal gain—in short, their abuse of power. In the Gospel of Luke, he declares:

"But woe to you Pharisees! For you tithe mint and rue and herbs of all kinds, and neglect justice and the love of God; it is these you ought to have practiced, without neglecting the others. Woe to you Pharisees! For you love to have the seat of honor in the synagogues and to be greeted with respect in the marketplaces.... Woe also to you experts in the law! For you load people with burdens hard to bear, and you yourselves do not lift a finger to ease them." (Luke 11:42–43, 46)

As uncomfortable as it may make many traditionalists, Christianity, in its earliest forms, engaged in the critique and deconstruction of a number of different religious cultures and systems, primarily Jewish, Greek, and Roman. If we truly seek to be "little Christs" (the literal translation of the word "Christians"), we must do the same in our own time and place. We must dismantle structures that cause damage, and we must minster to those who have been injured by them—including ourselves.

Many who have undergone the deconstruction process experience feelings of disillusionment, anger, and feelings of betrayal due to toxic theology or harmful church culture. Those feelings become especially complicated, however, when they are bound up with extreme internal emotional distress about displeasing God. These fears are often fed by religious systems that either dismiss the spiritual turmoil as a sign of weakness or else celebrate it as a mark of exceptional devotion—both of which can erode a person's mental health through shame cycles, self-deprecation, and a lack of personal agency. Deconstruction is a hard but necessary process for disillusioned and injured believers to develop healthy, life-giving relationships with God. The process is even harder, though, when an individual has never known faith separate from constant fear, nervousness, or anxiety.

This is why it is essential to understand not only what form of abuse is taking place but what tactics are being used to keep people entrapped in those toxic systems. Only then can an individual be liberated for life abundant in Christ. As Jesus declared in Luke 4:18, the Spirit of God has anointed him "to proclaim freedom for the prisoners and recovery of sight for the blind, to set the oppressed free." This is our sacred charge as believers, as well. Breaking down the way language and reasoning can be used to coerce and control as well as to combat such manipulation is more than just an intellectual exercise; it is a path to freedom. Jesus understood this. In fact, the most commonly used word in the New Testament translated as "salvation," *sōtēria*, literally means "deliverance" or "liberation." A life of salvation is a life of liberation from the weights that oppress our souls.

In Mark 12, we see this very technique of breaking down manipulative language played out quite literally. When the teachers of the law try to entrap Jesus with a *reductio ad absurdum* scenario—that is, a reduction to the absurd, or a hypothetical situation teased out to its most absurdly extreme application—he calls out their intentions. The Sadducees present Jesus with the following conundrum: if a woman marries a series of seven brothers in succession and each one dies before they have any children, to whom will she be married in eternity? The Sadducees, of course, are not asking for the sake of gaining an answer because this is not a real scenario with which they are faced. Instead, they want to

A life of salvation is a life of liberation from the weights that oppress our souls

catch Jesus in a technicality and thereby deem all his teaching invalid. But Jesus responds by asking: "Are you not in error because you do not know the Scriptures or the power of God?" He then proceeds to recount examples from the book of Genesis that invalidate their bad theology by identifying the false premise and systematically disproving it by pointing out the flawed reasoning that actually makes the arrogant religious leaders appear ignorant rather than enlightened. Jesus punctuates his argument with the exclamation: "You are badly mistaken!" (Mark 12:18–27).

But Jesus isn't done calling out manipulative techniques. Immediately, another highly significant exchange occurs:

> One of the teachers of the law came and heard them debating. Noticing that Jesus had given them a good answer, he asked him, "Of all the commandments, which is the most important?"
>
> "The most important one," answered Jesus, "is this: 'Hear, O Israel: The Lord our God, the Lord is one. Love the Lord your God with all your heart and with all your soul and with all your mind and with all your strength.' The second is this: 'Love your neighbor as yourself.' There is no commandment greater than these."
>
> "Well said, teacher," the man replied. "You are right in saying that God is one and there is no other but him. To love him with all your heart, with all your understanding and with all your strength, and to love your neighbor as yourself is more important than all burnt offerings and sacrifices."
>
> When Jesus saw that he had answered wisely, he said to him, "You are not far from the kingdom of God." And from then on no one dared ask him any more questions. (Mark 12:28–34)

Let's consider the implications of this exchange. When Jesus is challenged, he replies by quoting the Shema, a passage from Deuteronomy 6:4–5, which is regarded as one of the most sacred prayers in Judaism: "Hear, O Israel: The LORD our God, the LORD is one. Love the LORD your God with all your heart and with all your soul and with all your strength." But notice that when Jesus recites it, he makes one small alteration: "Hear, O Israel: The Lord our God, the Lord is one. You shall love the Lord your God with all your heart, and with all your soul, and *with all your mind*, and with all your strength."

Jesus wants his followers to be intellectually invested in their faith, not accepting blindly what they are fed. He wants them to have common sense rather than blind allegiance, and to think through the consequences of their religious behaviors and beliefs. His follow-up response about loving one's neighbor draws this out further: we are called to engage our minds in the service of loving God and loving our neighbors. On a simpler level, though, the addition Jesus makes to the Shema also points to the importance of *healthy* mental engagement in our faith. Loving God with all our mind doesn't mean obsessing to the point of dysfunction; it means celebrating the Creator who gave us the ability to imagine, invent, design, build, form, dream, love, celebrate, empathize, organize, praise, feel, long, analyze, evaluate, discern, and think critically. It means honoring and cultivating our healthiest thoughts, impulses, and meditations as gifts from, and to, God.

Finally, consider what the text says when the questioner affirms Jesus's responses: "When Jesus saw that he had answered wisely, he said to him, 'You are not far from the kingdom of God.' And from then on no one dared ask him any more questions" (Mark 12:34). A person who is willing and able to apply critical thinking skills to their faith not only draws near to God but also shuts down hostilities from those who seek to oppose and oppress them.

A person able to apply critical thinking skills to their faith not only draws near to God but also shuts down hostilities from those who seek to oppose and oppress them

My goal in the coming pages is not to convince anyone of anything, nor is it to pressure anyone into deconstruction or suddenly make abusers see the error of their ways. Obviously, if someone were to be convicted of their own toxic beliefs and committed to doing better, I would be thrilled. But I don't want to talk someone into something that they do not believe or that does not jibe with their conscience. What you believe is between you and God, and I would not presume to interject myself into that relationship. My goal is not to evangelize but to acknowledge. When you see what is at work externally, it's often easier to understand what is going on internally.

This book is not intended as a manual for "solving" or "curing" spiritual anxiety but as a way of calling out and dismantling some of the techniques, beliefs, and messages that have been used to control or manipulate people's religious behaviors by means of their spiritual scruples and emotions. It is an acknowledgment of the legitimacy of these anxious feelings and a guide to reexamining and reconsidering some of the most commonly weaponized scriptures.

That being said, if you find in reading this that your spiritual anxiety stems from the religious culture in which you were raised or from the ways in which you have been conditioned to experience God, you may also find relief in learning that your trauma response is a normal psychological reaction rather than a direct reflection of the state of your soul or your salvation. I want to offer en-

Through a deeper understanding of the way spiritual anxiety works, the discussion here may pour bravery into your soul and hearten you as you seek hope, health, and wholeness

couragement, perspective, maybe a little additional understanding, and above all, just a sense that, if you recognize yourself in some of these descriptions, you are not alone. "Encouragement," after all, comes from Old French, where it meant planting courage into someone—literally, making their heart (*cœur*) stronger for whatever they must endure. That is my prayer for this book: that, through a deeper understanding of the way spiritual anxiety works, the discussion here may pour bravery into your soul and hearten you as you seek hope, health, and wholeness.

As you move through this book, you will likely find that any one of the specific examples discussed in a particular overarching chapter theme (discipline, dogma, decoration, denial, degradation, diminishment, and domination) could just as easily have been covered in many of the others. These categories necessarily bleed into one another, overlapping and blurring boundaries—discipline and power imbalances often look very similar; so do shame and rejection, for example. The discussion here is focused less on the "what" than on the "how," and it will hopefully provide a kind of helpful shorthand for breaking these concepts down into piece-parts.

Spiritual anxiety can be dramatic and shocking or subtle and barely perceptible except through the long-term damage to an individual's emotional and spiritual health. There are many excellent resources available with a quick web search that will alert readers to behavioral warning signs and red flags of spiritual abuse, and I encourage anyone concerned to spend some time parsing such resources carefully. I want to repeat again, however, that it is important to remember that not all religious toxicity is deliberately abusive. Many well-intentioned people employ manipulative tactics without realizing either the mental or emotional impact of such teachings. They approach the subject that way because that is how *they* were taught. This does not make the impact less real, but it is important to acknowledge that not everyone who relies on these tactics does so from a place of ego, selfishness, or ill intent.

This book is not an attack on Christianity; it is a defense against abuses committed in the name of Christ. The intention here is to empower readers to be able to recognize certain behaviors and patterns as toxic that they may never have recognized as such before. Addressing the impact of such problematic approaches opens the door for healing. When we study the ways that Jesus used language, reason, and persuasion to promote love, acceptance, and affirmation, we can find paths toward healing the damage harmful theology may have done to our relationship with God and with other people.

When you are equipped with a fuller understanding of not only what is being done but how it is taking place, you can speak about it more freely and confidently. You can point to something tangible that invites discussion, debate, and dialogue. You can gently correct misguided teachings or you can boldly put abusers on notice. By equipping yourself with precise language to identify the behavior, calling out toxicity in real time, and doing the important work of better understanding the sources of your own spiritual anxiety, you are arming yourself to assert your freedom in Christ. It is a step forward in reclaiming your own mind and regaining your own power—"the power of God that brings salvation [*sōtērian*, liberation] to everyone who believes: first to the Jew, then to the Gentile" (Romans 1:16).

One of the strongest weapons abusers have is shame. If they can convince their victims that their pain is somehow deserved—that they brought it upon themselves because of their own stubbornness, hard-heartedness, ignorance, defiance, pride, or sin—the victims become easier to control. When a person feels shamed, they tend to stay isolated, silent, and compliant for fear that anyone should judge them for their perceived depravity. When you reject the shame, you also reject its control over you.

The Gospel of John opens with the famous statement: "In the beginning was the Word, and the Word was with God, and the Word was God." The term translated "Word" is the Greek "Logos," which literally means "word, speech, divine utterance." But it also carried another meaning in Greek philosophy. Logos meant a divine ordering or reason that creates sense from confusion or disorder. Here, John is rhetorically linking Jesus to the concept of Logos by presenting him as the manifestation of Truth that corrects false and problematic doctrine. As followers of Jesus, our charge is to do the same.

When you reject the shame, you also reject its control over you

Further in this same passage, John explains that Jesus is the light, and "in him was life, and the life was the light of all people. . . . The true light, which enlightens everyone" (1:4, 9). Light illuminates all it touches; it reveals what has been hidden, pushed away, or cast aside. Jesus shines to embrace and receive, not obfuscate or throw shade that limits what our vision includes or how far it reaches. And we are promised that, ultimately, "the darkness did not overcome it" (1:5). Which do we want to be a part of: the light that welcomes or the darkness that separates?

This book is for those who want to do more than just beg for scraps from the Master's table. It is about celebrating good people with tender hearts and vigilant consciences who want to love God and live their lives free from the constant fear of divine rejection—people who are striving to do their best in the name of God. It is for those who see beyond the whitewash on the tombs. It is for those who have witnessed a harvest of thorns and thistles rather than grapes and figs. It is for those who are tearing down the old assumptions and presumptions of their faith, and who seek to rebuild not with mass-produced bricks of bigotry, exclusion, fear, and legalism, but with beams of acceptance, inclusion, peace, and humility hewn by the Carpenter himself.

3

INVOLUNTARY INTERNALIZED
LEGALISM

Before we go any further, I want to make sure that we hit on a few of the most important takeaways relatively early on in case this book gets added to the "stack of good intentions" of unread and half-read books, which (at this point) you can't possibly hope to finish in this lifetime, no matter how strong the guilt or sincere the plans to do so. Don't feel bad. We all have one.[1]

But if we explore these points now, you will be armed with some essential insights at the outset of our discussion that will hopefully make you feel less alone and more empowered, even if it takes a little while to make it to the end of this book.[2] This will also allow us to consider the subsequent chapters in light of these issues and give you some basic vocabulary and strategies for what's to come. Think of it as "equipping the saints" (Ephesians 4:12) if "the saints" are people who are fed up with manipulative malarkey and Machiavellian mind games in the name of Christ—which actually seems pretty accurate.

The following chapters are closer examinations of how spiritual anxiety can develop under various circumstances, ways that it can be used to control both intentionally and unintentionally, and methods for flipping the script on misapplied and easily weaponized passages from Scripture. In order to do that, we have to start with a topic that nearly every conversation about modern, Western Christianity comes to sooner or later: legalism.

There is no question that Jesus railed against legalism, but how his example is regarded within modern Christianity varies greatly.

Some churches take a grace-filled, practical approach.

Some leaders talk about legalism in doubly problematic terms as something "the Jews" did but that Christians have magically transcended so it's not even something we have to worry about.

Some congregations take special pride in living so strictly "by the Book" that they make biblical literalism part of their identity without regard for time, culture, context, genre, hyperbole, or human decency in how they apply their interpretations.

Legalism is, in short, the "excessive adherence to law or formula" (Oxford English Dictionary) or a "strict, literal, or excessive conformity to the law or to a religious or moral code" (Merriam-Webster). In practical terms, legalism tends to function in one of two ways: either as a "slippery slope" logical fallacy or as a Rube Goldberg machine.

A slippery slope fallacy makes a series of if-then propositions that ultimately lead to a catastrophic or dire outcome far outside the realm of reasonable possibility: "*If A leads to B, and B leads to C, and C leads to D*," and so on down the line until *A* is presented as inevitably leading to *Z*, even if the end result is sometimes so far separated from the original conditions or intent as to be unrecognizable. (There is a more technical breakdown of this concept in the endnotes, if you really want to get into the weeds on how this all works.)[3]

Another way to think of legalism is as a Rube Goldberg machine. We've all enjoyed watching one of these devices play out: a dart pops a balloon, which sets off a line of dominoes that trip a mousetrap that launches a ball down a track until it falls in a small bucket that tips and triggers a pendulum that knocks over a weight that presses the button on a toaster to make breakfast. It is essentially an overly complicated and roundabout system for completing a very basic task, usually to comic effect. Legalism can work in much the same way, where unnecessary steps, constraints, and measures are artificially inserted and then must be completed in order to reach an otherwise fairly straightforward outcome. These impractical and often illogical complications impede progress to the desired goal or result, and the effect is usually either ironically comic or downright tragic.

We probably all have stories to share of legalism run amok, some of which may seem hilariously ludicrous and others utterly depressing. Among the more ridiculous examples I have personally encountered is hearing a person in leadership insist that another individual was not qualified to serve as an elder in the church because when the qualifications for elders are laid out in 1 Timothy and Titus, the texts say that the candidate's "children" must be well-disciplined. The man in question met every other qualification of character, ability, wisdom, experience, faithfulness, humility, and a strong marriage—except he only had one child and the biblical passages spoke of the conduct of the hypothetical nominee's child*ren*, plural. And this, it was argued, meant he did not meet God's standard for eldership.

A quick survey of a few friends turned up half-a-dozen other examples of legalism in under ninety seconds, including:

- a church youth group being made to sit through a presentation on dating that incorporated "an overhead slide telling us, in list form, the levels of 'intimate touching' and *exactly* 'how far was too far'";
- construction workers doing repair work on a church being forced to eat their lunches outside in July in Texas because when Paul admonishes Christians for getting drunk at the

Lord's Supper, he writes, "Do you not have households to eat and drink in?" (1 Corinthians 11:22), so eating inside the church building was considered unscriptural;

- a church whose members put their left hand behind their back when putting their weekly offering in the tray in order to comply with Jesus's words in Matthew 6:3–4: "But when you give alms, do not let your left hand know what your right hand is doing, so that your alms may be done in secret, and your Father who sees in secret will reward you";
- a person who was not allowed to voice concerns about harmful behavior by family members because "love keeps no record of wrongs" (1 Corinthians 13:5);
- a woman who was advised by her pastor that she had no biblical grounds to divorce her husband who had abandoned the family because she could not prove that he had committed adultery;
- a child who reported sexual abuse by a church leader being told to keep quiet because Hebrews 13:17 says to "obey your leaders and submit to them, for they are keeping watch over your souls and will give an account."

I'm sure you have your own heartbreaking or hilarious examples of legalism you could add to this list. The absurd, and sometimes seemingly arbitrary, enforcement of certain rules—both highly specific and overly general—can be one of the most frustrating and anxiety-inducing parts of any religious practice. Are you violating some unspoken law you've never heard of? Are you fully considering each and every possible aspect or imaginable contingency of an action before deciding whether or not it is acceptable? Are you choosing personal convenience over a strict adherence to God's will? Will your concerns be taken seriously by leadership or dismissed with the wave of a cherry-picked scripture?

These are examples of institutional legalism, but personal legalism operates a bit differently. Instead of applying stringent rules to the governance of the whole organization, personal legalism enacts them at the individual level, operating in two directions: outward (harshly judging other people) or inward (harshly judging oneself). It demands that things be done (or not done) according to a strict interpretation that leaves no room for even inadvertent error either because of highly specific and narrow constraints or because of overly broad and overarching restrictions that serve as a kind of "blanket ban" or "universal rule" in order to ensure obedience to God's will. But legalism is much more than just "salvation by works" theology. Whether it is directed outward or inward, legalism is ultimately about control: control of others by demanding certain beliefs and behaviors or control of God by creating an obligation of divine favor.

The first part of that statement is obvious, but the second part may be less apparent. Even when carried out with the very best and humblest of intentions, legalism is an attempt to manipulate God's favor by doing more than what was asked or by taking commands to such an extreme that they come at the cost of health, relationships, common sense, or common decency. It's a manifestation of prosperity gospel, which creates an if-then proposition to which God is bound: "*If* I do X, *then* God will bless me." The principle is, essentially: "If I leave absolutely no room for error, mistake, omission, or incompletion, then I will be on God's 'good side.'"

Legalism is ultimately about control: control of others by demanding certain beliefs and behaviors or control of God by creating an obligation of divine favor

We all know the problems that outward-facing legalism brings in terms of passing both burden and judgment onto someone else, but for the purposes of this book, I want to focus more on the issues arising from inward-facing legalism. When legalism becomes internalized, it can lead to spiritual anxiety.

Most legalists, of course, would not even consider themselves to be legalists; instead, they would regard their behavior as simply an articulation of their obedience, faithfulness, and religious duty—and possibly even as a privilege to demonstrate their devotion to their faith. If these feelings are overwhelmingly positive, then inward-facing legalism may actually be an important part of that person's individual spiritual expression.

The problem comes when the emotions associated with inward-facing legalism cause deep feelings of worry, confusion, stress, and even masochistic commitment to beliefs, practices, and relationships that are damaging to an individual's well-being. This launches a vicious cycle of invalidation ("I'm not living my life right.") to spiraling ("There is some secret sin in my life keeping me from God," or "These fears are proof my faith isn't strong enough.") to shame ("If I were a better Christian, this wouldn't happen," or "I'm not trying hard enough.") which leads back to the initial invalidating thought: "I'm not living my life right." The individual feels imprisoned by their own conscience, trapped by thoughts and behaviors but ultimately not able to curb them because of deep-seated fears that doing so might elicit God's wrath. This is a state that I call *Involuntary Internalized Legalism (IIL)*.

No, that's not any kind of formal terminology, and I deliberately avoided the word "condition" because it's certainly not an officially recognized ailment. But I think Involuntary Internalized Legalism is a useful term for helping to explain the way that many people with spiritual anxiety feel. They are entrapped by their own scruples, even if they know that such worries, concerns, and fears are irrational, excessive, or far outside the spirit of the law. That is what makes this type of inward-facing legalism so unique. It is not the result of a zealous individual choosing to hold themselves to a higher standard; it is the involuntary and often unwelcome presence of persistent self-conviction and self-doubt in matters of personal ethics and conduct.

Consider the anxiety-inducing scripture I mentioned in chapter 1: "Pray without ceasing" (1 Thessalonians 5:17). A reading of this scripture through the lens of IIL means that any pause in constant prayer is a violation of a divine command. A person with spiritual anxiety may end up "going to pieces" (*merimnaō*) in their attempt to obey this injunction while simultaneously trying to hold down a job, build relationships, and otherwise live their life. Anxiety feeds anxiety.

Because individuals who struggle with IIL have often been taught (whether by word or example) that a literal, legalistic interpretation of Scripture is the only acceptable guide for personal conduct, actions, or beliefs, then everything they experience is held up against that standard. Even if the individual has separated from the religious environment that initially fostered this oppressive theology, the framework for habitual self-condemnation very often remains in place.

Paul writes of this same struggle in Romans 7 when he describes the tension between sin and virtue that can exist when the mind wrestles with temptation. While it seems a bit harsh to term IIL as "sin" since it is a genuine effort to please God, it is certainly something that pulls the individual away from the peace and freedom of the gospel. The language of internal wrestling to free oneself from damaging behavior is poignant:

> For we know that the law is spiritual, but I am of the flesh, sold into slavery under sin. I do not understand my own actions. For I do not do what I want, but I do the very thing I hate. Now if I do what I do not want, I agree that the law is good. But in fact it is no longer I who do it but sin that dwells within me. For I know that the good does not dwell within me, that is, in my flesh. For the desire to do the good lies close at hand, but not the ability. . . . So then, with my mind I am enslaved to the law of God, but with my flesh I am enslaved to the law of sin. (Romans 7:14–25)

From the conversations and interviews I've conducted while researching this topic, I have found that people who struggle with IIL tend to have several of the following traits in common:

- They have been conditioned to believe in their own inherent unworthiness.
- They feel compelled to exhibit extreme piety to gain or maintain favor with God.
- They have been taught (either directly or indirectly) that faithful living must involve adhering to a "formula."
- They believe that nothing they do is ever enough, which leads to feelings of deep spiritual inadequacy due to being a disappointment to Christ.
- They fear losing salvation or divine favor if they stray from the controlling beliefs they have internalized, even if they no longer consider them necessary or correct.

These feelings are often coupled with a constrained sense of discernment. How do you know what voice is God's when so many other "biblical perspectives" feel misguided, incomplete, legalistic, dehumanizing, or just plain wrong? How do you hang on when faith begins to feel like a no-win proposition?

A common response to people struggling with discernment is John 10:4, in which Jesus states, "When he has brought out all his own, he goes ahead of them, and the sheep follow him because they know his voice." Simply put, the sheep know their Shepherd's voice. Sure. That's absolutely reasonable. But slinging that verse around like an ironclad guarantee vastly oversimplifies the matter; it's not a promise that Christ's will is automatically apparent if you just pray and listen hard enough, and the implication is that anyone who is struggling to discern the Shepherd's voice is *not* of his flock. That's not exactly comforting for people who are already anxious about their relationship with God.

If God's will were always perfectly clear, there would be no need for discernment; it would already be obvious and unambiguous. Yet 1 Corinthians 12:10 clearly tells us that discernment is a spiritual gift—which means that it comes more easily or instinctively to some people than to others. So what do we do when we've been taught to not listen to ourselves? Some faith traditions embrace the chronic practice of shaming intuition out of a person. That's not what they would call it, of course, but all the warnings against trusting in "the flesh" lead to a theology that strips away any sense of personal will and replaces it with dogmatic injunctions that may or may not be applicable to the situation at hand. It removes the agency but retains the blame.

One great spiritual practitioner who recognized the gift of intuition was Ignatius of Loyola. A soldier and the son of Spanish nobility, Ignatius was gravely injured in 1521 when a cannonball shattered his right leg in battle. During his convalescence, Ignatius experienced a religious conversion that eventually led him to cofound the Society of Jesus (known more commonly as the Jesuits), which eventually became the largest religious order within the Roman Catholic Church.

Some faith traditions embrace the chronic practice of shaming intuition out of a person

Just as significant to broader Christendom, however, were his *Spiritual Exercises*—a collection of his prayers, meditations, and essays on God that he published in 1548.

Of particular interest to Ignatius was the process of spiritual formation. He was highly attuned to the manner by which an individual discerns God's voice, receives a divine calling, and engages with personal religious expression. He observed closely the way many of his converts experienced this process, and he eventually developed a series of spiritual practices by which an individual can foster discernment of God's will and confident movement within a variety of good options in life.

Ignatian discernment, as the practice is called, is quite simple at its core. When comparing options of moral equivalence (that is, a choice not between right and wrong but between more than one possible good paths), the individual should pay attention to embodied emotion. Which option comes with a greater sense of lightness and peace? Which feels heavier or weightier? Ignatius

called these differing emotions "consolation" and "desolation."
He urged his followers to pursue God's will by prayerfully seeking a sense of consolation and trusting the Holy Spirit to work
within the individual to provide a feeling of tranquility, hope,
or orderliness in order to help guide them in the direction best
suited to their personal disposition, ambition, interests, goals,
and calling.

It seems pretty straightforward and commonsensical, doesn't
it? What could possibly be objectionable about working with
God to determine the best direction for your life? Unfortunately,
when you've been taught that listening to your own desires is giving into the flesh, a practice that recognizes that your own preferences have inherent value and that elevates your personal will
to a place of crucial importance in the discernment process can
feel dangerous. What's more, it can lead you to dismiss as mere
temptation what your soul is telling you is best. This is where IIL
does some of its most serious damage. No matter how far we may
have distanced ourselves from certain teachings, it's very hard to
unlearn something so deeply ingrained as the notion that there
is one right and righteous path and instead to learn to recognize
and celebrate the embodiment of spiritual promptings. That is,
if you've ever been introduced to such a concept as Ignatian discernment at all.

I grew up in Sunday school. I attended an evangelical college
that required a Bible or religion class every semester. I have long
struggled with "overanalysis paralysis" and have talked with pastors and Christian counselors about difficult decisions and my
challenges in making hard choices. I have been an active member in my local congregation my entire life. I have listened to So.
Much. Christian. Radio. And yet, even taking into account an inherent evangelical skepticism regarding anything Roman Catholic, I still had never heard of Ignatian discernment—or anything
like it—as a spiritual practice until I was a seminary student in
my early forties.

Oh, I heard about weighing options, making pros and cons lists, and certainly about praying over a matter for clarity. I definitely heard that I should "search the Scriptures for an answer." But no one ever suggested (to my recollection) that there was value in checking in my heart, mind, and soul to see what decision felt right. No one ever told me that my embodied emotions might have some wisdom worth considering. No one ever told me *to listen to myself* when it came to major life decisions. Instead, the suggestion was always, "What does the Bible say about that?" which usually translated to, "How can the Bible affirm the choice I think you should make?"

As a result, any time I felt consolation about a decision that didn't closely align with a traditional biblical response, I tried to squash that feeling down because I was convinced it was a sign of my rebellious, sinful nature trying to steer me wrong. If I struggled with desolation—or even just lacking peace—about a by-the-book legalistic option, I was warned more than once that I was "kicking against the goads," the same warning that Saul (before he was renamed Paul) hears from a heavenly voice on the road to Damascus as he resists the call of Christ (Acts 26:14).

To "kick against the goads" is an agricultural reference that means to defy the direction of the farmer's cattle prod. In my case, it was used to imply that any uncertainties I had were pricks of conscience that I was making an unbiblical choice rather than just natural questions or worries about a big decision. Never was it presented the other way around—that perhaps the "goads" were directing me toward something different than the strictest interpretation of biblical conduct and legalism. No, the goads were always a literal, legalistic view of Scripture, and any choice that deviated from them was an act of insubordination against God.

I know I was not alone in the experience. Many of us were coached in a similar way to automatically reject our intuition—our deep, inner capital-K Knowing—or even just our gut-feelings (because the gut, after all, is literally part of the physical body, which is not to be trusted). As I learned about Ignatian discernment, what struck me was not only that it took me until middle age before I ever heard of it as a legitimate approach to decision-making, but that *it took the Christian church 1,500 years to codify and validate such a basic, reasonable practice.* Of course there were proponents of similar ideas here and there throughout church history, some of whom left writings that helped to shape Ignatius's ideas, but the fact that this process wasn't broadly recognized as a valuable method of self-discovery for a millennium and a half is shocking. The fact that it is *still* not recognized as an acceptable practice by certain faith traditions is shameful.

Never was it presented the other way around—that perhaps the "goads" were directing me toward something different than the strictest interpretation of biblical conduct

Of all the clobber verses that have been weaponized to warn people against "trusting in the flesh," one of the most common passages is Proverbs 3:3–7:

> Trust in the LORD with all your heart,
>   and do not rely on your own insight.
> In all your ways acknowledge him,
>   and he will make straight your paths.
> Do not be wise in your own eyes;
>   fear the LORD and turn away from evil.

Here, many of us were taught, is indisputable evidence that we ought to ignore our feelings, our hunches, our experiences, our academic understanding of a topic, our rational analysis of a situation—anything that does not come directly and explicitly from the Bible. After all, as Jeremiah 17:9 warns us: "The heart is devious above all else; it is perverse—who can understand it?" The human heart is wicked and is not to be trusted, we are told.

The *only* place to find answers is in the Bible . . . as it is interpreted by certain preapproved and accepted leaders who usually fall in a pretty narrow demographic range of gender, race, age, and nationality.

This kind of proof-texting, or selectively applying verses to make a point, conveniently ignores the verses that indicate that maybe humans *do* possess the capacity to think, judge, and reason for themselves not as an act of rebellion, but as an act of wisdom, celebration, or even worship. In Job 38, God places the question plainly before Job: "Who has put wisdom in the inward parts or given understanding to the mind?" (v. 36) The implication, of course, is that the body that houses those "inward parts" and mind is actually capable of discerning truth. We see examples of this in the New Testament as well. As he opens his letter to the church in Ephesus, for example, Paul writes:

> I do not cease to give thanks for you as I remember you in my prayers, that the God of our Lord Jesus Christ, the Father of glory, may give you a spirit of wisdom and revelation as you come to know him, so that, with the eyes of your heart enlightened, you may perceive what is the hope to which he has called you, what are the riches of his glorious inheritance among the saints, and what is the immeasurable greatness of his power for us who believe, according to the working of his great power. (Ephesians 1:16–19)

If the human heart is hopelessly, irredeemably corrupt, why would Paul waste any time in praying for the "eyes of your heart" to become "enlightened" so that the believers could better "perceive" their calling from God through "a spirit of wisdom and revelation"? What is this passage if not a recognition of the capacity for human beings to grow in wisdom and prudence, even while God works behind the scenes on behalf of God's faithful? James 1:5 has a similar message: "If any of you is lacking in wisdom, ask

God, who gives to all generously and ungrudgingly, and it will be given you." Why bother praying for wisdom if we don't have the capacity for it and aren't supposed to use it because we should be drawing our answers solely from the Bible and not from our own thoughtful contemplation?

There are some readers for whom this discussion will seem pointless and obvious. *Of course* we are supposed to utilize our God-given intellect; no one *actually* thinks we're just supposed to chuck our minds out the window and look *only* to the Bible for direction and guidance, right?

. . .

[Awkward silence.]

. . .

Many Christian faith traditions have a healthy culture of encouraging independent thought and prayerful discernment. But others . . . don't. Very few of those would actually say so, of course (though some might), but when it comes down to brass tacks, they will still prioritize biblical literalism over a more subjective approach—the law takes priority over life or logic. And, unfortunately, this kind of thinking is especially difficult for people who struggle with IIL. While they clearly recognize the disconnect between a legalistic response and a rational one, they often feel compelled to follow the legalistic response instead, even if it results in further harm—which can, in turn, lead to deepening feelings of self-loathing or deep spiritual frustration.

If you stop reading at this point and take nothing else from this book, let it be this: *It is not a sin to listen to your intuition.* You will not lose your salvation for protecting yourself or others from dangerous, predatory, or abusive situations. Paying attention to cues of concern, discomfort, suspicion, or the condition known most commonly by its scientific name of "the heebie-jeebies" is not, *in any imaginable way*, "surrendering to the flesh" or "acting without faith." It is, in fact, just the opposite; it is perceiving, listening to, and reacting to the mental signals that God has instilled in your brain to indicate the possibility of threats to your safety or well-being. Can intuition be wrong? Of course. But can it also prove very, very right? Absolutely. This doesn't mean that we should never take risks or venture outside our comfort zone, or that our own culturally conditioned prejudices or preferences may or may not be at work. But it certainly does mean that we should give weight to that inner voice that says, "Hang on a second. Something doesn't feel right" without feeling guilty about it.

It is not a sin to listen to your intuition

In fact, in order to emphasize this point, I think it is essential to introduce the Jewish concept of *pikuach nefesh* (literally, "saving a life"), which I discussed in detail in *Gaslighted by God*. The idea behind "saving a life" is, simply, that

> moral law comes secondary to the preservation of human life—and when in doubt, a faithful person is supposed to err on the side of caution, with life coming before the law. In other words, it is permitted to call 9-1-1 on the Sabbath even though dialing a phone is normally forbidden on that day under Jewish law. Or if a person is starving and only unkosher food is available, they can eat it without becoming unclean. The purpose of the law is to give life, not to allow death to prevail over a technicality.

> In fact, not only are these violations of law permitted, they are considered a greater act of holiness than adhering to the commandments. A person who places higher priority on saving a life is considered more pleasing to God than one who avoids doing so in an effort to preserve his or her own religious purity. In fact, the principle of *saving a life* is so sacred that when two people must choose which one violates a

religious law to save a life, the more righteous or religiously strict individual is supposed to have the *honor* of doing so.

This extends to the personal level, too. If someone has a condition like diabetes or is on medication that requires food or drink, life takes precedence over religious dictates, even during a fast or on a high holy day. The principle behind this reasoning is common sense: God cares more about the health of God's people than about the minutiae of the law. If food is required for preserving health, then a reasonable amount is permitted, no questions asked.[4]

This definition is followed by a number of instances from Scripture in which the philosophy of "saving a life" is invoked, including examples in the Gospels in which Jesus clearly prioritizes life over the law.

What is more, this prioritizing of health over holiness is supposed to be carried out free from guilt, shame, or even moral agony. Actions that protect and preserve life are innately holy. Listening to your intuition as a means of protecting yourself or someone else from harm or exploitation is grounds for commendation, not condemnation. Anyone who tries to convince you otherwise has made an idol out of their own holiness.

Actions that protect and preserve life are innately holy

A quick glance at church history reveals that Christianity has a habit of fetishizing suffering. From gripping tales of the martyrs greeting death happily to the early Christian theologian Origen castrating himself in the early third century CE as a means of showing his devotion; from medieval penitents wearing hair shirts or mystics praying for the wounds of Christ to manifest on their own bodies; from Puritans shunning all earthly pleasures to modern conversations about how trials purify us for greater glory—much of the rhetoric around Christian suffering has led many believers to believe they should actively seek it out. While suffering can certainly lead to spiritual growth and maturity, some people become seemingly addicted to it, declining to take action that might remove themselves from their difficulties because they have been taught to believe that they are glorifying God by remaining in their pain rather than seeking ways to resolve it. For people shaped by legalism or authoritarianism, pursuing health or safety by raising questions, challenging toxic power systems, leaving abusive situations, or simply standing up for oneself may feel like moral rebellion.

For people shaped by legalism or authoritarianism, pursuing health or safety by raising questions, challenging toxic power systems, leaving abusive situations, or simply standing up for oneself may feel like moral rebellion

So how do we make that leap from the anxiety that comes from deep-seated IIL to a more liberated perspective? How do we give voice to our most honest beliefs when we've been taught that our truest self is fundamentally evil? How do we shed the learned fear that finding ourselves means losing our soul?

Perhaps the first step is to alleviate the pressure to make the "right" choice—the choice that God needs us to make to put us on the path to God's highest good for our life, the choice that the whole heavenly host is rooting for us to pick. Until we are sure about what the singularly "right" choice is, we may feel incapable of making any decision at all; after all, when uncertainty strikes, we often hear Psalm 27:14, which tells us "Wait for the LORD; be strong, and let your heart take courage; wait for the LORD!" Unfortunately, as we all know, God does not seem to have any particular urgency to work according to human timetables. Sometimes, praying, fasting, reading Scripture, and seeking counsel turn up nothing. So what do we do when waiting for the Lord to reveal the "right" path yields no answer at all? After all, the existence of a "right" choice implies that there is only one correct answer that is God's best and that is in accordance with God's will. This, then, implies that if we make the wrong choice, everything else that follows will be less than God's best and out-side of God's will. So, you know, *no pressure*.

Perhaps one healthy response to dealing with the challenge of discernment is to remove it from binary terms. Instead of pinning all our faith on the "right" choice, we can instead pray for God to make clear the "best" choice. If we miss the "right" choice, it implies that any other choice we make is the wrong one, which will derail God's entire plan for our lives and everything from that moment forward is simply whatever God was able to cobble together from scraps. If we miss the "best" choice, how-ever, it means that there are still other shades of good and better paths available to us. "Best" implies a hierarchy of choices, where there may be one superior choice among any number of good ones, and even if we miss it, we still have a multiplicity of life-affirming, positive options at our disposal.

Obviously, there are certain instances where there truly is a straightforward right choice and a straightforward wrong one, like, "Should I cheat on my taxes?" or "Should I be kind to the new neighbors who are different from me?" or "Should I use the break room microwave to heat up fish?"

Far more often, however, what we actually face is an array of options of varying value. Many decisions, such as deciding which car to buy, which committees to serve on at church, or even what to do about a difficult family situation, rarely have a single "cor-rect" answer. Even a decision that sets you on one path as op-posed to an entirely different one, such as which school to attend or which job to take, doesn't usually come with an unambiguous set of "right" and "wrong" options.

For those who are natural people pleasers or who have been conditioned to perceive their value as being tied to their perfor-mance, this can be a difficult mental pivot. Even if we know that there are multiple options that could work out well, we still want to choose the "right" one to avoid letting everyone down. It's almost as if we are on *Let's Make a Deal* and the entire heavenly host is in the studio audience, yelling for us to select one particular door because, in their omniscience, they know how to avoid the one that hides the Zonk. We find ourselves faced with the weight of right or wrong, inside God's will or out of it, sheep or goats[5]—maybe even heaven or hell—with every single decision we make. The human soul was not created to exist in a state of perpetual crisis.

Yet that is exactly what IIL does to us; it leads us to pin eternal consequences to temporal choices and entraps us with artificially inflated stakes. By lessening those stakes whenever possible, we remove a lot of unnecessary pressure and show ourselves grace. When you are trapped in a world of Involuntary Internalized Legalism, it can feel like you were created only for unquestioning obedience to a formula when in reality you were created to thrive in the love of an infinite God who gifted you a capacity for knowledge, discernment, curiosity, wonder, imagination, kindness, ambition, passion, expression, connection, engagement, peacefulness, and wholeness. You were created for life, not for the law.

The human soul was not created to exist in a state of perpetual crisis

Whatever you are struggling to discern as the "right" path to living out your faith, remember that God's best for you is not a life hemmed in by fear. God's best for you is not being trapped by unnecessary impediments to Christ's grace. God's best for you is not a constant fear of rejection. God's best for you is not living a lie. God's best for you is not a theology that leads you to hate yourself. God's best for you is not a life defined by spiritual trauma.

You were created for something so much more beautiful, profound, and liberating than this, but there is no shame in struggling through spiritual anxiety on your journey toward it—because that shame isn't yours. It was a burden placed on you by someone else, and the fact that you internalized it is evidence of how profoundly you love God and how seriously you take your spirituality. Please keep that in mind as we move forward through this book. The root of the problem lies not with you but with the toxic systems that have complicated your birthright as a child of God to live a life of grace, love, and freedom.

4

DISCIPLINE—
CONTROL THROUGH FEAR

Content warning: discussions of corporal punishment,
suicidal ideation

The Murdstones—Edward and his sister Jane—loom large in
the pages of *David Copperfield*, Charles Dickens's 1850 coming-
of-age masterpiece. Clara Copperfield, David's loving, youthful,
widowed mother meets the handsome and seemingly charming
Mr. Murdstone at church. Despite the misgivings of her faithful housekeeper, Clara marries Mr. Murdstone, who promptly
moves his older sister into the house. Together, the siblings rule
the once-happy home with the iron rigidity typical of Dickensian
villains. Through a combination of physical violence and psychological manipulation, the Murdstones reduce Clara to a state of
anxious, terrified obedience and young David to a state of confused, nervous misery.

The cruelty of brother and sister, as David observes in his narration as a middle-aged man looking back at his childhood, was
not merely that of harsh personalities, but also a cruelty that

darkened the Murdstone religion, which was austere and wrathful. I have thought, since, that its assuming that character was a necessary consequence of Mr. Murdstone's firmness, which wouldn't allow him to let anybody off from the utmost weight of the severest penalties he could find any excuse for. Be this as it may, I well remember the tremendous visages with which we used to go to church, and the changed air of the place. Again, the dreaded Sunday comes round, and I file into the old pew first, like a guarded captive brought to a condemned service. Again, Miss Murdstone, in a black velvet gown, that looks as if it had been made out of a pall, follows close upon me; then my mother; then her husband. . . . Again, I listen to Miss Murdstone mumbling the responses, and emphasizing all the dread words with a cruel relish. Again, I see her dark eyes roll round the church when she says "miserable sinners," as if she were calling all the congregation names. Again, I catch rare glimpses of my mother, moving her lips timidly between the two, with one of them muttering at each ear like low thunder. Again, I wonder with a sudden fear whether it is likely that our good old clergyman can be wrong, and Mr. and Miss Murdstone right, and that all the angels in Heaven can be destroying angels. Again, if I move a finger or relax a muscle of my face, Miss Murdstone pokes me with her prayer-book, and makes my side ache. (chapter 4)

This strict discipline in the name of religion is carried over to the way Mr. Murdstone runs the home. "Firmness, I may observe," David tells the reader, "was the grand quality on which both Mr. and Miss Murdstone took their stand. . . . [I]t was another name for tyranny; and for a certain gloomy, arrogant, devil's humour, that was in them both. The creed, as I should state it now, was this. Mr. Murdstone was firm; nobody in his world was to be so firm as Mr. Murdstone; nobody else in his world was to be firm at all, for everybody was to be bent to his firmness."

David illustrates this point by describing a time when his nerves caused him to forget some lines of his lesson. Mr. Murdstone, who has been preparing a cane with which to beat the small boy, corners the child:

> "David," [Murdstone] said, making his lips thin, by pressing them together, "if I have an obstinate horse or dog to deal with, what do you think I do?"
> "I don't know."
> "I beat him."
> I had answered in a kind of breathless whisper, but I felt, in my silence, that my breath was shorter now.
> "I make him wince, and smart," [said Murdstone] "I say to myself, 'I'll conquer that fellow'"; and if it were to cost him all the blood he had, I should do it...."
> ... God help me, I might have been improved for my whole life, I might have been made another creature perhaps, for life, by a kind word at that season. A word of encouragement and explanation, of pity for my childish ignorance, of welcome home, of reassurance to me that it was home, might have made me dutiful to him in my heart henceforth, instead of in my hypocritical outside, and might have made me respect instead of hate him. I thought my mother was sorry to see me standing in the room so scared and strange. (chapter 4)

At the conclusion of the book, some thirty years and almost sixty chapters later, David runs into an old family acquaintance, Dr. Chillip, at a roadside inn, and the two reflect on days gone by. Eventually, the doctor mentions that Mr. Murdstone, having driven David's mother to an early grave, has once again remarried a cheerful, kindhearted woman, and "that her spirit has been entirely broken since her marriage, and that she is all but melancholy mad" (chapter 59).

Here, David asks the doctor the most damning question of all about Mr. Murdstone:

> "Does he gloomily profess to be (I am ashamed to use the word in such association) religious still?" I inquired.
>
> "Mrs. Chillip," he proceeded, in the calmest and slowest manner, "quite electrified me, by pointing out that Mr. Murdstone sets up an image of himself, and calls it the Divine Nature. . . .
>
> ". . . [W]hat such people miscall their religion, is a vent for their bad humours and arrogance. And do you know I must say, sir," he continued, mildly laying his head on one side, "that I DON'T find authority for Mr. and Miss Murdstone in the New Testament?"
>
> "I never found it either!" said I. (chapter 59)

Fear has been the most reliable way to control others since the dawn of time. Some of the earliest written accounts of human history document the exploits of kings and armies over other nations or the enactment of treaties where a weaker nation pledges its allegiance to a warlord for the sake of self-preservation. Off the battlefield, fear is still an effective way to control the masses by drawing their attention to the power of the unknown and inescapable; in religions around the globe, this often takes the form of rituals and symbols that invoke both the mystery and inevitability of death.

Because of the emphasis on a final judgment and the eternal destiny of the soul, Western Christianity quickly developed its own distinct form of *memento mori* (Latin for "remember that you must die"). By the early Middle Ages, hellmouths became a prominent motif in Anglo-Saxon art. Exactly what their title implies, hellmouths were gaping jaws of a grotesque animal or monster opened wide to swallow the souls of the damned. This visual device rapidly spread throughout Europe and was used widely in medieval art and architecture. Hellmouths also became standard set pieces for liturgical dramas and morality plays designed to bring to life stories from the Bible and cautionary tales about the perils of sin.

In the late medieval period, the *danse macabre*, or "dance of death," emerged as a trope in European art, which was an allegorical portrayal of death as an inevitable, inescapable pageant always unfurling around us that might envelop anyone at any time. On church walls across the continent, elaborate murals and frescoes of grinning skeletons parading and pirouetting through towns alongside the living highlight the undeniable fact that death is omnipresent, even in the midst of life. Woodcut illustrations in some of the earliest printed books feature this same motif—the terrible contrast of death and life that sought to remind the viewer of their own impending judgment.

Many of these same images continued to shape religious and cultural sensibilities for centuries. Ominous inscriptions from personified Death and skulls adorned with flowers feature prominently in a number of Italian and Spanish Renaissance paintings and seventeenth-century Dutch still lifes. Winged skulls appear on the earliest colonial gravestones in North America. Their somber, almost ghoulish presence contrasts greatly with more modern portrayals of *calvaeras*, or highly decorated "sugar skulls" popularized at the turn of the twentieth century by the whimsical illustrations of José Guadalupe Posada in honor of the Day of the Dead first celebrated in Mexico.

Though certain symbols have been reclaimed and rehabilitated in various cultures and practices, the traditional intention of *memento mori* was to shock the viewer into a contemplation upon their own mortality, followed by sober reflection or tearful repentance for sin. It was an attempt to control behavior through fear by forcing the viewer to feel dread for their immortal soul. These methods may seem rather transparent or even crass to modern viewers, but that does not mean they aren't still employed today—and not even in an altogether different form.

Whether it is the specific descriptions of each type of sinner who will suffer eternal torment or the rantings of a hellfire-and-brimstone preacher in a tent revival, this kind of preaching is a staple of the Western Christian mythos. Even more lurid, books (and the movies they inspired) depicting violent, horrific scenes of chaos at Armageddon are among the top grossers of the last fifty years. This kind of "rapture porn" (as it has been not-so-affectionately dubbed by people who grew up with it) is designed to do exactly what the medieval hellmouth, *danse macabre*, and Grim Reaper symbolism were trying to do for previous generations of believers. The goal is, quite literally, to "scare the hell out of you" and direct your thoughts heavenward instead.

These modern *memento mori* certainly achieve their objective. They have terrified generations of readers into a state of panicked repentance and hypervigilant "watchfulness" for the Second Coming of Christ. They have justified violence toward children in the name of "breaking the will to save the soul." They have rooted their message in a hell-avoidant theology rather than a Christ-focused one. And they have led to alienation, anxiety, and abuse among many of those exposed to such teachings. There is much debate on the theology of hell and which translations and cultural influences may have impacted our modern understanding of it. I'm choosing not to parse those here because the issue at hand is not hell itself but the spiritual anxiety caused by those who wield the idea of eternal damnation as a means of extracting obedience to a prescribed set of behaviors that may or may not actually be in line with the heart of God.

Christine[1] is one such believer who grew up surrounded by end-times ideology in her mainline Protestant church outside of Dallas. Her family had moved to the area from the East Coast so that her father could attend a large, prominent seminary that put a great deal of emphasis on dispensationalism, "so the Rapture was very,

very present in our lives," she explains. Now a lawyer in her mid-thirties, Christine looks back at her teenage years in the church youth group with a combination of sadness and gallows humor:

> I joke about it now, but if I got home from school and no one was there, one of my first thoughts was, "Oh my goodness—the Rapture happened, and I was left behind." My dad might have run to the hardware store for something to fix the lawn mower or my mom went to the grocery store, and my rational brain knew that, but until I saw someone or got a phone call or found a note, that was on my mind. I was worried until something objectively quelled that fear.
>
> I had all the books in the *Left Behind* series for kids—what were there, thirty or something?[2] It's a lot. My mom read all the books for adults. My parents were always watching the news, looking for signs of the antichrist because they were certain we were living in the end-times. We even used clay to make the creatures from the end-times prophecy in [the book of] Daniel. My parents believed that every generation had an antichrist in it, just in case *that* was the end-times, because the devil doesn't know when the Second Coming is going to happen. Only God does. I mean, you've got to make everything make sense, so there you go: an antichrist for every age. Problem solved.

Her church, and others like it, leaned heavily on fear as an evangelistic technique. "Every year at Halloween, we couldn't celebrate Halloween itself because it was the 'devil's holiday,'" Christine explains:

> But we would do a fall festival with Halloween-adjacent stuff like hay bales and pumpkins and leaves, and then the youth would be bused over to another church nearby that put on a "hell house," which was like a haunted house but it was

simulation of what hell was supposed to be—lots of people running around in *Scream* masks supposed to be demons and people with pitchforks, horns, and red paint on their faces. There were black lights and lots of screaming. Each room had the consequences of a different sin played out: people getting drunk or overdosing on drugs.

One room I remember vividly had a hospital bed with a young girl on it. She had had underage, premarital sex and gotten pregnant, and now she was miscarrying. There was a lot of red paint that was supposed to be blood. You just stood there and watched each scene unfold and then the demons would shuffle you to the next room.

The next to last room was really bright—it was supposed to show the stark contrast between heaven and hell. It was really light and there was happy music playing and the disciples and the apostles and Jesus were there, and God with a white beard (because that was obviously what God looked like, right?) and someone presented the Roman Road or some other series of scriptures that laid out the plan of salvation. Then you went into the last room where there were volunteers who would talk and pray with you if you wanted to be saved. It was all very clearly laid out as, "Do this, or this hell house is what is waiting for you."

Hell houses weren't the only scare tactic Christine's church employed, however. This was the early 2000s; the recent wave of school shootings—especially the one at Columbine High School in Colorado in 1999—was very much in the news. "After the shooting at Columbine, there was a lot of talk about being willing to die for your faith because if you reject Christ with a gun to your head, are you really a true Christian?"

The result of these discussions was that her church staged a mock shooting scenario one Wednesday night. Several people burst in yelling things about Christians and waving guns. The youth leader then stood up and explained that it wasn't real, but that it should make everyone think about what they would do in a similar scenario. "It was just a few minutes," Christine says. "Just long enough to scare the shit out of you. Then there was an altar call, and we were all challenged to consider what we would have said."

"I never knew the answer to that," she adds, "and it sort of ate at me."

The result of growing up steeped in a culture that used fear as currency was that faith had little to do with a relationship with Jesus, and everything to do with "just checking boxes. Faith is entirely transactional at that point," Christine explains. "As long as you don't breach the contract you made with God, you're in. You accept Christ because you don't want to end up in hell. . . . I grew up hearing 'Once saved, always saved,' but there were lots of things that Christians wouldn't do or shouldn't do, but people did anyway, so you wouldn't actually know for sure if you 'made it' until it was too late."

Christine's experience was far from unique; in fact, a number of people I spoke with shared similar memories. Some recalled visiting or volunteering to work in hell houses and the absolute conviction they felt at the time that this was how God wanted them to reach lost souls. One person even described a hell house that included a scene in an abortion clinic, with the aborted babies appearing at the end in the heaven room. Another shared stories of being shown films about the end-times at youth group lock-ins that were "basically horror movies" with nightmare-inducing demons and monsters and "so much blood."

"There are ways to talk about unpleasant realities in the world and the fallout from sin that don't involve exposing children to deeply scarring images or experiences," one person remarked. "I can't believe some of the awful things my parents were okay with me watching because it was in church so it was supposed to be teaching me valuable lessons. All it really did was plant horrible images in my brain that I couldn't unsee. That didn't make me love God or serve my neighbor more; it just made me feel afraid—all the time."

Several people I spoke with mentioned ominous lyrics in certain hymns that have troubled them in retrospect. "Jesus Is Coming Soon" was by far the most commonly mentioned; a number of people marveled at the fact that their church sang "many will meet their doom"[3] in a sprightly, four-part harmony every week as if that was a perfectly normal way to acknowledge (even celebrate?) eternal damnation.

Personally, the hymn that most stoked *my* anxiety was Eliza E. Hewitt's "When We All Get to Heaven." The sentiment is lovely, but as someone who lived in perpetual fear of losing my salvation, around the age of ten I started singing the chorus "*If* we all get to heaven" so that I wasn't being too presumptuous in case we didn't all make the cut—myself included.

I was also extremely worried about Matthew 12:31: "Therefore I tell you, people will be forgiven for every sin and blasphemy, but blasphemy against the Spirit will not be forgiven." As it turns out, I was not alone; a number of people I spoke to raised similar anxieties about this specific passage. What, exactly, does "blasphemy" mean, and what if you unwittingly or unwillingly commit it—is your soul just toast from that moment forward?

The term in Greek refers to using abusive language in the sense of slandering someone or disparagement by declaring something to be the opposite of its true nature. This verse has been parsed and debated for two millennia and there is still no clear-cut, commonly accepted explanation of exactly what it means. Does it refer to words spoken against the Holy Spirit, or (perhaps more convincingly) to actions done in the name of the Holy Spirit that go contrary to the nature of God, or is something missing from the context that might change its meaning altogether? With time, I have come to accept that the best we can do is to live our lives in such a way that we honor the Holy Spirit dwelling within us; accept that God knows our hearts, thoughts, and motivations; and trust that the grace of Jesus either covers every sin or it doesn't. But for most of my life, such a response would have been unthinkable. There simply was no room for nuance, mystery, or mercy.

Laura was part of a Christian pop band as a teenager in the 1990s but now works in a completely unrelated field, though she still attends church regularly and leads discipleship classes. As a middle schooler, she was badly bullied while grieving the loss of her grandmother, who had been like a second mother to her. "I said that I wanted to die, which I'm sure was very difficult for my parents to accept and handle, but in my mind, which I'm sure I didn't articulate well at the time, I thought, 'If I die, then I know I'm going to heaven. Jesus loves me, and my grandma loves me, and they're all going to be there, so it's a safe place.'"

Her parents took her to a child psychologist, who suggested that maybe Laura was under too much pressure at home. "They yanked me out of there," Laura said. "They didn't like the implication that there might be anything wrong with their parenting." Instead, her mother suggested Laura sit down with their pastor.

> Obviously, my mom was trying to do the right thing. None of what happened was her fault at all, but the pastor was older and a very black-and-white thinker. I explained everything to him the best I could at that age, and he said something that left me with nightmares for a long time. He said, "Well, you know, if you kill yourself, you're going to hell." In the church I grew up in, they believed that's what would happen because there wouldn't be the opportunity to repent for that act before you died. That terrified me, and I sat with that shame and guilt for a long time, not wanting to burden my parents with it. I didn't get any kind of counseling after that until I was in college, when there was a free student counseling center.

Instead of asking questions about why Laura was experiencing the emotions she was feeling or trying to understand what might be at the root of her young mind trying to make sense of a lot of turmoil, grief, and sadness, the pastor went straight for a response designed to scare Laura away from suicidal ideation. The result was an even deeper emotional wound that plagued Laura for years as she battled against her own internal monologue of confusion, guilt, and fear.

Another source of a great deal of anxiety was communion; this came up in interviews with almost everyone I spoke to from a Roman Catholic background. "You can't partake of the Eucharist if you are in a state of mortal sin," one person explained. "And I was taught that can be anything from having killed someone to using birth control with your spouse to being divorced."

It's definitely not only a source of Catholic anxiety, though. Communion is a "closed ritual" in many faith traditions, meaning that it is offered only to those who have completed the appropriate rites within the church; this has been the case in Christianity since at least the second century CE. But whereas some churches celebrate communion as a shared memorialization between committed believers of the grace and reconciliation made available in the resurrection, others regard it almost like a dare. Every week growing up, I listened to a different man from the congregation read the instructions for the Lord's Supper given in 1 Corinthians 11, and always ending with verses 27–29:

> So then, whoever eats the bread or drinks the cup of the Lord in an unworthy manner will be guilty of sinning against the body and blood of the Lord. Everyone ought to examine themselves before they eat of the bread and drink from the cup. For those who eat and drink without discerning the body of Christ eat and drink judgment on themselves.

In my mind, I imagined an "unworthy" person's soul shriveling up and turning to dust just like the Nazi sympathizer Walter

Donovan, who drinks from a false grail in *Indiana Jones and the Last Crusade*. And, it turns out, I was not alone.

"I was scared to death every time I went to take the little cup out of the tray," a friend remarked to me. "It felt like a test."

Another added, "I was too busy worrying that I wasn't being mindful enough of Christ and eating and drinking 'judgment unto myself' to actually think about the forgiveness and freedom Jesus was offering."[4]

Some fear, of course, can be a good thing. After all, fear is what has kept us alive long enough to continue the species: *Don't walk too near the edge of that cliff. Avoid those unfamiliar berries. Run away from snakes that make that shake-y noise with their tails.* There are some people who truly believe that fire-and-brimstone sermons, hell houses, and gory Rapture films are serving a similar purpose of saving lives and souls. But there is also a word for someone who takes pleasure in inflicting terror, pain, or humiliation on others: sadist.

Fear has been used to control people since the dawn of human history, but it seems especially horrific when it is done in the name of religion. The Spanish Inquisition, the various witch hunts in Europe and North America, the use of whips and metal collars to punish and restrain people under chattel slavery—these were all done in the name of saving souls for Christ (and possibly making some material gains on the side). This is, of course, not to imply that someone in a demon costume prodding you with a plastic pitchfork is on par with someone burning you at the stake or torturing you into subservience, but the principle behind the actions is the same: the manipulation of emotions for the sake of compliance. Playing up the fear of damnation or using the threat of extreme discipline in order to extract complete obedience and submission is an abuse of power designed to keep those in authority *in control*. The system protects the system.

But *how* does that system prime individuals to internalize messages of acquiescence? As we explore the issue of control through fear, I'd like to spend some time walking through a few of the biblical stories that are commonly invoked in these discussions: Moses getting water from the rock; Nadab and Abihu offering "strange fire" in the temple; Uzzah and the ark of the covenant; Achan and the hidden plunder; and Jephthah's oath.

These characters and stories are often held up as cautionary tales whose inclusion in the Bible is intended to illustrate to future generations the importance of following God's word to the letter. In many cases, however, we have been taught to read those stories through an agenda-driven lens that obscures their fuller meaning or implications. Simply by applying a new lens—either by stripping the old one and rereading the text without timeworn presuppositions or by considering the passage in its broader context—we may find alternate interpretations that paint a much different story than the one we've always been taught to find there.

Please allow me to pose a simple question: Why was Moses not allowed to enter the promised land?

In one of the greatest acts of apparent injustice in Scripture, we see that Moses, the man God called to confront Pharaoh, to produce the plagues, to lead the enslaved Hebrews out of Egypt and through the Red Sea, to receive the Ten Commandments, to guide the people through forty years of wanderings in the wilderness, to intervene on behalf of the people with God multiple times, to commission the ark of the covenant and the tabernacle—that man is forbidden from crossing the Jordan River into the promised land. Why?

As probably anyone who ever attended Sunday school or VBS can tell you, it's because instead of asking the rock to produce water, as God instructed, Moses struck it with his staff (Numbers 20:12).

And that, kids, is why it is essential that we follow God's word to the letter. Then we all went forth, a little more terrified of the Bully in the Sky who was just itching to punish us for the slightest deviation or misinterpretation or frustrated outburst.

It's a convenient, easy lesson on obedience—but that's not the full story. Numbers 20 recounts the infamous incident of Moses and Aaron at the rock of Meribah. Miriam has just died and been buried, and now the people are (reasonably) panicking, as they find themselves in the middle of the desert with no water to grow food, let alone to drink for survival:

> So they gathered together against Moses and against Aaron. The people quarreled with Moses and said, "Would that we had died when our kindred died before the LORD! Why have you brought the assembly of the LORD into this wilderness for us and our livestock to die here? Why have you brought us up out of Egypt to bring us to this wretched place? It is no place for grain or figs or vines or pomegranates, and there is no water to drink." Then Moses and Aaron went away from the assembly to the entrance of the tent of meeting; they fell on their faces, and the glory of the LORD appeared to them. The LORD spoke to Moses, saying, "Take the staff, and assemble the congregation, you and your brother Aaron, and command the rock before their eyes to yield its water. Thus you shall bring water out of the rock for them; thus you shall provide drink for the congregation and their livestock."
>
> So Moses took the staff from before the LORD, as he had commanded him. Moses and Aaron gathered the assembly together before the rock, and he said to them, "Listen, you rebels; shall we bring water for you out of this rock?" Then Moses lifted up his hand and struck the rock twice with his staff; water came out abundantly, and the congregation and their livestock drank. But the LORD said to Moses and Aaron, "Because you did not trust in me, to show my holiness before the eyes of the Israelites, therefore you shall not bring this assembly into the land that I have given them." These are the waters of Meribah, where the Israelites quarreled with the LORD and through which he showed himself to be holy. (Numbers 20:2–13)

CHAPTER 4

On its face, the "God demands literal obedience" interpretation is understandable, but this story is more complex than this overly simplified and moralized version most of us have been taught. First, let us consider that in Exodus 17:5–6, Moses *was* instructed to strike a rock for water, so his repetition of that action in this later instance is not at all unreasonable nor particularly rash. More significantly, however, when the history of the rebellion and subsequent wanderings of the Hebrew people is recounted in Deuteronomy 3:23–27, there is no mention of the rock-striking incident at all. Instead, Moses explains that when he asked God to let him cross the Jordan, "The LORD was angry with me on your account and would not heed me. The LORD said to me, 'Enough from you! Never speak to me of this matter again!'" (26). The sin that resulted in Moses's denial was the sin of the people, which God placed on Moses as their emissary. This is reinforced in Psalm 106:32–33, when the rebellion of the people is again vicariously shouldered by Moses:

> They angered the LORD at the waters of Meribah,
>> and it went ill with Moses on their account,
> for they made his spirit bitter,
>> and he spoke words that were rash.

Moses was not denied entry to the promised land because he failed to follow instructions but because he failed in leadership

In other words, Moses was not denied entry to the promised land because he failed to follow instructions but because he failed in leadership. The story is indeed a cautionary tale, but not about the high value of legalistic obedience; it is a warning to those in power of a religious body that they will be held to a higher standard.

The story of Nadab and Abihu's deaths may also be familiar as one trotted out in the name of radical obedience. According to Exodus 28:1, Aaron and his four sons (Nadab, Abihu, Eleazar, and Ithamar) were appointed by God as the first priests in the tabernacle established for the Hebrew people during their years in the wilderness. Nadab and Abihu had an especially privileged position in that they were among the select group who, along with Moses and Aaron, were permitted to ascend Mount Sinai to witness the presence of God without harm (Exodus 24:1–2, 9–11). But some time later, these two priests did something in the course of worship that resulted in dramatic consequences and made their names forever synonymous with divine punishment:

> Aaron's sons Nadab and Abihu took their censers, put fire in them and added incense; and they offered unauthorized fire before the LORD, contrary to his command. So fire came out from the presence of the LORD and consumed them, and they died before the LORD. (Leviticus 10:1–2 NIV)

This short, unembellished story has been parsed for millennia to examine every minuscule detail of what that "unauthorized" fire might have been. For branches of the faith that place a heavy emphasis on traditions, such as specific ways of dressing or a highly codified worship style as a hallmark of devotion, this story is often held up as proof that introducing something new to religious practices is both dangerous and sinful. Even in less tradition-driven denominations, however, it is often taught as yet another example of why anything other than radical, literal obedience to God's commands will result in swift spiritual (if not physical) death.

But in the rush to use this story as a means of demanding obedience, toxic religious systems tend to overlook a crucial fact: It is not a story about average people who displeased God in their everyday lives, but about priests who misused their positions of authority.[5] The story of Nadab and Abihu is not about a layperson making a misstep; it is about God's response to religious leaders who overreach the parameters of their power.

It is also possible that the story of Uzzah, who was struck dead by God for touching the ark of the covenant, has a similarly misapplied moral. In 2 Samuel 6:3–9 and 1 Chronicles 13:7–11, Uzzah and his brother Ahio drive the oxcart that transports the ark to Jerusalem on King David's orders after its decades-long exile from the center of Jewish worship. The celebration takes a tragic turn, however: "When they came to the threshing floor of Nacon, Uzzah reached out his hand to the ark of God and took hold of it, for the oxen lurched. The anger of the LORD was kindled against Uzzah, and God struck him there, and he died there beside the ark of God" (2 Samuel 6:6–7).

The story of Nadab and Abihu is not about a layperson making a misstep; it is about God's response to religious leaders who overreach the parameters of their power

The seemingly unnecessary violence toward this well-intentioned act seems highly unnecessary; even David "was angry because the LORD had burst forth with an outburst upon Uzzah" (2 Samuel 6:8). Countless sermons and commentaries have sought to parse the reasoning behind this apparent injustice, with the conclusion inevitably falling into one or both of the following camps: Uzzah was killed either because (1) he was in violation of the clear directives given in Numbers 4 because he was transporting the ark by cart rather than by special poles, or (2) because God ordered no one to touch the ark—no exceptions. It's a chilling story; when we fail to take God's commands seriously, we must pay the price. It doesn't matter that Uzzah was showing reverence in trying to keep the ark from hitting the ground. "God demands our obedience," according to this reasoning, "not our excuses."

Interestingly, however, the story of Uzzah may be less about zero-tolerance obedience and more of a warning against entitlement in religious practice. You see, for the past twenty years, the ark had been stored in the home of Abinadab, who just so happened to be the father of Uzzah and Ahio (1 Samuel 7:1–2). Perhaps God's anger was kindled not because Uzzah tried to prevent the ark from falling but because he had assumed a posture of special license or personal ownership toward the sacred object that had been with his family for so long that he believed the rules no longer applied to him. After all, if the punishment had to do with the mode of transportation, why was Ahio not also struck down? It was only the person who presumed special privilege by touching the ark who was punished.

Is this not a pattern we have seen repeated over and over in our own culture ad nauseam? A person assumes that their position of leadership in the church affords them special privileges that they condemn in others, like televangelist Kenneth Copeland, who lives a notoriously lavish lifestyle that includes private jets (which he claims allow him to remain closer to Jesus and protected from demons) and has a personal net worth of somewhere between $300 million and $760 million.[6] Or maybe nepotism is at play, and when a person assumes the legacy of a prominent relative, they proceed to treat it as their own personal source for wealth and pleasure, like Jerry Falwell Jr.'s debauched and tabloid-worthy presidency of Liberty University, the evangelical Christian college his father co-founded in 1971.[7] What if Uzzah was acting out of a similar sense of carte blanche or inherited entitlement because of his family's ties to the ark? What if the story is actually an admonition against acting out of privilege? What if the lesson we are meant to take from Uzzah's death is not that the road to hell is paved with good intentions, but that those in power who place themselves above the rules are special targets for God's wrath?

What if the story is actually an admonition against acting out of privilege?

What are we to make of God's wrath, after all? In an effort to rehabilitate religion from old traditions that were blatantly rooted in scare tactics, well-intentioned people will often point to Ecclesiastes 12:13: "The end of the matter; all has been heard.

Fear God, and keep his commandments, for that is the whole duty of everyone." The point of this passage, as it is explained from this angle, "doesn't mean to be afraid of God, but to revere God."

The only problem is that the verb, *yera*, translated here as "fear," literally means to hold something in awestruck terror. It comes from the word *yare'*, which is the same verb used more than three hundred times throughout the Hebrew Scriptures to mean literal fear (e.g., Genesis 3:10, when Adam and Eve hid from God after they sinned; and 1 Samuel 7:7, when the army of Israel is afraid of the Philistines).

When the discussion of fear in Ecclesiastes 12:13 is invoked, however, it is rarely done so with an eye toward its fuller context. In conjunction with the verse that follows, it reads: "The end of the matter; all has been heard. Fear God, and keep his commandments, for that is the whole duty of everyone. For God will bring every deed into judgment, including every secret thing, whether good or evil" (Ecclesiastes 12:13–14). The reason we are to fear God is not because God is inherently terrible but because God can bring every hidden thing to light. *In other words, the thing we ought to be afraid of is not God but the revelation of our own hypocrisy.*

Now, I freely admit that the idea of having all our inner thoughts broadcast absolutely ratchets up anxiety for people who already struggle with feelings of being spiritual failures—unless you consider the matter this way: Those who struggle with spiritual anxiety have usually made a habit of confessing their sins to God frequently (even constantly); therefore, their sins and shortcomings *are not hidden.* The people who actually have something to fear are those who have been deluding themselves, hiding their motives, or lying to God about the state of their hearts and minds. It is the people who abuse power under the guise of

It is the people who abuse power under the guise of doing God's will who have the most to lose and the most to fear when what is done in secret is exposed

doing God's will who have the most to lose and the most to fear when what is done in secret is exposed.

Turning aside from stories of leadership accountability, let us now consider two often-invoked biblical stories that pose far more complicated and challenging questions surrounding divine discipline and unhesitating obedience: Achan and Jephthah.

Joshua 6–7 recounts the story of Achan, who secretly withheld some gold, silver, and a beautiful garment taken in the fall of Jericho, despite orders that all plunder must be turned over to God. The impact of this act is felt by the entire nation when it loses the subsequent battle of Ai because divine favor was withdrawn as a result of Achan's sin. Through the casting of lots, the guilty party is finally unmasked, Achan confesses to the crime, and the contraband goods are found buried beneath his tent:

> Then Joshua, together with all Israel, took Achan son of Zerah, the silver, the robe, the gold bar, his sons and daughters, his cattle, donkeys and sheep, his tent and all that he had, to the Valley of Achor. Joshua said, "Why have you brought this trouble on us? The LORD will bring trouble on you today."
>
> Then all Israel stoned him, and after they had stoned the rest, they burned them. (Joshua 7:24–25 NIV)

Is there any person who grew up attending church who does not recall being taught this story as a child? It seems it is trotted out any time there is a discussion of noncompliance, secret sin, or why some prayers go unanswered. Achan, his children, and even his domesticated livestock are all stoned to death and their carcasses burned outside the camp. "And that," the lesson concludes, "is the price for disobeying God's commands."

"Even his children and animals?"

"That's what the Bible says. There is no room for sin among God's chosen people."

And so we are sent off into the world, clutching our Sunday school worksheets and story Bibles and wondering if the cookie we snuck before dinner last night means God wants our entire family—including Fluffy and Fido—dead. This is the same God, by the way, who we were taught commanded "Thou shalt not kill" (Exodus 20:13) and also the same God who is, supposedly, the very essence of love (1 John 4:8).

And we wonder why people feel confused, conflicted, and concerned about how they might incur God's wrath.

We see a similarly problematic story in the account of Jephthah and his daughter in Judges 11–12. Jephthah was an unlikely leader. The son of a prostitute who was driven out of the family by the sons of his father's wife, Jephthah worked as an armed bandit before attacks from the Ammonites led the elders of his former community to invite him back, promising to make him ruler of Israel if he succeeded in defeating their enemies. Jephthah agrees and succeeds in driving back the warring tribes. But in the midst of his campaign, he makes a vow to God, swearing, "'If you will give the Ammonites into my hand, then whatever comes out of the doors of my house to meet me, when I return victorious from the Ammonites, shall be the LORD's, to be offered up by me as a burnt offering" (Judges 11:30–31).

According to the book of Judges, "Jephthah crossed over to the Ammonites to fight against them, and the LORD gave them into his hand" (11:32). Upon his return home, however, the first thing to greet him was his only child, a daughter, who is celebrating his victory with music and dancing. When Jephthah realizes his predicament, he tears his clothes in grief, but his daughter responds:

> "My father, if you have opened your mouth to the LORD, do
> to me according to what has gone out of your mouth, now

that the LORD has given you vengeance against your enemies, the Ammonites." And she said to her father, "Let this thing be done for me: grant me two months, so that I may go and wander on the mountains and bewail my virginity, my companions and I."

"Go," he said, and he sent her away for two months. So she departed, she and her companions, and bewailed her virginity on the mountains. At the end of two months, she returned to her father, who did with her according to the vow he had made. She had never slept with a man. (11:36–39)

Jewish and Christian apologists alike have wrestled with the complexities this story introduces. Many take it at face value as a warning against making rash oaths. Others point out that the Hebrew of Jephthah's vow could be translated "whatever comes out of the doors of my house to meet me, when I return victorious from the Ammonites, shall be the LORD's, *or will be* offered up by me as a burnt offering"; according to this interpretation, Jephthah's daughter takes two months to mourn giving up married life and motherhood before being consecrated to serve in the tabernacle as a virgin prophetess. And, of course, there are some religious leaders who draw ringing parallels to the story of Abraham's willingness to sacrifice Isaac when God tests him and commend Jephthah for maintaining his promise even at great personal loss to himself.*

Never mind that God reiterates throughout the Bible the vileness and depravity of child sacrifices, mentioning more than twenty times in the Hebrew Scriptures the evil of this practice "which I did not command, and it did not come into my mind" (Jeremiah 7:31). And yet, somehow, there are those who see fit to

* Interestingly, what one rarely hears in toxic church environments regarding this story are discussions about one group of people's bodies bearing the consequences of others' decisions. (For more on control through power imbalances, see chapter 10.)

elevate this story as illustrative of the kind of extreme obedience of God expects of us—as if the greater evil would have been to let the innocent party live than to refuse to participate in a horrific act of violence in God's name.

For those who have been controlled by narratives designed to invoke mortal fear at the thought of anything short of legalistic adherence to the Bible as a code of conduct, it is worth considering this: In the case of both Achan and Jephthah, any preacher who spends more energy trying to explain why the stoning of innocent people or sacrifice of a child is justifiable rather than on the horror of the act itself and the cultural anxieties the story reveals is someone whose moral judgment should be called into question. In defending the Bible's inerrancy, they have convicted God of immorality.

In defending the Bible's inerrancy, they have convicted God of immorality

Some people will argue that it is irresponsible to read twenty-first-century values onto ancient texts, but it is equally irresponsible to enforce ancient values in twenty-first-century society and call it integrity.

As we consider what should be an immutable truth—that violence carried out upon children is expressly and unambiguously contrary to the heart of God—we must also consider the way that church-sanctioned extreme physical discipline has been invoked as a way of controlling children and adults alike through fear.

"Christian domestic discipline" is a concept that is alive and well in certain circles, which argue that "male headship" gives men both the right and responsibility to carry out corporal punishment on every member of their household seen to be in rebellion. Lest anyone suppose that this is an old practice that no one actually believes in anymore, a quick online search reveals advocates actively publishing defenses and how-to guides on the practice (including public humiliation and punitive spanking of wives—separate from any BDSM or other sexual practices)—as recently as a month prior from when I am writing this in December 2022.

Though we will discuss misogyny in the name of God in chapter 9, it is important to acknowledge that manipulation through fear on the basis of gender is alive and well in some religious traditions. For now, however, I want to focus on discipline as a means of control through fear for children.

Michael, a middle-aged father of two, recalls his own strict upbringing in a fundamentalist Christian family that relied heavily on corporal punishment for maintaining order. "Three of the four people who looked after me as a kid [parents and grandparents] hit me with wooden spoons, paddles, or belts," he explains. "They were all professing Christians who read the Bible and prayed over me before those beatings, and they said it was their duty as Christian parents to discipline me however they needed to to make sure I didn't fall away from God in rebellion."

The physical abuse continued throughout Michael's adolescence. His father, especially, he says, would fly into rages that were all explained away as being one of his God-given rights as head of the household. "I remember being a sophomore in high school and being afraid to get undressed in the locker room because I didn't want anyone to see the bruises and welts they left," Michael says:

I wasn't a bad kid. I wasn't getting into trouble. This was just for typical dumb kid stuff like forgetting to take out the trash or losing my gloves or something. And every time he'd say, "I'm doing this because I love you. I'm doing this because this is what the Bible says parents are supposed to teach their children right from wrong."

Well, what's that going to do to a kid except make them scared all the time? If [an adult] is going to live by a book that says it's okay to whip an eight-year-old kid with a belt—not just okay but their *right*—just because he lied about doing his homework, he *might* start doing his homework or he might start lying more so he doesn't get beat again. And then he starts hating himself because he's lying all the time and God hates liars, so now what? . . . You don't see how a God like that could ever love you.

Michael describes a childhood that left him terrified of God's punishment and equally terrified of God's love because the two looked indistinguishable. "You've seen what his 'love' supposedly looks like," he says. "You end up either with a lot of anger or you just keep being scared your whole life, because those feelings have to go somewhere."

Michael's story is, unfortunately, not uncommon. It seems every few months, some new story hits the headlines of children discovered locked in a home and subjected to extreme, even deadly, religious discipline. But there are far more stories that never make the news—stories less sensational but every bit as real and every bit as damaging for the victims' physical and emotional well-being. Stories inside our own communities, our own churches, and even our own families.

Over the past thirty years, a number of studies have been conducted on the sharp rise in literature on faith-based authoritarian parenting from the early 1970s to mid-1990s—essentially codified texts of disciplinary practices long practiced in certain religious circles. The problem with these manuals and books is that, as one such study cited, "contemporary understandings of biblical 'literalism,' and their elective affinity with both 'authority-mindedness' and beliefs that human nature is fundamentally sinful" serve to normalize and promote "conservative Protestant childrearing practices that diverge sharply from those recommended by contemporary mainstream experts."[8]

The study went on to outline various approaches advanced by half-a-dozen prominent Christian parenting and family advocates. The article summarized their philosophies as follows:

Because children initially understand God in terms of parental images, conservative Protestants suggest that children will infer God's view of them based on the treatment they receive from their parents. . . . These writers are quick to point out that parents should teach their children by example that God is loving, merciful, and forgiving. . . . At the same time, however, because God's punishment of sin is understood as inevitable and consistent, they also believe that parental discipline should embody these characteristics as well. . . . Given such convictions, conservative Protestants argue that the experience of loving physical discipline (1) helps the child to develop an appropriate, accurate image of God, and (2) underscores the importance of obedience to His authority. Thus, corporal punishment is believed to demonstrate to the young child that deviation from biblical principles will provoke consistent and inevitable reproof from authorities in this life and from God in the next ("the wages of sin is death"). By contrast, obedient children who are able to avoid chastisement are said to learn that a strict adherence to biblical principles will ensure God's blessing.[9]

What are we to make of the anguish that fear-based control can generate? It is clearly meant to manipulate our emotions into a strong response, but is the resulting mental and spiritual suffering truly pleasing to God? The response it elicits is almost certainly not the sincere repentance by which we ask for and receive forgiveness so that we might move forward with our lives. Much more likely, it instead invokes churning emotions and ongoing agony over our shortcomings. It is a state of continual soul-turmoil that leaves us exhausted, miserable, and heartsick. We want to believe that there is a place of safety and rest for us within God's will. We want to release the angst we have lived with for far too long. We want to believe that whatever we were taught about fearing God was misguided.

Even when we catch a moment of peace or a breath of reprieve, at some point, that chiding, nagging voice inevitably comes back: *But the Bible says . . .*

Does it, though? We've already considered a number of cases where maybe the Bible doesn't actually say what we've been taught to believe it does. I'd like to propose to you one more: the most popular verse among those who subscribe to extreme discipline in the name of God is Proverbs 13:24, which states, "Those who spare the rod hate their children, but those who love them are diligent to discipline them." The Hebrew word translated here as "rod" is *shebet*, which can mean a rod or club, as it is used in Exodus 21:20, where punishment is demanded of anyone who kills their "male or female slave" after beating them with a *shebet*.[10] This passage should turn the reader's stomach for a number of reasons, but focusing strictly on the discipline aspect, it should trouble us that the verse in question is implying that a child ought to be beaten with an implement recognized as being capable of causing death.

Interestingly, though, *shebet* can also be interpreted to mean "scepter" (Genesis 49:10; Numbers 24:17) and even "tribe," as it is used more than twenty times in the Hebrew Scriptures. Scholars believe that the word originally meant a branch, so its metaphorical application to describe the family groups (or "branches") of the people of Israel makes sense. It is interesting to consider how the verse might read if this latter definition were applied instead: "Those who avoid the tribe hate their children." Suddenly, instead of corporal punishment, the verse encourages turning to the community for guidance and correction. Rather than a passage that promotes child abuse in the home, it becomes another form of the African proverb: "It takes a village to raise a child."

This interpretation also makes sense paired with the second half of the verse, which asserts that "those who love them are diligent to discipline them." The word translated "discipline" is *shachar*, which literally means to search or seek diligently. It is the same verb used in Proverbs 8:17, where Wisdom personified says, "I love those who love me, and those who *seek me diligently* find me," and again in Proverbs 11:27, which states, "Whoever *diligently seeks* good seeks favor, but evil comes to the one who searches for it." David uses *shachar* in Psalm 63:1, when he writes: "O God, you are my God; *I seek you*; my soul thirsts for you; my flesh faints for you, as in a dry and weary land where there is no water." This word, which has been rendered in English as "discipline" and twisted to justify abuse, actually conjures up images more akin to the good shepherd seeking the lost sheep in Matthew 18. The implication is that the child is being lovingly pursued to bring them back into the fold with the rest of the community with whom they have relationships rather than beaten with a weapon in order to break their spirit.

How differently this scripture reads simply by changing the lens through which it is interpreted. For those who would insist upon biblical literalism, the words have not changed at all—only the values we read onto them. It still implies that a loving parent will provide their child with attentive and swift guidance, direction, and correction; the only difference is the spirit behind these actions. The essence of the verse has not changed, just the method. This reading is certainly not the traditional one, but— *what if it were?* How differently might Christian history have played out—how differently might your own story have played out—if Proverbs 13:24 had been translated as a passage advocating restorative justice rather than an easy and convenient justification for asserting power over someone more vulnerable?

If your relationship with faith (or with people of faith) has been grounded in fear, it will probably take some work to overcome that conditioning. If you can't yet release your fears, let down your defenses, or find peace in the presence of the Divine— that's okay. By kicking into overdrive, your mind is doing exactly what it was created to do in order to protect you in dangerous situations, and it's not easy to override biology. And fear is not a sin. Just know that the fear that was forced upon you by someone

The words have not changed at all—only the values we read onto them

else is *their* failure, not yours. If what 1 John 4:18 says is true, that "there is no fear in love, but perfect love casts out fear; for fear has to do with punishment, and whoever fears has not reached perfection in love," then if the way someone expresses "love" is actually causing a chronic, unhealthy anxiety about God, it's probably not perfect and it's probably not from God—no matter what they claim.

Micah 4 lays out a beautiful vision of a peaceful world in which there is no violence, and the people "shall beat their swords into plowshares / and their spears into pruning hooks" (4:3). In this renewed creation, people are eager to approach the temple in order to learn and grow (4:1–2). They are taught, corrected, and blessed by the grace and wisdom of godly instruction in a manner compatible with this world of utter tranquility. And in the end, they rest peacefully "under their own vines and under their own fig trees, and *no one shall make them afraid. For all the peoples walk, each in the name of its god, but we will walk in the name of the LORD our God forever and ever" (4:4–5, emphasis added).

In this new Eden, where God's people are gathered together, there is no fear *specifically because of* the sovereign presence of God. It is the act of walking with God that brings about this state of peace, nothing else—not scare tactics, not violence, not condemnation, not threats, not punishment, not manipulation, not fear. Just God. Only God.

5

DOGMA—CONTROL
THROUGH INDOCTRINATION

Zora Neale Hurston was one of the preeminent voices in the Harlem Renaissance, the intellectual revolution of African American culture that flowered in the Harlem area of upper Manhattan in the 1920s and 1930s. Pulling from her own childhood experiences in Eatonville, Florida, a predominantly Black town outside Orlando, Hurston was a profoundly gifted scholar, writer, and filmmaker. As a literary anthropologist and ethnographer educated first at Barnard College and then Columbia University at a time when educational opportunities for women of color were limited, Hurston dedicated her life to documenting the folklore, customs, and dialects of formerly enslaved people in the Deep South, capturing their voices and traditions in her numerous novels, plays, poems, and academic articles.

One of Hurston's most famous and influential works is her 1937 novel of female self-discovery, *Their Eyes Were Watching God*. In it, the protagonist, Janie, struggles to find her authentic self after being shaped and controlled for so long by the people and circumstances that surround her. Some had acted out of selfish motives and others from a legitimate dread of the world, but these manipulations were always done under the guise of order, protection, or looking out for Janie's best interest.

As a middle-aged Janie reflects on the course of her life thus far, she has a realization about the grandmother who raised her. Nanny's own life had been shaped by the combined traumas of slavery, rape, and the lived experience of a woman of color in the Jim Crow era, so her fear-based response of trying to shape and control every aspect of Janie's life made sense. Janie, however, can now see the profound damage that such a tight, insulated view of life could have on an individual who was deliberately shut off from so much of the world and so severely chastised when she sought more:

> She had been getting ready for her great journey to the horizons in search of *people*; it was important to all the world that she should find them and they find her. But she had been whipped like a cur dog, and run off down a back road after *things*. It was all according to the way you see things. Some people could look at a mud puddle and see an ocean with ships. But Nanny belonged to that other kind that loved to deal in scraps. Here Nanny had taken the biggest thing God had ever made, the horizon—for no matter how far a person can go the horizon is still way beyond you—and pinched it in to such a little bit of a thing that she could tie it about her granddaughter's neck tight enough to choke her. She hated the old woman who had twisted her so in the name of love.[1]

Whatever Nanny's intentions or the forces that shaped her thinking, Janie finds herself almost forty years old and barely able to imagine a life where she makes her own decisions. That capacity had been drilled out of her before she could even fully understand what it really meant. Janie made impulsive decisions here and there, but always under the influence of someone else. She had never learned how to become an independent, whole person with thoughts and opinions of her own that she could confidently express out loud. In trying to protect her, Nanny had stripped Janie of the chance to question, explore, and develop curiosity about the world beyond her own experience.

Sometimes, our own deeply held beliefs lead us to controlling or limiting the world of those with less power; other times, however, they can lead to the willful rejection of anything that does not fit the convenient or comfortable narrative by which we live— even at the cost of basic human decency or compassion for suffering and struggling souls.

In 1968, Colombian writer Gabriel García Márquez published a short story entitled "The Very Old Man with Enormous Wings," in which a decrepit angel tumbles to earth during a rainstorm and lands in the muddy yard belonging to Pelayo, Elisenda, and their baby. Because the celestial visitor is so different from everyone's expectation of what an angel should look like—weak, injured, dirty, speaking in a foreign tongue, and responsible for only disappointing miracles—they first want to club him or at least send him away. Eventually, however, they decide to keep the angel locked in a chicken coop and charge admission to see him. Some neighbors propose ideas for making the angel a vastly powerful political or military leader, while the local priest of this coastal backwater is disappointed that the angel "did not understand the language of God or know how to greet His ministers."[2] The priest writes to his superiors for advice, but they only seem concerned with what value they can draw from a parade of meaningless questions and the settling of pointless doctrinal debates that do not relate to the more pressing issue regarding the treatment and fate of the injured angel: "They spent their time finding out if the prisoner had a navel, if his dialect had any connection with Aramaic, how many times he could fit on the head of a pin, or whether he wasn't just a Norwegian with wings."

Not long afterward, a carnival comes through town with a sideshow that features a woman transformed into a spider for disobeying her parents. The villagers' interest and concern shift to this more sensational (and cheaper) form of entertainment and edification. Still, Pelayo and Elisenda have made enough money off of the angel for Pelayo to quit his job and establish a side venture, for Elisenda to purchase an extravagant new wardrobe, and for the family to build "a two-story mansion with balconies and gardens and high netting so that crabs wouldn't get in during the winter, and with iron bars on the windows so that angels wouldn't get in." The old angel, however, remains nothing more than a prisoner in their yard whom the child is warned not to approach (even though he does anyway).

After several years, the angel has regained his health and begins miraculously appearing in the house, though the family drives him back out to the yard with brooms. Finally, one day, as Elisenda is preparing lunch, she notices the old angel testing out his wings before flying clumsily away. She makes no effort to stop him; in fact, "Elisenda let out a sigh of relief, for herself and for him, when she watched him pass over the last houses . . . no longer an annoyance in her life." Her family has extracted what value they could from the celestial visitor, unwelcomed because his presence and undeniable reality upended so much of what the villagers *wanted* to believe about the heavenly realm.

People love being right almost as much as they hate being wrong. One of the very first stories in the entire Bible is of Cain murdering Abel because he was angry that Abel's sacrifice was more acceptable than his own. Whether it is seeking approval from our parents, friends, teachers, bosses, religious leaders, or even God, we want assurance that we are on the side of power.

This is one reason why conspiracy theories are so popular; people want to believe that they are the ones who have it all figured out, who broke the code, who peeked behind the curtain, who are smarter than everyone else, who are somehow "special-er," who are on the winning side. In religious circles, this kind of "anointed one" thinking leads directly to dogmatism, arrogance, and even fanaticism. We see it all the time. People claim that they uncovered a secret code in the Bible or figured out the exact date of the Second Coming; celebrity pastors insist that their hot take on some issue is the only thing standing between you and the blessings you long for; denominations claim that their approach to salvation or style of worship are the *only* tickets to heaven—as if God were a puzzle to be solved and human existence were an escape room that must be cracked before we can make our exit to the next life.

There's nothing wrong with pushing back against mainstream thought or trying to "do faith" better than the status quo; that's the point of the books like this one, after all—to challenge lazy, incomplete, or toxic teachings that have taken over many churches and redefined Christianity as something far removed from the heart of Christ. But spiritual abuse occurs when a person, organization, or system presents a narrow set of subjective beliefs as the boundaries of reality and then demands strict and unquestioning adherence to it. That's where the line between doctrine and indoctrination becomes blurred. No longer are people allowed to think for themselves; they are handed a confining, blindered view of reality and told that any other perspective is dangerous, untrue, or inherently sinful. And if those ironclad beliefs are ever challenged, it usually does not end well for the dissenter.

In 1615, fifteen women in the town of Leonberg, Germany, were charged with witchcraft and brought to trial on the order of Lutherus Einhorn, the *vogt*, or administrative lord, of the city. Germany had been Protestant for nearly a century at that point, yet many practices had not changed at all—including execution for those found guilty of witchcraft. Among the accused was a woman named Katharina Kepler, who had supposedly given another woman a potion that made her sick after the two had a disagreement. The real reason for Katharina's arrest, many people believed, was actually the theological beliefs of her son, the esteemed astronomer and mathematician, Johannes Kepler.

The younger Kepler had run amok of Lutheran authorities for advocating the same ideas that would soon land Italian astronomer Galileo Galilei in trouble with the Catholic Church: heliocentrism, or the theory that the earth orbits the sun rather than the other way around.

In 1539, Martin Luther had learned of the heliocentric theory Nicholas Copernicus was developing and condemned it before Copernicus's findings were even published. Kepler's defense of those ideas some seventy years later cost him a university teaching position because his theology was deemed too problematic and in violation of Lutheran doctrine at the time.

Unwilling to deny what he knew was fact, despite his deep personal faith, Kepler continued his astronomical study and eventually discovered, among other landmark findings, the three laws of planetary motion. Nevertheless, he was excommunicated by the Lutheran Church in 1613 for advocating the theory that the moon was a solid body, which church leaders maintained stood in contrast with Genesis 1:16: "God made the two great lights—the greater light to rule the day and the lesser light to rule the night—and the stars."

Katharina Kepler's arrest for witchcraft in 1615 was seen as a political move intended to intimidate, humiliate, and discredit her son, who defended her at her trial. Eight of the women arrested with her were found guilty and executed, but Katharina was spared and went to live with her son in Linz, some 250 miles to the west in Austria. When she finally returned home almost four years later, Katharina was arrested again and held in prison for over a year with threats of torture. She never confessed to any of the charges against her, nor was any credible evidence ever produced, and her son was finally able to arrange her release in October 1621. Katharina died six months later, regarded by the local religious leaders as collateral damage in their effort to control a man who believed in a creation that did not fit their own vision of the Creator.

The persecution of the Kepler family by religious authorities raises a fundamental truth: When believers are called to be faithful, this does not mean faith in the institution itself but in the thing the institution represents. As many Christians love to remind each other, "You can't 'go to church'; you *are* the church. The building is not the church—the people are." In the same way, the institution itself or denominational affiliation is not the one to Whom we owe our ultimate allegiance. We don't worship the name on the sign. (At least, we're not supposed to.)

But this is where discussions about dogma can get sticky because we generally choose our religious affiliations based, at least in part, on the philosophies and practices that make them unique from other bodies of worshippers within the same broader body of faith. So, to some degree, we are all making dogmatic choices based on what we hold to be the "right way" to be in Christian community with other believers, worship God, and live our faith. Doctrinal differences are not inherently abusive, but the ways in which they are shared, advanced, or enforced can be.

When we speak of "Christian orthodoxy," this usually implies matters of belief that are considered fundamental to the religion itself. What we don't always consider is that these various beliefs were not all firmly established during the lifetimes of Jesus or the apostles, or even in the first few centuries after they lived. This is true even for issues as seemingly basic to modern believers as the nature of Christ (fully man? fully God? fully God *and* fully man? a fifty-fifty split? a man chosen by God to take on a divine role?) or which of the multiplicity of Christian writings that were circulating throughout the Mediterranean by the fourth century CE, from Spain to Syria, Turkey to Tunisia, Egypt to Ethiopia, should be included

When believers are called to be faithful, this does not mean faith in the institution itself but in the thing the institution represents

in what eventually became known as the New Testament. These topics were all studied, debated, and written on over hundreds of years while multiple ecumenical councils of church leaders from various locales met every few decades to debate the latest controversy, hammer out the wording of assorted creeds, and establish a set of overarching doctrines that we now take for granted as the basic tenets of Christianity. In fact, as various denominational movements and schisms up through the present day show us, many of these terms are *still* not universally agreed upon.

The point is that "Christian orthodoxy" is not a simple, clear monolith that was unambiguously established once and then grew steadily more corrupted or deteriorated over the following two thousand years. This is important to establish when critiquing dogma in the church. No one is saying that unless Christianity throws out every single core belief it is too controlling. Of course there need to be certain uniting beliefs in addition to different personal or denominational interpretations; the problem comes when people use those differences as a basis for exclusion, rejection, division, or damnation.

It is true, however, that there have *always* been differing doctrines on which beliefs and practices are orthodox and which are not, and on who gets to set the terms of orthodoxy in the first place. Each denomination, sect, or independent congregation absolutely has a right to operate according to the principles that it believes are the best reflection of what God wants for the church. But here's the catch—individuals have that right as well. And what's more, every church and every person has the right to believe and operate according to their conscience *so long as the expression of their religion does not cause harm to someone else.* As the old saying goes, "Your rights end where mine begin." And harm can be difficult to quantify.

Many of us come from environments where independent thinking was forbidden (or at least discouraged) in favor of the dictates of the group, or more specifically, the leaders of the group. To be part of the community meant to believe exactly as the rest of the community believed. It was an "us versus them" mentality where "us" meant "our very specific and prescriptive set of beliefs" and "them" meant anyone outside that bubble, including—maybe *especially*—other people who also claimed the name of Christ. Expressions like "Our God works wonders" often mean just that: "Ours, not yours." It is an "ours" with limits, boundaries, and constraints. It can imply exclusive ownership *of* rather than humble belonging *to*.

When your reality is filtered through such a belief system, it is difficult to conceive of anything different as safe, acceptable, or true. Sometimes we entertain private questions or doubts, but their implications are often too scary to explore openly. Usually, it is not until we create some separation from our environment that the familiar is allowed to become just unfamiliar enough that we are able to see it with fresh eyes. Then we are finally able to examine what we were taught with a more objective eye. That is what indoctrination does: it normalizes certain beliefs and practices so that they go unchecked. Often, it takes an outsider (or at least an outside perspective) to see things more clearly and recognize red flags that everyone inside has simply accepted as reality. And since outsiders are not to be trusted in dogmatic environments, the system has a built-in method of self-preservation.

Indoctrination is effective because it is baked into every aspect of how a group operates and defines itself, presenting the leaders' interpretation of the world as objective reality. It appeals to our inherent need to belong, to have a place and identity—humanity's innate sense of tribalism: "We exist because we are *this*, not *that*." Sometimes the ideological distinctions are obvious, such as unique ways of dressing, but other times, they are much more subtle—slight tweaks designed to subtly reinforce the prevailing notions of orthodoxy within a group.

I discovered this one Sunday in my mid-twenties, when I was visiting a new church that was a different denomination from the one in which I had been raised. The congregation was singing the old favorite "To God Be the Glory" by the indefatigable hymn writer Fanny J. Crosby, and I had been feeling right at home until we reached the last lines of the second verse: "The vilest offender who truly believes, / That moment from Jesus a pardon receives." *Well, that's not right,* I thought to myself. *Leave it to these upstarts to get the words wrong. How embarrassing for them.*

First thing when I got home, I looked up the lyrics online, eager to prove to myself that the version I had grown up singing was the correct version sanctioned by both Jesus and Ms. Crosby. Confidently, I typed in the name of the hymn and scrolled to the end of the second verse, which I was absolutely certain *actually* said: "The violent offender who truly obeys / That moment may enter the heavenly way."

Except . . . I was wrong. With my trusty old denominational songbook in one hand and at least thirty images of hymnals and lyrics sites on the World Wide Web in front of me that confirmed the version I had encountered in church that morning, I was forced to reach the deeply uncomfortable realization that my religious forebears had altered the lyrics of the beloved old hymn to align more closely with their denominational doctrine.

You see, I grew up in a faith tradition that takes a hard stance on baptism by immersion as the moment of eternal salvation, not the moment of belief or repentance. In fact, we took the act of immersion so seriously that a common debate was over what would happen if a person got in a car accident and died on the way to church to get baptized. Would they still go to heaven if they had the intent but had not actually been immersed yet? In such a circumstance, had they truly obeyed the command Peter gives the crowd at Pentecost in Acts 2:38 ("Repent and be baptized every one of you in the name of Jesus Christ so that your sins may be forgiven, and you will receive the gift of the Holy Spirit")?

By way of a somewhat humorous illustration of how seriously this topic was regarded, I was baptized one summer at church camp when I was thirteen. I went forward during the evening worship service and was immersed in the lake a few minutes later. Just a few hours later, around 2:00 a.m., a girl in my cabin rolled out of her top bunk and crashed to the floor with a loud thud and an (understandably) surprised screech. Thankfully, she was fine. But as we were all climbing back into bed afterward, a friend turned to me and said, "When I heard the noise and the shout, my first thought was JESUS IS BACK—*and Tiffany was saved just in time!*" My lifelong devotion to Jesus would not have been enough to save me in that scenario; only the act of getting dunked in the lake the previous evening had done the trick to prepare my soul for the Second Coming. If I had merely "believed" (according to Ms. Crosby's lyrics) and not also "obeyed" (according to our hymnal's edits) my soul would have been in jeopardy had the person descending from on high that night actually been Jesus returning in glory rather than an eighth grader worn out from canoeing and lanyard weaving.

My point here is not to debate the finer points of salvation theology but to illustrate the hair-splitting thinking that dominates so many of our lives and leaves no room for grace. I know I seem to be picking on my own tradition, but that's because it's what I know. The truth is, we all have our "wacky doctrine" stories from our various denominational backgrounds. Granted, maybe not every denomination changed entire lines of traditional hymns in order to "correct" the theology, but every tradition definitely has its own quirks and idiosyncrasies that range from merely eye-rolling to deeply problematic.

That's part of what bonds us as a Christian family—just like a biological family, we're all weirdos in our own unique ways. Baptists put out a lot of altar calls. Catholics like incense. Pentecostals speak in tongues. The Churches of Christ don't use musical instruments. Episcopalians love their prayer book. Methodists are really into writing hymns (and singing every single verse). Lutherans publish *a lot* of congregational cookbooks. The problems arise when one group decides that its particular oddities are the only kind of weirdness that God likes and then makes those quirks prerequisites for salvation and turns ideas into idols. Such dogma is often presented as an all-or-nothing deal; rejecting one part of it is the same as rejecting all of it. The metaphor I often heard as a child was, "If I gave you a glass of water that had a drop of poison in it, would you still drink it? That's what we do when we don't accept *every piece* of God's truth—every point of doctrine we get wrong is another drop of poison added to the glass." Is it any wonder so many

The problems arise when one group decides that its particular oddities are the only kind of weirdness that God likes and then makes those quirks prerequisites for salvation

of us grew up terrified of exploring dissenting opinions when the act of doing so was equated with voluntarily ingesting arsenic? The only way to guarantee the safety of our metaphorical water was to consume *only* what was provided to us after being filtered through our specific denominational pipe system. Anything else, we were taught, is both corrupted and corrupting.

Former child reality TV star Jinger Duggar Vuolo, whose family was the subject of the program *19 Kids and Counting*, summed up this constant nervousness in an interview with *People* magazine in 2023:

> "Fear was a huge part of my childhood . . . I thought I had to wear only skirts and dresses to please God. Music with drums, places I went or the wrong friendships could all bring harm."
>
> Even when her family went to play a sport called broomball, Vuolo says she felt "terrified" she might be defying God's will. "I thought I could be killed in a car accident on the way, because I didn't know if God wanted me to stay home and read my Bible instead."

Describing the doctrines of the movement of which her family was a part, she said that the principles were rooted in "fear and superstition and leave you in a place where you feel like, 'I don't know what God expects of me.' . . . The fear kept me crippled with anxiety. I was terrified of the outside world."[3]

For many people brought up in such a controlling, authoritarian environment, even the act of asking questions can be dangerous. When you're told, "That's not what we believe," the indication is that if you don't believe the same things, you are not included in that "we." You automatically become an outsider, and outsiders are capital-L Lost. As Jinger Duggar Vuolo said, the "outside world" becomes a place of terror; the only safe place is wholly contained within the ironclad walls of preapproved dogma that ensures a sharp separation between "us" and "them."

But what about the parable of the banquet in Luke 14? Jesus shares this story at a Sabbath meal he has been invited to in the home of a high-ranking Pharisee. He knows that the Pharisees are "watching him closely," so after healing a man afflicted with severe swelling, Jesus chooses to make a statement that will challenge the Pharisees who are plotting against him. As usual, when addressing religious leaders, Jesus makes a pointed statement against people who live in echo chambers, surrounding themselves only with those who are like-minded and who reinforce the power structures already in place.

First, Jesus speaks to his host, telling him that when he holds an event, he should not focus on inviting friends, family, and influential people, "in case they may invite you in return, and you would be repaid. But when you give a banquet, invite the poor, the crippled, the lame, and the blind. And you will be blessed because they cannot repay you, for you will be repaid at the resurrection of the righteous" (Luke 14:12–14).

Then Jesus addresses the whole party, sharing a parable that illustrates his point:

> "Someone gave a great dinner and invited many. At the time
> for the dinner he sent his slave to say to those who had been

invited, 'Come, for everything is ready now.' But they all alike began to make excuses. The first said to him, 'I have bought a piece of land, and I must go out and see it; please accept my regrets.' Another said, 'I have bought five yoke of oxen, and I am going to try them out; please accept my regrets.' Another said, 'I have just been married, and therefore I cannot come.' So the slave returned and reported this to his master. Then the owner of the house became angry and said to his slave, 'Go out at once into the streets and lanes of the town and bring in the poor, the crippled, the blind, and the lame.' And the slave said, 'Sir, what you ordered has been done, and there is still room.' Then the master said to the slave, 'Go out into the roads and lanes, and compel people to come in, so that my house may be filled. For I tell you, none of those who were invited will taste my dinner.'" (vv. 18–24)

The parable is about creating community and building togetherness, even with those who are different. Notice that "the poor, the crippled, the blind, and the lame" are not second thoughts, invited only after the first round of guests has declined. When the host asks the slave to collect them, the slave tells him that *it has already been done*. When the host "invited many" (v. 16), he appears to have included those social outsiders from the start.

The people who choose not to attend are too consumed with their own way of doing things to celebrate and build relationships with others. Even the man who has been recently married—the one who has, perhaps, the most valid excuse for missing the event—is so focused on his own life that he shuts himself and his new wife off from community. Rather than bringing her to the banquet so she can celebrate her new place in society and possibly even in her new village, he opts to keep her home and away from places where she could meet other people and form relationships.

The generous rich man quickly loses interest in people who prefer to reject a welcoming table and, in response, only opens his gates wider and pulls up more chairs to the feast. He is not picky about who or what or how people come; he does not seem to discriminate based on the way they approach his feast. His main criterion is that they *want* to come, *want* to feast with him and others, *want* to be part of a celebration that includes every sort of person. The host's party is happening with or without the standoffish friends; the people who choose to miss it do so on their own account, not God's.

Unfortunately, many Christians are not content to be a guest at the feast; they want to act as host, herald, and bouncer, too—setting the guest list, delivering invitations, and working the door. It is far too easy for people who occupy the most powerful position in an authoritarian system—be it a church, organization, family, or even just a specific cultural setting—to insert themselves into the role of God. Their word is law, their leadership goes unchallenged, and their personal preferences masquerade as divine mandates. They demand total obedience because it is the only way to maintain strict control within the established power structure.

> *The host's party is happening with or without the standoffish friends; the people who choose to miss it do so on their own account, not God's*

This is why spiritual anxiety can be so oppressive for people trapped in dogmatic environments. Despite false claims of humility, many authoritarian leaders have set themselves up as God-manifest in the relationship structure; therefore, any disagreement with them is portrayed as a disagreement with God, and any challenge to their authority is the same vanity that supposedly drove Lucifer to rebel against heaven (Revelation 12:7–9). The weight of sin—particularly a willful, intentional act like questioning leadership—is especially heavy for people who struggle with Involuntary Internalized Legalism because it means that the sin was a deliberate violation of personal religious scruples.

Many of us raised in Protestant traditions were taught that all sin—any sin—keeps us from God's presence and is, therefore, equal. For people who struggle with spiritual anxiety, this can be a terrifying prospect because it means that every single mistake during the day, every impatient thought that comes into your head, every unkind word you choke down, every sin of omission places you on the same footing as a serial killer, despotic dictator, or child abuser.

The primary justification for this thinking is usually Matthew 5:21–22, when Jesus is preaching to an assembled crowd and tells them, "You have heard that it was said to those of ancient times, 'You shall not murder'; and 'whoever murders shall be liable to judgment.' But I say to you that if you are angry with a brother or sister, you will be liable to judgment; and if you insult a brother or sister, you will be liable to the council; and if you say, 'You fool,' you will be liable to the hell of fire."

That's a pretty unambiguous statement, but (as always) we need to consider these comments in their broader context. They follow the Beatitudes as part of the Sermon on the Mount—the sermon Jesus preached outlining how to shift our hearts toward kinder, more compassionate living. In this sermon, he also broadened the definition of adultery (lusting after someone who is not your spouse) and narrowed the terms of divorce (only for infidelity). Anger may lead to harm against another; lust reduces a person's value to their sexual availability; divorce was, essentially, a sentence of poverty and desperation in a world where women held very few rights. The reason that Jesus challenged these traditional definitions was not to entrap the sinner into a debt impossible to pay but to illustrate the responsibility we have toward other people—an idea very much in line with the southern African philosophy of *ubuntu*, a Bantu word that captures the idea of a shared humanity where each individual's personhood is bound up in the humanity of others. It

Matthew 5 is not a blanket declaration that all sin is equal, but a reminder that we can diminish the humanity of others in ways that don't even require physical action

is an ancient concept that became more widely known outside of the African continent during South Africa's anti-apartheid struggles of the 1990s. Though Jesus obviously did not use the word *ubuntu*, his teachings are centered in this same notion that the way we treat one another is an essential and inextricable part of the created order. In short, Matthew 5 is not a blanket declaration that all sin is equal, but a reminder that we can harm, disrespect, and diminish the humanity of others in ways that don't even require physical action.

So, no. All sin is not equal. But Jesus's forgiveness is. So is grace; it is doled out with equal potency, simply in different amounts. Consider the parable Jesus shares with his dinner host in Luke 7:

> "A certain moneylender had two debtors; one owed five hundred denarii, and the other fifty. When they could not pay, he canceled the debts for both of them. Now which of them will love him more?" Simon answered, "I suppose the one for whom he canceled the greater debt." And Jesus said to him, "You have judged rightly." (vv. 41–43)

Debt is debt. Sin is sin. But amounts and degrees vary widely, as Jesus recognized. This is an aspect of theology where Protestantism may have grossly "overcorrected" in its break from Catholicism. Roman Catholic theology separates sin into two major categories: mortal and venial. While Catholic theologians recognize that every situation and circumstance is different and therefore decline to draw up a hard and fast list for each category, the general definition of mortal sins is that they are major, grave, and put the soul at eternal risk if the sinner does not seek reconciliation with God before death. Venial sins are all the rest. It might be helpful to think of it as the difference between breaking the law and breaking a household rule. All sin is sin, and it all requires forgiveness, but violent assault and missing curfew generally do not chalk up the same ranking on the eternal tally sheet.

We all inherently know this. Intellectually, we recognize that perpetrating genocide should not carry the same eternal consequences as lying about sneaking a cookie before dinner. Jesus even says to Pilate in John 19:11, "You would have no power over me unless it had been given you from above; therefore the one who handed me over to you is *guilty of a greater sin*" (emphasis added). Yet how many of us have heard at least one sermon on the idea that God cannot abide the presence of sin, and any sin at all, no matter how minor (though in this view there is no such thing as a "minor" sin), cuts us off from the presence of God without the blood of Jesus?

Part of being a rational and nominally moral human is a basic sense of proportion. "In for a dime, in for a dollar" hamartiology (philosophy of sin) runs deeply contrary to everything we know about a God who claims to value justice as one of the most important earthly values. If you honestly believe that pinching your sister when you were ten is equal to murder, sexual assault, genocide, child exploitation, animal abuse, wanton desecration of the earth, and so on—you need to reevaluate your understanding of God.[4]

But spiritual anxiety can also result from a struggle to reconcile off-base teachings not just with logical reasoning but also with willful ignorance. As Kepler and Galileo both experienced firsthand, sometimes people of faith deny facts in favor of comfortable traditions that maintain the status quo and help to separate "us" from "them," in whatever way that designation is meaningful. Intellectual dishonesty of any kind is almost always agenda-driven; an individual hears or sees whatever they want and either ignores or dismisses the rest. At its best, it's confirmation bias; at its worst, it's self-deceit for the sake of comfort, convenience, or control. This is a kind of logical fallacy called a "straw man argument," in which an opponent's idea is oversimplified or presented out of context in order to make the refutation of it look like the only reasonable response. There is no room for

nuance or nonpolarized thinking; in essence, it creates a carica-
ture of the argument.

For example, a person using a straw man argument may say,
"The theory of evolution teaches that all life on earth is the result
of pond scum that got lucky over millions of years. If you think
that you are nothing more than some hairless monkey and God
is just the product of some old campfire tales thousands of years
ago, be my guest. But personally, I have a little more respect for
the human soul than that and come judgment day, we will see
who is right." Here, they present the matter as if the *only* two
options are a literalist interpretation of Genesis or a complete
rejection of God—and that anyone who believes otherwise is at
risk of losing their faith entirely.

Scott, a sales rep for a large company and a deacon in his
church, recalled a science quiz he took in "fourth or fifth grade"
in his Christian homeschool group in the 1990s:

> It had questions like, "True or false: Satan uses radiocarbon
> dating and dinosaur fossils to trick people into believing in
> evolution." It was just so anti-science. I mean, I believe God
> created the world, but not six thousand years ago and not in
> six days. But you wouldn't believe the sleepless nights it took
> to get me to there—to get me to believe that letting go of a
> literal belief in Genesis didn't make the whole Bible untrue,
> right up to the resurrection. . . . I thought letting go of one
> thing meant everything would be like dominoes, because
> that's what I'd been taught—either it's all true or none of it
> is. And I was just so scared of seeing my entire faith collapse.

Dogmatic views around divorce constituted another topic
that came up quite often in these interviews. There were people
who were publicly reprimanded in their church for not finding
ways to save their marriages; others were shamed for leaving marriages that were abusive but did not technically meet the bibli-

cal stipulations of adultery. One woman, Elizabeth, spoke of her mother's reaction to the news of her divorce, and the fact that their parent-child relationship seemed to hinge on the church's stance on the issue:

> Mom was a "you have to follow these rules" kind of person. Women should have their heads covered to be doing things correctly in worship. You have to be right with the church in order to partake of Communion. You have to follow these exact rules in order to have that promise of eternal life—there was a lot of talk of what would happen if you don't follow these rules. I'd try to talk to her about different things like the service element of faith, and she cared about that but it all had to be in the context of traditional churchgoing.
>
> . . . I had a terrible marriage that should never have happened. And when I got divorced, it was like the end of the world for my mother since that is just not acceptable within the church, and that put us in a whole new era of our relationship. . . . We had a really difficult day one day just after that, when my divorce hadn't been announced yet. I was home for the holidays, and we were getting ready to go to church on Sunday. And Mom takes me aside, right at the beginning of Mass, and says, "I'm so glad you're here, but you need to know you're not allowed to take Communion." And I just felt like, "So why am I here?" It was a difficult time. My mom is no longer with me and, to her dying day, I think she regretted that I wasn't right with the church. So no surprise, I have a lot of spiritual anxiety.

Elizabeth explained that no matter the church's stance on an issue, it's hard to ever fully get past feeling like you've disappointed your mother or to hush that tiny voice in the back of your head that questions whether her concerns about the state of your soul might have some truth to them after all. And despite

Elizabeth's marriage being unhealthy and unstable, the fact that her mother seemed to prioritize institutional doctrine over her relationship with her daughter was a deep and lasting wound.

One woman I spoke with for this book, Julia, experienced personal targeting as a result of running afoul of a dogmatic leader. She was raised in a midwestern Catholic family but always struggled with the idea of easy or intrinsic religious belief. Julia talked about how her doubt was treated by some people in the church as a stubborn rejection of truth, but the irony is that compared with certain people of faith, Julia felt that *she* was not the person committing willful ignorance. We will explore more of Julia's story in chapter 8, but I want to highlight her experience of basic facts standing in opposition to doctrinal teaching.

As an adult, Julia still fostered respect for the institution that had been such an important part of her life, and she was offered a teaching position at a religious university despite being open about her agnostic views on religion. "I regularly ate lunch with nuns, and we talked about it. Everyone knew, and we got along just fine. It wasn't an issue," Julia shrugs. She loved her job and her students until "there was a sea change."

For years, a beloved religious leader had headed up the school, operating under a set of core values that included hospitality toward all students, whatever their religious beliefs or affiliation—including none at all. But when that leader retired, a new leader was brought in who, in Julia's words, "only had religious experience—not real-world experience." The university took a hard pivot. Philosophy classes were eliminated, and all students now had to take three religion courses about the school's denominational doctrine, no matter their major or faith. The university's new president even appointed a group of especially pious students who reported back to the administration on the religious condition of the campus as they observed it.

As a biologist teaching courses in anatomy and physiology, Julia came under fire:

In a class like that you obviously teach the systems of the body, including the reproductive system. I tried to orient things towards the students who, in that class, were probably going into nursing or occupational therapy, physical therapy, or going to be doctors. I'd tell them, "You're going to be dealing with patients who use birth control. You need to have an understanding of this so you know the different types and how they work. I am *not* here advocating or denying. I am not here saying yea or nay. And I'm not judging: I'm giving you facts." And then we talked about the different forms of birth control, how they worked, and what their effectiveness was. I talked about the big picture—how one of the problems with birth control pills is that some of the products end up in wastewater, which is problematic because there's an environmental impact. I mentioned the things that had an impact before conception and things that had an impact after conception, so that if you believe life begins at the moment of conception, you can be aware of what different approaches do for preventing conception versus preventing implantation. We didn't talk pros or cons—we just talked about what was out there and its impacts on the human body. . . . And the department knew what I was teaching; I didn't try to hide any of it because I didn't feel the need to hide it. I wasn't advocating for anything except giving students relevant information, and everyone knew it and was fine with it. . . .

But I had one student—I got fired for one student—she showed up in my office with a shoebox of pamphlets, telling me how wrong I was for saying natural family planning was anything less than 95 percent effective. I tried to explain to her the various challenges—that most women don't have perfect twenty-eight-day cycles, which make it harder to track; how sometimes the egg lives longer; sometimes other biological factors can impact things; sometimes you're married and just want to have sex with your husband and you forget that tomorrow is the day you're ovulating. I explained that the 95-percent figure was just theoretical. The real-life numbers are different because of any number of different factors, and I just wanted students going into medical professions to be aware of that. Well, she got mad and went to the president. . . . They "chose not to renew my contract" even though I'd been at the school for years and my student evaluations were consistently outstanding.

I loved my students. I loved teaching. But I was out. . . . And the guy who came after me . . . he only talked about the immorality of birth control in anatomy and physiology classes—which is what the new administration wanted. But it isn't going to serve the students.

The reason Julia was given for her dismissal was that she had not yet completed her PhD, although she was further along in her degree than other faculty members who were not let go. She had come to terms with her religious doubts and the fears they conjured up years earlier, but that experience served as a blazing reminder of why she had left the church in the first place: "It made me feel even more strongly that blind obedience to an institution is wrong."

Another woman shared her experience of listening to her evangelical pastor's fast and loose relationship with facts in his sermons: "I'd just be sitting there, and shaking my head going, 'No, that's not true.'" Eventually, she noticed that this was a pattern. The pastor would start preaching something from the Bible that seemed reasonable, but then would launch off onto his own pontifications that were full of factual errors. There were several instances, but as an example, one Memorial Day weekend, the pastor was preaching on God and country. He cited Thomas Jefferson's 1801 letter to the Danbury Baptist Church, where the phrase "separation of church and state" first appears:

He said, "This letter is misquoted all the time. People end the statement there and never get to the end of the letter." Then he put up a huge slide on the screen and said, "The line keeps going. It actually ends like this 'But that wall of separation is only meant to go one way. It's meant to keep the government out of the church, not the church out of the government.'"

I thought, "I've never heard of that, and I was a poli-sci major as an undergrad, but maybe I'm wrong." So I went home and went straight to the Library of Congress site and pulled up the letter and—no, I wasn't wrong. That quote was not there. I emailed him and said, "Can you point me to your source material because I've never seen this version of this letter before, and I'd like to read it." I thought that was the most nonthreatening way that I could possibly address the issue to gently call his attention to the fact that the information he had was inaccurate.

But I got nothing. It was crickets. He'd responded to some of my emails before when I'd had questions about sermons and stuff, but he was just silent now. And then, on the Fourth of July, he restated it. The slide went back up there, and I just sat there, shocked. . . .

But the pastor didn't care. To me, if one of your parishioners brings a concern to you about your "facts," and you don't address it, and then you say the same thing again from the pulpit, you don't care. You just don't care.

((((●))))

If your religious identity hinges entirely on absolute doctrinal "rightness," evangelism can *only* mean convincing others of your rightness, too. After all, if you are one of the few people special enough to have "figured out God," the only way to win more souls to God is to get them to replicate your steps exactly so that they, too, can crack the code. This means asserting control over their body and mind for the sake of their soul.

You see, anxiety can work both ways. When people within a system are desperate to hold onto power or preserve a status quo that keeps them in a privileged position, they are revealing their own anxieties—anxieties that their preferred way of being is threatened. In order to safeguard what they don't want to lose, they have to make other people believe it is the right way. In a religious context, this means that the only way to protect what is pleasing to them is to convince others that it is pleasing to God, so they wrap their preferences in dogmatic language of "defending the truth" and "fighting for what's right" or else crying persecution. They create an alternate reality designed to force people into sharing their views.

I struggled to understand this for years. There I was, desperately afraid of sinning by using God's name in vain, even if I was just repeating a line from a book in my head, rather than recognizing that people who used hate and fear to control others while trumpeting themselves as the "true followers" of Christ were far guiltier of using God's name in a profane context. It's spiritual sleight of hand; if you can get people to look the other way, focus on something else, worry about their every move, maybe they won't notice the way culturally normalized legalism is being used to keep them in line.

The faith tradition in which I grew up has deep roots in the American South, where teetotaling on religious grounds is very common. In many congregations, any inconvenient mention of alcohol in the Bible, such as Jesus turning water into wine at Cana (John 2:1–11) or Paul encouraging Timothy to "take a little wine for your stomach" (1 Timothy 5:23) is explained away as a medical necessity due to a lack of clean drinking water. The idea that there could be such a thing as the responsible consumption of alcohol in a social setting is simply not entertained.

> It's spiritual sleight of hand; if you can get people to look the other way, focus on something else, worry about their every move, maybe they won't notice the way culturally normalized legalism is being used to keep them in line

CHAPTER 5

One evening when I was in graduate school and studying ancient Greek, I attended a Bible study where the lesson was centered on the idea that *oinos*, the word for "wine" in the New Testament, referred only to grape juice, not fermented wine. The class leader kept circling back to the expression "one drink drunk," meaning that even a single sip of an alcoholic drink was a sin and that there was no biblical evidence that Jesus ever touched or consumed fermented wine in any form.

While it is true that *oinos* can refer to any type of beverage squeezed from grapes, it does not exclusively (or even primarily) refer to a nonalcoholic drink. When the leader opened the floor for questions, I asked about the implications of this interpretation on verses like Ephesians 5:18, which talks about *oinos* leading to drunkenness—indicating that the word must refer to literal wine at least some of the time. Rather than answering my question, the leader responded with one of his own: "Let me ask you something. If you don't believe that one drink is one drink drunk, then how many drinks does it take for *you* to get drunk?"

This seemed like an odd response, but I answered honestly, having never tried alcohol myself: "I don't know. I've never been drunk."

The leader looked surprised for a moment, started to say something, then turned away to call on someone else, leaving my initial question unresolved. I was confused by his challenge to me and abrupt pivot from our conversation until I realized that he had been trying to trick me into giving a self-incriminating reply. Any answer I could offer that indicated I knew how many drinks it took to get me drunk would mean that I had been drunk in the past and therefore lacked the moral fortitude to debate him on this point. This kind of *ad hominem* attack (literally, "to the person") is a rhetorical fallacy in which the arguer tries to discredit the opponent's argument by discrediting the individual while sidestepping the argument. Rather than confronting the facts, they attack the challenger's character in an effort to distract from the actual issue. This is a common technique used in a variety of settings, including religious ones, for keeping people loyal to a set of beliefs by discrediting the behavior of anyone who questions them.

When we discuss the relationship between thoughts and actions, it is important to recognize the distinction between orthodoxy, orthopraxy, and orthopathy. Orthodoxy means "right thinking"—a person's beliefs are in line with what the community considers acceptable and true. Orthopraxy, on the other hand, means "right acting"—that a person's behavior conforms to the established and approved norms of society. Orthopathy (in a theological context) refers to "right feeling"—that one's motivations are pure. Theologically speaking, however, the distinction isn't quite so simple. They are obviously linked—thoughts steer actions, and actions are governed by motivations—but it's a little more complicated than that. Orthodoxy covers the "correctness" of a person's religious principles—principles that include certain types of behaviors. Orthopraxy and orthopathy, however, refer not only to the behaviors themselves, but also to the way that they are carried out—whether they are done in the "correct" way as prescribed by culture, tradition, specific beliefs, and one's own emotional attunement.

Behavior is generally easier to control from the outside than beliefs because it is visible; you can see what someone is doing and correct, compel, or constrain them according to the desired outcome. Beliefs are harder to control because it is impossible to know exactly what a person is thinking; you can browbeat someone into verbal agreement, but there is no way of knowing for sure whether they have actually accepted your way of thinking and feeling or whether they have simply given up open disagreement. Nothing is more terrifying to authoritarian leaders than the realization that they cannot assert absolute control over their victim's mind, which is why they rely so heavily on indoctrination.

In religious settings—especially in systems that prioritize belief over everything else—"right thinking" becomes absolutely essential, and anyone who fails to hold the "correct" beliefs may

Nothing is more terrifying to authoritarian leaders than the realization that they cannot assert absolute control over their victim's mind, which is why they rely so heavily on indoctrination

be seen as a threat both to themselves and to the broader community. This is why people with spiritual anxiety and especially those who struggle with IIL have such a difficult time pulling their religious sensibilities out of crisis mode. Even if their behavior is completely above reproach, their inner life—their thought life—may not fall

into line as neatly with the orthodoxy of their community. What's more, people wrestling with these issues often feel like hypocrites upon discovering that their thoughts are misaligned with their actions when they rely on external compliance to mask any unorthodox thoughts, ideas, or questions. This can then launch the vicious cycle we discussed in chapter 3: invalidation ("I'm not living my life right"); spiraling ("There is some secret sin in my life keeping me from God," or "These fears are proof my faith isn't strong enough"); and shame ("If I were a better Christian, this wouldn't happen," or "I'm not trying hard enough"), which leads back to the initial invalidating thought: "I'm not living my life right."

Belief and behavior are indelibly intertwined. "Right thinking" counts for very little if it is not then translated into some kind of outward expression rooted not in fear, power, or shame, but in love. Dogmatic obedience to doctrine without regard for motivation or impact is merely legalism played out in yet another form. Throughout the New Testament, circumcision—the ritual required of all Jewish males as an external sign of the covenant between God and God's people—is often used as a metaphor in discussions of law versus grace. Therefore, when Paul writes in Galatians 5:6, "For in Christ Jesus neither circumcision nor uncircumcision counts for anything; *the only thing that counts is faith working through love*" (emphasis added) or "faith expressing itself in love" (NIV), he is arguing that liberation comes not from prescriptive beliefs themselves but from the manifestation of gratefulness for our covenant with God and the outpouring of that gratefulness into the world.

In fact, evidence suggests that orthopraxy and orthopathy, much more than orthodoxy, were the primary conditions for acceptance in early Christian communities. The *Didache*, an early church manual that dates from the late first century (making it contemporary or within one or two generations of the canonical books of the New Testament, including the Gospels), lays out rules for proper Christian living, basic procedures for rituals such as baptism and communion, and guidelines for communal order in worship and administration. It outlines the moral behaviors that Christians are expected to follow (not engaging in murder, adultery, pedophilia, sexual misconduct, idolatry, etc.), but nowhere does it delineate a required set of doctrinal beliefs.

This trend is reinforced by the *Apostolic Tradition*, a text generally accepted as dating from around 220 CE and the most comprehensive record of church practices from the first few centuries of the faith. Probably composed in Rome, the *Apostolic Tradition* was circulated widely throughout the Christian world, including Egypt, Ethiopia, and Syria. It includes several discussions of the screening process by which potential converts were to be evaluated for admission into the broader body of believers. Book 20:1–2 states:

> They who are to be set apart for baptism shall be chosen after their lives have been examined: whether they have lived soberly, whether they have honoured the widows, whether they have visited the sick, whether they have been active in well-doing. When their sponsors have testified that they have done these things, then let them hear the Gospel.[5]

Interestingly, this is just one of several sources from the first few centuries after Jesus that indicate that anyone interested in conversion to Christianity was not permitted to listen to preaching from the Gospels until they had appropriately demonstrated a commitment to "right acting." Learning the finer points of doctrine followed baptism, but it was orthopraxy, not orthodoxy, that was given primacy in the churches. On that basis—a demonstrated commitment to engaging marginalized populations like the widowed and ill—was a person welcomed into fellowship, not on the basis of whether they professed identical beliefs as the church leaders. Remember, this was an era when many of those now-standard beliefs were still being debated and codified.

Many modern adherents of strictly dogmatic theology point to Romans 12:2 as proof of the need to shun the outside world and be absorbed completely into the confines of whatever set of beliefs they insist are required for salvation-liberation: "Do not be conformed to this age, but be transformed by the renewing of the mind, so that you may discern what is the will of God—what is good and acceptable and perfect." But that's not actually what the verse is saying at all. It is encouraging believers *not* to get locked into traditional ways of thinking due to comfort, misplaced loyalty, or the fear of new ideas. Instead, the charge is to be transformed or changed (literally, *metamorphousthe*, from which we get the word "metamorphosis") by renewing the mind not for the sake of conforming to external beliefs but in order to use one's own discretion or judgment to determine the will of God with regard to what is *agathon* (intrinsically or inherently good), *euareston* (gratifying, well-pleasing), and *teleios* (complete, mature) in God's sight.

It is significant, too, that the word for "renewing" (*anakainōsis*, meaning to be made fresh or changed to be made anew) appears just one other place in the New Testament, in Titus 3:5, which happens to fall right in the middle of another favorite passage invoked by authoritarian leaders to demand total conformity to their own belief systems. Here, the letter states that its readers should be subject to rulers and authorities, to be obedient, to be ready for every good work, to speak evil of no one, to avoid quarreling, to be gentle, and to show every courtesy to everyone. For we ourselves were once foolish, disobedient, led astray, slaves to various passions and pleasures, passing our days in malice and envy, despicable, hating one another. But when the goodness and loving kindness of God our Savior appeared, he saved us, not because of any works of righteousness that we had done, but according to his mercy, through the water of rebirth and *renewal* by the Holy Spirit. . . .

I desire that you insist on these things, so that those who have come to believe in God may be careful to devote themselves to good works; these things are excellent and profitable to everyone. But avoid stupid controversies, genealogies, dissensions, and quarrels about the law, for they are unprofitable and worthless. After a first and second admonition, have nothing more to do with anyone who causes divisions, since you know that such a person is perverted and sinful, being self-condemned. (Titus 3:1–11)

The framework we are usually given for understanding this verse is, essentially, that we are to be submissive to leaders because we were clueless schlubs before we were given correct instruction. But read the passage again. The thing that saves us is *not our doctrine but God's mercy* (v. 5). What's more, look at the kind of person who is being criticized in the passage: "foolish, disobedient, led astray, slaves to various passions and pleasures, passing [their] days in malice and envy, despicable, hating one another" (v. 3) and those who engage in "stupid controversies, genealogies, dissensions, and quarrels about the law" (v. 9).

This sounds less like someone thoughtfully engaging with their faith and more like it is describing someone who practices willful ignorance, who elevates their preferences as required practice, and who takes pride in their rejection of others over legalistic minutiae that ultimately doesn't matter. The concern is that such behavior will result in people causing "divisions" (v. 10) by segregating themselves from whoever does not agree with them. The letter then calls upon its readers to use their common sense in these situations, "since *you know* that such a person is perverted and sinful, being self-condemned" (v. 11, emphasis added). What spiritual abusers intend as a verse of self-validation is actually a verse of self-incrimination.

Galatians 5:22–23 lists the fruit of the Spirit as love, joy, peace, patience, kindness, goodness, faithfulness (*pistis*: trust), gentleness, and self-control. Nowhere is listed doctrinal rigidity.

It can be terrifying to dismantle structures you once thought were unassailable and to separate eternal truth rooted in the heart of God from someone's opinions packaged as truth and rooted in their ego. If your worldview was shaped by strict dogma rather than grace-filled freedom, by walls rather than horizons, by indoctrination rather than the incarnation, it is completely natural to experience spiritual anxiety as you sort through all the beliefs that were forced upon you. Often, the most intimidating part of all of this is having to acknowledge problematic or toxic attitudes or beliefs that you once embraced in your own life. If you look back on your past self and feel uncomfortable about who you were, that's actually a good thing because it means you are not the same person now that you were five, ten, twenty years ago. It means you were brave enough to engage in the sometimes painful honesty of admitting you needed to grow—and then actually putting in the hard work of doing it. The person who *doesn't* cringe a little when they regard their past self is the one who should probably be the most embarrassed because it likely means they haven't grown at all.

> *It can be terrifying to dismantle structures you once thought were unassailable and to separate eternal truth rooted in the heart of God from someone's opinions packaged as truth and rooted in their ego*

When the emotions of this process get overwhelming—fear, confusion, anger, despair, betrayal—remember two vital points: (1) You don't have to get it all right; in fact, it's impossible to do so. Differing opinions are not poison, no matter what you may have been taught—and grace is the ultimate antidote anyway. And (2) as you seek out truth, examine each idea to see if it is one that leads you to a less legalistic set of beliefs, a bigger banquet table, a less fearful view of the world, a deeper love for all of creation, or a wider understanding of who God is and how God operates. If it doesn't—if it makes you feel more constrained, controlled, coerced, or cut off from God, it's probably something other than truth.

6

DECORATION—
CONTROL THROUGH PRAISE

Content warning: discussions of disordered eating

In *The Joy Luck Club*, the 1989 novel by Amy Tan,[1] four mothers and four daughters weave their stories together into a rich tapestry of celebration, heartache, confession, and trauma surrounding the complexities of life for Chinese American immigrant families. One of the daughters, Lena St. Clair, narrates to the reader about her lifelong struggle with guilt, pleasing, and swallowing her emotions in order to hold onto love.

It starts with a childhood grudge Lena holds against a bully named Arnold who lives in their apartment building. Lena's mother warned her that a plate with food left on it at mealtimes prophesied a marriage to a "bad man," which Lena's adolescent mind decides is personified in Arnold. As Lena struggles with disordered eating in the form of anorexia, her mother's nagging about uneaten food only makes Lena hate and fear Arnold more because she does not want to marry a man like him. Several years later, Arnold's sudden death from a complication with measles plants a secret fear in Lena that she is somehow responsible because of her angry thoughts toward him, even though she knows this is entirely irrational. But that night, she sneaks a tub of ice cream to her room and gorges herself until she throws it back up as a way of somehow making amends by punishing her body.

This anecdote lays the groundwork for Lena's complicated worries and fears about love (and ice cream). It segues into a description of Lena's failing marriage with a man named Harold, whom she met when they were working at the same architecture firm. When they first started meeting one another for lunch, they split the bill fifty-fifty—a habit that continues into their growing relationship. She longs to be generous without accounting, to be able to give to one another freely instead of always consulting the balance sheet to make sure things are fair. But Harold finds Lena's apparent practicality attractive, so she never broaches the topic for fear he would no longer find her special.

Though she loves their footing as equals, Lena never feels able to voice her concerns because her continued compliance is rewarded as their relationship moves forward. She first encourages Harold to start his own architecture firm, which he is able to afford only after he invites her to move in so they can save on rent. True, her half of the rent is now more than she was paying on her much smaller place, but she agrees because she wants to support his dream and longs for assurance that the relationship is secure. Then, when Harold is faced with a noncompete clause from his old company, Lena is the one who gives him the idea to pivot to a different area of design that proves wildly successful. Soon, they are married, and Harold finds himself president of a rapidly growing business—and still splitting every expense, bill, and spending choice fifty-fifty even though he makes eight times Lena's salary. And through it all, he has never stopped to notice that she never touches the ice cream he brings home every Friday, and for which she pays half.

Lena laments:

Now that I'm angry at Harold, it's hard to remember what was so remarkable about him. And I know they're there, the good qualities, because I wasn't that stupid to fall in love with him, to marry him. All I can remember is how awfully lucky I felt, and consequently how worried I was that all this undeserved good fortune would somehow slip away. When I fantasized about moving in with him, I also dredged up my deepest fears: that he would tell me I smelled bad, that I had terrible bathroom habits, that my taste in music and television was appalling. I worried Harold would someday get a new prescription for his glasses and he put them on one morning, look me up and down, and say, "Why, gosh, you aren't the girl I thought you were, are you?"

And I think that feeling of fear never left me that I would be caught someday, exposed as a sham of a woman.[2]

Lena feels exploited not because she begrudges contributing financially to the relationship, but because the relationship is not rooted in authenticity. The traits that Harold praises and culti- vates in Lena are draining life from her. She offers them willingly because she loves him, but also because they help her feel as if she is worthy of his love for her. If she speaks up or pushes back, she risks no longer being seen as pragmatic—the very thing that made her so valuable as a partner in Harold's eyes. As a result, she has kept silent for the better part of a decade, feeling her anxiety and resentment grow each time she agrees to something that draws her farther away from her own honest feelings.

((((●))))

Sometimes, spiritual anxiety comes not from feelings of inade- quacy or failure but from the opposite—from praise and celebra- tion over a person's extreme dedication to spiritual practices or to the work of the church.

A person who prays continually or reads their Bible for hours every day may be held up as an example of what true devotion looks like. Someone who spends every spare minute volunteering at the church building, serving on committees, putting together Sunday School lessons, preparing Communion plates, or coordinating church activities is often honored by a round of applause or a gift card to Applebee's at the end of VBS. There is absolutely nothing wrong with these behaviors; in fact, they *should* be celebrated and recognized for how they embody a life of devotion and for what they contribute to the life of the church. Thank God for people who worship with tender hearts and who find fulfillment in servant leadership.

The problem is that not everyone who does these things *wants* to do them; some people with spiritual anxiety feel trapped in positions of obligation. The more devotion they show or the harder the work, the more they are praised, so they double-down on their efforts not because they are addicted to the positive attention (which is a separate issue) but because it is a signal that they must be in God's favor if their behavior is celebrated by the church. As their efforts increase, so does the approval. The more their seemingly positive behaviors are praised, the more the behavior is reinforced as being praiseworthy. It can quickly become a vicious cycle with each validation acting as another turn of the screw until the individual feels imprisoned by their own good deeds as the only way to stay on God's side, maintain their place in the church, or temporarily appease the nagging whisper that says, "You're not enough." The very thing that is burning them out or breaking them down is the same thing that is fueling their superhuman efforts.

The very thing that is burning them out or breaking them down is the same thing that is fueling their superhuman efforts

This paradox is captured well in the Greek word *phármakon*, the root of the English word "pharmacy," which can mean either curative medicine or poison, depending on the context.[3] It is a kind of autoantonym—a word that means both itself and its opposite. For example, "to cleave" can mean either "to separate" or "to cling to"; "oversight" can mean either "supervision" or "a lack of attention"; "sanctioned" can mean both "permitted" and "forbidden." As the word's use changed with time, so did its associations. In the same way that *phārmakon* can be both toxin and cure, praise for spiritual striving can both soothe and stir up feelings of spiritual anxiety.

While praise can sometimes prove to be a double-edged sword despite the very best of intentions behind it, it can also be used as a means of manipulation. Burnout in religious settings is so common as to be cliché; leaders and laypeople alike can feel discouraged, exhausted, and drained by the constant demands that naturally come with church work or expressions of faith. Couple that with the emotional demands of spiritual anxiety, and circumstances are ripe for deeply unhealthy habits to develop that are rooted in a sense of guilt, shame, or Involuntary Internalized Legalism. When someone recognizes that they can extract value from someone else—whether consciously or not—by applauding their behavior, the potential for exploitation is immense. This is not to say that positive reinforcement is not a good and effective parenting or leadership tool; it is, and it is far superior to most other approaches. But when praise is used to control behavior by playing off a person's sense of guilt, religious obligation, or innate desire to please other people or God and connects external performance or production to salvation, it becomes abusive.

When praise is used to control behavior by playing off a person's sense of guilt, religious obligation, or innate desire to please other people or God and connects external performance or production to salvation, it becomes abusive

Now, ego can certainly come into play; it is a rare person who doesn't long to be recognized as special at some point, and our "spiritual ego" is no exception. Obviously, there is nothing inherently wrong with enjoying being celebrated or recognized for one's contributions or the use of one's gifts in service of God. Unfortunately, ego can also lead us to "perform" for the sake of recognition rather than for purer motives. Individuals who struggle with IIL may find this tension especially challenging, as they often compulsively second-guess their own motivations and intentions past the point of a healthy self-audit and into the realm of self-loathing. Unfortunately, abusive leaders can often detect an individual in such a state and exploit it for their own purposes.

One of the stories that seems to come up most often in discussions around achievement-based spiritual anxiety is the parable of the talents. There are actually two versions of the parable shared in the Gospels; the more commonly cited version appears in Matthew 25, while the longer and more complicated version appears in Luke 19. The story, in summary, is that before a wealthy ruler leaves on a trip, he calls some of his slaves to him and entrusts them with coins (called "talents") of varying amounts. Upon his return some time later, the slave to whom he gave the most talents has worked hard to double the amount; the same is true of the slave to whom he gave a middling amount. The slave entrusted with only one talent, however, brings it forward and confesses that he feared the rich man's wrath and shrewd reputation; because of that, he hid the coin but now is ready to return it, unspent. The wealthy man then berates this slave and strips him of the one talent, giving it instead to the slave who had earned the most, declaring, "For to all those who have, more will be given, and they will have an abundance, but from those who have nothing, even what they have will be taken away" (Luke 19:26).

Many of us were raised on this story as biblical proof that we needed to cultivate whatever gifts God had given us for the sake of the kingdom. (The English word "talent" meaning "aptitude" or "ability" comes directly from this parable.) It's not a bad takeaway; after all, no one wants to see potential squandered or misdirected.

The challenge, however, comes when we internalize the story to the point that we begin to commodify *ourselves*, evaluating our worth as people and as believers in terms of what we produce. This way of thinking is very common in people who struggle with spiritual anxiety. They are constantly plagued with questions like, "Am I doing enough with what God gave me?" or, "If I'm not using my talents in a way that directly serves the church, will God be displeased with me?" These emotions are reasonable if we understand the wealthy enslaver to be God. The thing is, neither version of the parable makes this connection; in fact, they both seem to indicate otherwise.

In Matthew 25:24–28, the character of the wealthy man is revealed in highly unflattering terms:

> "Then the one who had received the one talent also came forward, saying, 'Master, I knew that you were a harsh man, reaping where you did not sow and gathering where you did not scatter, so I was afraid, and I went and hid your talent in the ground. Here you have what is yours.' But his master replied, 'You wicked and lazy slave! You knew, did you, that I reap where I did not sow and gather where I did not scatter? Then you ought to have invested my money with the bankers, and on my return I would have received what was my own with interest. . . . As for this worthless slave, throw him into the outer darkness, where there will be weeping and gnashing of teeth.'"

Not only is the rich man known to be of severe temperament and engaging in morally dubious business dealings, but he also berates his slave for not investing the money in a bank to earn interest—a practice expressly forbidden under Jewish law. Deuteronomy 23:19–20 makes it clear that Jews were not to charge one another interest and could only charge fair rates for foreigners.

Nearly half-a-dozen other scriptures in the Hebrew Bible condemn the charging of interest in one form or another, as well. While the text does not state whether the fictional wealthy man, his servants, or the bankers in question were Jewish or gentile, it does seem surprising if Jesus would have cast God in the role of someone engaged in a controversial practice whose sole purpose was the accumulation of material wealth. The passage concludes with the command for the slave to be cast out of his home and into a hellish darkness—all for the sin of not doing enough with some silver.

Now consider the way the wealthy man is portrayed in Luke's version of the parable. It opens this way: "A nobleman went to a distant region to receive royal power for himself and then return. . . . But the citizens of his country hated him and sent a delegation after him, saying, 'We do not want this man to rule over us'" (Luke 19:12, 14). The events play out like the version in Matthew with the single-talent slave making a similar accusation against the ruler's unscrupulous business ethics, and the ruler admitting to the charge before demanding to know why his money was not loaned out for interest. The parable concludes with the nobleman declaring, "as for these enemies of mine who did not want me to rule over them—bring them here and slaughter them in my presence" (v. 27).

Is this violent, unprincipled ruler who is motivated by gaining "royal power for himself" really consistent with the image of the loving father Jesus worked so hard to cultivate throughout his ministry? Does the parable somehow feel "off" when read in that light? What if this reading is nothing more than a reflection of our cultural values, while the parable in Jesus's day may have carried a very different moral for the audience?

What if the story isn't about demanding more from God's servants but demanding repentance from those whose primary goal is to obtain wealth? Rather than centering the servants as the source of the story's moral lesson, what if we are instead meant to see an admonition against those who value people based only on what they can produce? After all, in both versions of the parable, it is only the servant who was given a single talent who has the courage to name the wealthy man's misconduct. Since when does Jesus side *against* the poor? Since when does Jesus side *against* those who call out corruption and speak truth to power? What if the parable of the talents could be a warning against exploitation?

Consider the position of the story in each gospel. In Matthew, the parable comes on the heels of the parable of the ten virgins (25:1–13). This particular story opens by Jesus declaring "The king-

What if the parable of the talents could be a warning against exploitation?

dom of heaven will be like . . ." and goes on to describe ten young women who form a wedding party; five bring oil and five do not. Those who run out are forced to leave their post to buy more, during which time the bridegroom arrives and the wedding party

begins without the five who left. The parable of the talents starts directly afterwards with the transitionary term *hōsper,* meaning, "Even as" or "Just like," but it does not draw a direct parallel to the kingdom of heaven the way the previous parable does. It is a bit ambiguous; perhaps it is meant to function in the same metaphorical way as the story above it; perhaps it is meant to be its own lesson in how we ought to live in this world while anticipating the next; or perhaps it is meant to buttress the words of Jesus that immediately follow, which happen to be a description of the judgment of the nations, when the Son of Man praises the righteous for offering him food, water, clothing, care, and comfort:

> Then the righteous will answer him, "Lord, when was it that we saw you hungry and gave you food or thirsty and gave you something to drink? And when was it that we saw you a stranger and welcomed you or naked and gave you clothing? And when was it that we saw you sick or in prison and visited you?" And the king will answer them, "Truly I tell you, just as

you did it to one of the least of these brothers and sisters of mine, you did it to me." (25:37–40)

The righteous here are those who give without counting the cost or extracting value from the vulnerable and powerless. They are the ones who seek out the poor and powerless in order to elevate them and restore their dignity.

We see this theme played out even more clearly in Luke 19, where the parable of the talents is situated between two significant events. The first is when Jesus calls out to Zacchaeus, the vertically challenged tax collector who has climbed a tree in order to get a better view. Responding delightedly to the opportunity to host Jesus in his home, Zacchaeus

> hurried down and was happy to welcome him. All who saw it began to grumble and said, "He has gone to be the guest of one who is a sinner." Zacchaeus stood there and said to the Lord, "Look, half of my possessions, Lord, I will give to the poor, and if I have defrauded anyone of anything, I will pay back four times as much." Then Jesus said to him, "Today salvation has come to this house, because he, too, is a son of Abraham. For the Son of Man came to seek out and to save the lost."
>
> As they were listening to this, he went on to tell a parable, because he was near Jerusalem and because they supposed that the kingdom of God was to appear immediately. (19:6–11)

Jesus then begins the parable of the talents. Notice several significant details in this short passage:

1. Zacchaeus honors Jesus by *giving away* the money he hoarded on behalf of a cruel master (Rome). Already, we see someone acting in a way that is contrary to the master's orders in the parable.
2. Jesus points out that he came "to seek out and save the lost."

Who is lost in the parable that Jesus then tells? It's not the people who doubled their money while the master was away; it's the servant who refuses to play by the unscrupulous master's rules. *He* is the one who is cast outside the gates—and *this* is who Jesus seeks and saves.

3. Who, then, is the master corrupted by power? Is it God, or does it make more sense to imagine that Jesus might be referring to the Pharisees, who are "grumbling" (v. 6) at Jesus's willingness to flip the script on the importance of influence, control, riches, and social standing?

Considering the context in which Jesus is sharing the parable of the talents (the home of a civil servant of the colonizing empire) and the audience who is listening and responding (religious leaders who are able to cast out and destroy those who refuse to abide by the systems that keep them in power), which interpretation makes more sense?

The second point to consider with regard to the parable's position in the gospel comes as Luke continues the story from this point. Leaving the home of Zacchaeus, where he shared the parable of the talents, Jesus rides into Jerusalem, weeps over the city, and makes one of his boldest stands against exploitation and corruption when he forcibly cleanses the temple of the money changers and those who are treating it as a marketplace (Luke 19:45–46). Thematically, the parable is sandwiched between events that critique monetizing people and profiting from the work of God's kingdom. Does it make more sense, therefore, to read it as a story that promotes a similar message or as one whose moral is the exact opposite of the stories around it?

Maybe it's not about commodifying ourselves for the sake of Christ at all

What if the parable of the talents was never about what God demanded from us but was, instead, a warning against the religious elite who treat people as something from which value must be extracted and who toss out anyone who bucks the system? So many of us have been taught that if we fail to live up to our potential—however that is measured—God is angry with us (at best) or hell awaits us. But maybe it's not about commodifying ourselves for the sake of Christ at all. Suddenly, the pressure to "perform" in the church or maximize our output for God is lifted—and doesn't that seem a bit more in line with Jesus's overall message and vibe?

In *No Future without Forgiveness*, Bishop Desmond Tutu's powerful account of the effort to bring reconciliation to South Africa following decades of racial violence and injustice under apartheid, he notes that "we can never give up on anyone because our God was one who had a particularly soft spot for sinners." Tutu encourages his readers to imagine the sheep that the Good Shepherd leaves the ninety-nine to pursue not as "an attractive, fluffy little lamb" (since those rarely go astray), but instead as a

> troublesome, obstreperous old ram. This was the one on which the Good Shepherd expended so much energy. When he found it, it is highly unlikely to have had beautiful fleece. It would almost certainly have been thoroughly bedraggled and perhaps fallen into a ditch of dirty water and was thus smelling to high heaven.[4]

Tutu's point, of course, is that God seeks even those who we might feel are hardly worth the effort, but I think his thoughtful parsing of this parable raises another point particularly applicable to the discussion here. The Good Shepherd pursues the stinky old sheep despite its filthy, snarled coat; the love he has for it has nothing to do with the material value it represents. His concern is for the sheep itself and its physical well-being, not the potential price of its wool. God's love for us has nothing to do with what we can offer; our worth to God is so much more than whatever value can be extracted from us.

Our worth to God is so much more than whatever value can be extracted from us

There is an interesting example of this in Acts 16, which states:

> One day as we were going to the place of prayer, we met a female slave who had a spirit of divination and brought her owners a great deal of money by fortune-telling. While she followed Paul and us, she would cry out, "These men are slaves of the Most High God, who proclaim to you the way of salvation." She kept doing this for many days. But Paul, very much annoyed, turned and said to the spirit, "I order you in the name of Jesus Christ to come out of her." And it came out that very hour.
>
> But when her owners saw that their hope of making money was gone, they seized Paul and Silas and dragged them into the marketplace before the authorities. (vv. 16–19)

It didn't matter that the message the enslaved woman was shouting was true and drawing attention to the evangelists; she was being exploited, and Paul's frustration was mounting as the situation grew more and more volatile. When Paul casts the spirit out of the woman, her enslavers are upset because it quashed not her message of liberation through Christ but rather their means of commodifying the woman. Paul, however, prioritized the woman's humanity rather than her witness, recognizing that she needed deliverance from her abuse, even though she was proclaiming God in the process.

In Matthew 12:18–22 and Mark 11:12–14, 20–24, the Gospel writers share an odd story about Jesus cursing a fig tree because it had no fruit on it, even though "it was not the season for figs" (Mark 11:13). The story has been interpreted a variety of ways; both Matthew and Mark include a lesson about faith and confident prayer, but the story is often invoked as a warning that God has a right to demand a harvest from creation at any time. Those unable to demonstrate their usefulness by their yield run the risk of being cursed to wither. In other words (according to this interpretation), our value to God lies in our ability to commodify our existence for the sake of the kingdom. Such an interpretation overlooks one very important detail in the story, however; Matthew 12:18 and Mark 11:12 both take care to note that Jesus approached the tree because "he was hungry."

This one simple line gives us a vital detail for understanding the story. Yes, believers are called to produce fruit, but Jesus wanted those figs to savor and enjoy, not to sell in the marketplace. The church is not a divine sweatshop, and we are not workers whom God exploits for profit. After all, think about the story of the woman with the jar of costly perfume who used it to anoint Jesus. Everyone present was shocked by the extravagant gesture, but do you remember who, specifically, the Gospel of John says complained about the "wasted" value of her offering? Judas—the same disciple who turned Jesus over to the authorities for thirty pieces of silver, so . . . *maybe not the best model for our own attitudes and behaviors* (John 12:4-6; Matthew 26:15).

The church is not a divine sweatshop, and we are not workers whom God exploits for profit

What is more, Jesus was concerned with taking care of the physical body, not exclusively the eternal state of the soul. When he had a real, tangible, physical need—like hunger—he sought to resolve it. Jesus could preach deep, existential sermons and offer profound philosophical insights on life, and he could also be immensely practical. Sometimes the pragmatic, pedestrian necessities of life are shoved to the side in favor of grand gestures and hyperbolic statements of faith that perhaps weren't Jesus's intent at all.

In Luke 10, Jesus shares the parable of the good Samaritan, where a traveler is accosted by bandits. Bloodied and left for dead, the man languishes in the road as both a priest and a Levite (a member of the priestly tribe) go out of their way to avoid him. The only person who stops to help is a Samaritan—that is, a descendant of the people of the northern kingdom of Israel who were considered by most in Jesus's day not to be true Jews because of their mixed heritage with gentiles and because they had a few key differences in points of religious law. Jesus explains:

> "But a Samaritan while traveling came upon him, and when he saw him he was moved with compassion. He went to him and bandaged his wounds, treating them with oil and wine. Then he put him on his own animal, brought him to an inn, and took care of him. The next day he took out two denarii, gave them to the innkeeper, and said, 'Take care of him, and when I come back I will repay you whatever more you spend.' Which of these three, do you think, was a neighbor to the man who fell into the hands of the robbers?" He said, "The one who showed him mercy." Jesus said to him, "Go and do likewise." (Luke 10:33–37)

It is a simple but powerful story that calls upon the listener to reconsider not only their own prejudices and cultural biases, but also advocates for deep compassion toward those in need. This is a story that gets held up as an example of selfless service, but it is also a story that can lead some people to go to exhaustive measures out of concern for "doing enough" on behalf of their struggling neighbor. For the spiritually anxious, this kind of conscientious concern is often praised as evidence that they "have a heart for service," but it can also rapidly lead to burnout, deprioritizing of one's own family, neglecting personal responsibilities, and other unhealthy outcomes as they strive to "go and do likewise."

For anyone who has ever found themselves challenged to the point of physical, emotional, or financial exhaustion by this story, it is important to remember that the good Samaritan did not undertake the injured man's care himself. He took him to the inn, made arrangements, *and then continued on his way*. He stayed just one night, and then left the victim in the hands of someone who was able to provide adequate attention and meet the man's needs. Yes, the Samaritan provided funds and made plans to check back in on the injured traveler, but he did not abandon his other obligations in looking after the needs of the unfortunate stranger.

There are those for whom this kind of ministry is life-giving, and they are truly gifts to humanity. But not everyone can or should throw themselves into tireless service in every situation that presents itself. Most people can't effectively operate at such a demanding level of caretaking and all-encompassing investment in someone else without falling short in other areas where they have been called to stewardship.

Please don't misunderstand my meaning: I am *absolutely not* saying that we should only do the bare minimum in order to avoid being inconvenienced by someone else's pain. I *am* saying that people who struggle with the anxiety of wondering whether they've done enough can take comfort in the fact that one of the Bible's primary examples of radical hospitality also had boundaries around his involvement. The Samaritan did what he could, he carried on, and he was still remembered as "good."

Maybe a helpful way to think of it is to consider the checkout line conundrum. Imagine you are standing in line with a cartful of groceries when you happen to notice that the person behind you just has a carton of milk. "Would you like to go ahead of me?" you ask. "I don't want you to have to wait behind me when you've only got one thing." The person thanks you, is rung up, and goes on their way. As that transpires, however, a mother with a sobbing baby and a toddler in the middle of a meltdown joins the line behind you. You can see she has a package of diapers in her basket and a look of sheer exhaustion in her eyes. She clearly needs a win today. "Why don't you go next?" you suggest. She gratefully accepts your offer and steps up to the register. Meanwhile, you notice that the person behind her holding a sandwich and soda is anxiously checking his watch, clearly nervous about making it back to work before his lunch hour ends. "I don't have anywhere to be," you offer, stepping aside to make room in the line. Behind him, you notice someone else with a cart full of ice cream. Your groceries are mostly nonperishables, so they will be fine sitting out awhile longer. If you're called to put others ahead of yourself, wouldn't the godly thing be to let that person get their Ben & Jerry's rung up as quickly as possible? . . .

Do you see where this is going? It is wonderful to recognize needs and accommodate them as you can, but at some point, *you have to be able to leave the store*. That's not selfish, snobbish, or sinful. It's simply being a human in the world who has needs and responsibilities of your own. People may try to shame you for not doing more, but how do you even quantify something as subjective as "enough" when considering your responsibility to humanity, to the earth, and to God?

It is certainly true that we are so much more empowered to act for the cause of justice than we tend to realize, and we should all examine our lives for ways in which things that are meaningless can be traded for the sake of alleviating suffering and combating evil. The challenge for many people with spiritual anxiety, however, is that this burden is one that is almost impossible to quiet or pause for the sake of mental rest. It sits heavily on their shoulders at all times, overwhelming them with hopelessness that their efforts will never be enough. That there is always more they could be doing. Always greater lengths to which they could go. Always one more mouth to feed, person to rescue, soul to save. Add on to that all the reminders that Christian work is supposed to carry the weight of eternity with it, and the prospect of "godliness" becomes crushing.

Sure, you can argue that that is where grace through the resurrection comes in to cover our deficiencies, but grace by itself can't feed the hungry, rescue the hurting, stop genocide, or protect the earth. People acting *through* grace are necessary to make those things happen. People who still have lives and families and jobs and dogs to walk and birthday parties to attend and relatives to visit and houses to maintain. People who are not sinning if they buy their child extrainsulated gloves for the winter or get their cat the "nice" litter that doesn't stick to their paws or watch a football game instead of cleaning up a polluted river every weekend. People who are not sinning if they don't invest every single cent and every waking moment into solving the world's problems. Otherwise, how do you justify *any* form of rest or joy with all the suffering in the world? How do you justify a Sabbath? How can you ever believe you've done anything even approaching "enough"?

This is the exhausting and disheartening realization that it is not enough to be "enough." In other words, meeting the requirements is not sufficient; you feel you must exceed them. You must do more than what is expected in order to feel you have given sufficient time, attention, energy, resources, or dedication. And because you know you could always do more, you always *seek* to do more. Even the most zealous preacher would be hard-pressed to agree that anyone could realistically dedicate every breath to furthering the message of Christ—with no moments of levity, no conversations about the weather, no action that doesn't somehow directly further the kingdom of God. Some may certainly try, but that kind of single-minded fanaticism is simply not possible in any sustainable way. But the religious rhetoric of our faith certainly doesn't reflect that. So much Christian media leans into the message of wholehearted, all-in, "no backsies" selling out to Jesus. It sounds great—unconditional love, radical forgiveness, countercultural service. This is the way we serve as Christ's hands and feet to the world. But "godliness" is an infinite proposition; there is always some way to be *more* loving, *more* forgiving, *more* devoted, *more* Christlike. It is a state that can never be achieved—a Sisyphean task of endlessly falling short, no matter how well we do. This isn't about the impossibility of earning salvation through a works-based theology; this is about the gnawing fear that, ultimately, we will always know we could and should be doing more. Yet we are told that no matter what we do, it's not sufficient. Sermons, hymns, faith blogs, and devotional books remind us that we are wholly unworthy of Jesus's blood and God's grace, so how could we even dare to think that any devotion we offer, no matter how all-consuming, can ever be enough—that *we* can ever be enough?

Perfectionism, which is a very common trait among people with spiritual anxiety, is also a very common trait among people who have suffered trauma, especially in their childhood.[5] While it is certainly true that there are some personality types that naturally exhibit perfectionist tendencies, it is also true that perfectionism can be a trauma response—just like spiritual anxiety. It is a mental reaction to a highly stressful situation in order to cultivate acceptance and praise or to avoid punishment. Over time, if the pattern persists, these reactions may become adaptations to prolonged exposure to excessively demanding or distressing environments.

Dawn, a historian and homeschool mother of four, shared the moment when, at forty years old, she suddenly recognized the root of her perfectionism:

> I was reading an article where the man being interviewed said "I don't give things up forever." He was speaking in regard to dietary stuff, but it hit me that when I want to make changes in my life, in my mind, I always go immediately to whatever the perfect version of that thing is. Like, dairy is a problem for me? I'll be vegan. Yoga is good for me? I'll do it every single day forever. And that is not only unsustainable but wildly impractical across the board. When I think about it even a second longer, I realize moderation is much better and I adjust my expectations of myself quickly. But why do I always knee-jerk to whatever is the hard-core version of what I'm interested in? And then it hit me: "Be perfect, as I am perfect" [Matthew 5:48].
>
> Now I know that's not what it means . . . but that's the underlying rubric that zero sin is the goal, not just harm-reduction. And a large portion of my life was spent with that

message on repeat: If you think something is the "right" thing to do, you should attempt to do it perfectly. And any sin at all—no matter how small—means you are failing to hit the mark, which is the perfection of Christ. He covers you when you fail and everything, but you still have to have perfection as the unachievable aim in the first place.

So when I want to improve something about myself, I unintentionally knee-jerk to whatever the perfect version of that is in my head, even if I quickly pivot to a reasonable response. . . . I didn't even realize it was attached to a weird church root until my brain went there reading the article.

Imagine how distressing it is for a person struggling with spiritual perfectionism—the deep-seated fear that their value to God and the church is tied directly to how well they perform—to hear verses like Isaiah 64:6, which tells us that our righteous deeds are like "filthy rags." This passage, which is a favorite one for dismissing people for not doing "enough" while simultaneously shaming them to try harder, may actually communicate something different than how it is often invoked. Consider the way that the verse reads in several of the most popular translations:

> But we are all as an unclean thing,
>> and all our righteousnesses are as filthy rags
> and we all do fade as a leaf; and our iniquities,
>> like the wind, have taken us away. (KJV)

> All of us have become like one who is unclean,
>> and all our righteous acts are like filthy rags;
> we all shrivel up like a leaf,
>> and like the wind our sins sweep us away. (NIV)

> We have all become like one who is unclean,
>> and all our righteous deeds are like a filthy cloth.

CHAPTER 6

We all fade like a leaf,
> and our iniquities, like the wind, take us away.
> (NRSV updated edition)

We have all become like the unclean;
> all our righteous deeds are like a menstrual rag.
All of us wither like a leaf;
> our sins, like the wind, carry us away. (CEB)

The translations are all incredibly similar with one notable exception: Our righteous deeds are like . . . *what?* Really, Common English Bible? That's the translation you went with? As it turns out, that's actually the most accurate interpretation of the Hebrew. This term, *begged 'idim*, refers specifically to the cloths that women used to catch menstrual blood. Isaiah 64:6 is saying, in essence, that our righteousness is like a used Maxi Pad, which is . . . quite a statement. Let's take a minute to break that down.

First, it is astounding that in the twenty-first century Western church, we are still so squeamish about the natural functions of a woman's body that every single major English translation of the Bible (with the exception of the CEB) deliberately avoids the menstrual terminology. We will address a few ways historical angst about femaleness and female bodies have played a part in the rhetoric of faith in chapter 10, but for now, it's fair to ask what kind of Victorian prudishness is dictating our culture when, despite the fact that at any given time approximately one quarter of all women of reproductive age are menstruating, we still treat menstruation as so taboo and shameful as to use euphemisms when it appears in a nonmedical or ritualistic context in the Bible. On the other hand, if we accept that people *are* mature enough to talk about menstruation without fainting from embarrassment or repulsion, Isaiah 64 seems to be implying that the divine design of a woman's body is so inherently appalling as to be equated with sin.

But perhaps this passage could be understood differently from how most translations make it appear. The filthy rags are deemed such not because they are putrid and rotting but because they are *ceremonially* unclean in a kosher sense. The word used in the first line of the verse to mean "unclean," *tame*, is the word used throughout the purity laws in Leviticus. Therefore, the ritual uncleanliness of the rags in Isaiah 64 must be regarded as something more spiritually significant than simply dirty cloths; the fact that the *begged 'idim* are specifically used for menstruation may shed light on a deeper symbolic significance.

Menstruation occurs when there is the possibility of life but the egg goes unfertilized or fails to implant. Obviously, ancient peoples did not know the intricacies of human ovulation, but they certainly understood that a woman's menstrual cycle stopped during pregnancy. Therefore, when her monthly bleeding began, it was clear that there was no new life growing in her womb. Menstruation symbolizes both missed potential and a chance to try again.

Let us also examine the other similes used in this same scripture, which employs the Hebrew poetic technique of parallelism where ideas rather than words are "rhymed" by matching them. The reader is reminded that everyone dies, as does a leaf; but although the leaf is no longer living, it is still active in the wind—the same wind to which our sinful drifting from God is compared. But consider the imagery: wind is something invisible that still feels active and alive, just like quickening in pregnancy, when the mother can feel the baby's movements inside her womb even though she cannot see the baby itself. What's more, the word for "wind" (*ruach*) is the same word for "breath," such as in Genesis 7:15 to refer to every animal that has the "breath of life." It also can mean "spirit," like in Genesis 1:20, when the "Spirit of God moved upon the face of the waters" (KJV) or "a wind from God swept over the face of the waters" (NRSV updated edition). What if the parallelism in this passage is highlighting menstruation as missed potential for bringing physical life into the world just as sin is a missed opportunity for bringing spiritual life into the world? Menstruation is the process that allows the body to purge itself in order to prepare to try again to bear life. Rather than reading this verse as a *condemnation* of our efforts, perhaps we can understand it as an *invitation* to reengage with sincere hearts. Our righteous deeds fall short of what is needed for a new creation (as they always will), but they are also what allow us to keep trying. Our insufficient but sincere efforts are evidence of the fruit we hope to one day nurture.

How does such a shift in perspective change our feelings of spiritual anxiety? Does this view of the verse comfort rather than needle a troubled conscience that already feels insufficient to the call of love and service extended by Christ's liberation—as if the deck has been stacked against it from the start? After all, if praise (however unhealthy) can temporarily soothe our anxieties about giving, doing, and being all we can be, criticism can stir them up. Hebrews 10:24 says that we ought to "consider how to provoke (*paroxysmon*) one another to love and good deeds." The word literally means to stir up or incite, and it actually appears in Acts 15:39 in reference to the disagreement between Paul and Barnabas over the presence of John, who was also called Mark, on their mission trip, which resulted in the evangelists parting ways. It would appear (on the surface, at least) that this kind of unpleasant agitation is exactly what believers are called to do. If we consider the passage from Hebrews 10 in context, however, a different picture arises.

Verse 22 tells us that we should approach the presence of Christ "with a true heart in full assurance of faith, with our hearts sprinkled clean from an evil conscience and our bodies washed with pure water." The word "evil" (*ponēras*) is ultimately derived from the root-word *ponos*, meaning "pain-ridden." Right away, therefore, we see that our consciences should be at peace, not hurting or troubled. Second, the "provocation" of verse 24 is supposed to lead us toward "love and good deeds," not "fear and obligation." Finally, verse 25 urges believers to take part in "encouraging one another." The word translated "encouraging" is *parakalountes,* which comes from the word *paraklētos,* meaning one who helps, comforts, or is a legal advocate. It is the same word used five times to refer to the Holy Spirit (John 14:16, 26; 15:26; 16:7; 1 John 2:1). In other words, we are called to be a comforting presence to one another, not agitators or disturbers.

In fact, we can even take this one step further. The word translated as "Satan" in most English-language Bibles is actually just a transliteration of the Hebrew word *satan*, meaning "accuser" in the sense of someone who functions like a prosecuting attorney. This is apparent in his role in the book of Job, where *satan* appears before God in the celestial courts to argue Job's guilt. By using the word *paraklētos*, with its legal overtones, to describe the spirit of God that dwells within us, the Holy Spirit is set in direct opposition to that which accuses us and tries to find us guilty of offending God. This means that anyone who tries to stir up our conscience to make us believe that we are unworthy or inadequate stands opposed to the work of the *paraklētos,* and anyone who has driven away the sense of God's presence stands aligned with the other side.

Perhaps the thought of the Comforter at work in you can help calm your worries, relieve your fears, counter any accusations against you, and be a source of peace and reassurance. And when you do begin to feel anxiety over your "enough-ness" or controlled by agenda-driven praise from others, it may help to separate what are legitimate pricks of conscience from what are external manipulations by considering the source and perhaps the agenda of the controlling party. But even if the struggle remains—even if you find the pressure of praise too deeply engrained in the way you approach your spirituality to ever be fully free of it—perhaps you can still hold fast to the knowledge that your value to God is inherent, not conditional. You serve a loving Master who is not impressed by those who accrue earthly metrics of success, but by those who have the courage to reject the manipulations of people who live only for their own gain.

7

DENIAL—
CONTROL THROUGH REJECTION

King Lear, one of Shakespeare's bleakest tragedies, is also considered one of his greatest. Driven by a combination of vanity and insecurity, King Lear calls his three daughters to him, inviting each to share how much she loves him in return for a portion of his property. The first two ramble effusively, gushing obediently (but ultimately insincerely) about their great affection for their father. Lear is flattered by the display and happily anticipates the speech of his youngest daughter, Cordelia, with whom he has always been closest.

After each of her sister's speeches, Cordelia nervously wracks her brain to figure out what she can possibly say that will please her father and demonstrate her devotion without damaging her integrity. To the shock of everyone present, when her turn finally comes, Cordelia refuses to speak, recognizing that her love for her father is too valuable and sincere to treat as a cheap token to be traded for wealth or power.

Angry, humiliated, and hurt, the old man casts out his youngest daughter and divides his kingdom between the older two, who, predictably, mistreat and reject their father now that they have gotten what they wanted from him. They beat, blind, and drive out the king, who wanders the countryside, desperate, broken, and driven mad by grief.

During his travails, Lear is visited occasionally by a character known as the Fool, a court jester. The Fool is the one character aside from Cordelia who is brave enough to speak truth without apology to the king. Some scholars speculate that both Cordelia and the Fool may have originally been played by the same actor, as they serve a similar function and never appear onstage at the same time. Lear even affectionately refers to Cordelia at the end of the play as "my poor fool" (5.3.306). Although the Fool's biting observations sometimes anger Lear, the character's advice is usually wise and the Fool's perspective almost always proves prescient. As Regan, one of the evil sisters, remarks: "Jesters do oft prove prophets" (5.3.71).

Eventually, Lear is led to an encampment where Cordelia has raised an army to defend her father. In his blinded, injured state, he does not even recognize his daughter at first but simply accepts her kind ministrations until his senses return and the two are reconciled. In the end, all three daughters die, as does the old king as he brokenheartedly cradles the body of his youngest—the one who was most loyal—in his arms.

Let's review that plot one more time to see if anything sounds familiar:

A loving child who nervously but bravely refuses to play political games for the sake of material gain is rejected as disloyal in favor of the children who merely *claim* to be loyal, despite evidence of their pettiness, greed, jealousy, and self-serving ambitions. The father casts his lot and makes his home with the flatterers who, having exploited what he had to offer, proceed to disfigure him beyond recognition until the once-great king ends up lost, broken, and alone in the wilderness, confused and disoriented by the storms raging around him. There, he encounters the child he rejected, now thriving despite being banished from her father's realm.

It is only then that the king realizes that this child—the one who refused to surrender her integrity by offering lip service rather than true loyalty to his ideals—is the one who is ultimately willing to prove her love in a way that actually matters. She is the only child willing to suffer and fight to save her father's kingdom from those who exploited it for personal gain and power.

If we think of Lear as Western Christianity and Cordelia as dissenting Christians who refuse to comply with misguided demands that have nothing to do with true loyalty to their Parent's kingdom, we suddenly have a pretty strong metaphor for the way many current believers feel.

They have watched their siblings in Christ make flattering speeches and showy displays of affection—what Cordelia calls "glib and oily art" (1.1.224)—that are nothing but shallow gestures completely disconnected from genuine love and humility. Anyone who protests is considered an enemy and cast out. Disagreement is mistaken for disloyalty and vain ambition; after all, it is a universal human tendency to read our own motives onto our rivals. Dissenters are rejected and accused of all sorts of misdeeds. Eventually, the church as the body of Christ is twisted, disfigured, misused, and exploited for the sake of power and profit before being tossed out altogether.

Western Christianity is left wandering in the stormy wilderness, hurting, struggling, and deeply wounded. It cries out for justice, wondering why creation is in turmoil around it and trying desperately to understand what went wrong. What it cannot see is the fact that those who were rejected as disloyal may very well be the ones who actually had the most love for the kingdom and what it was supposed to represent. They are often the ones fighting on the margins not to destroy the kingdom but to preserve it—to end oppression, to put a stop to abuses, to bring peace and restoration to everyone.

But it is a sad pattern throughout history that those who dare to speak truth to power are often threatened with rejection—even if their objections stem from a sincere and earnest love. As Cordelia observes, "We are not the first / Who with best meaning have incurr'd the worst" (5.3.4–5).

Nor, of course, was she the last.

((((((()))))))

Massachusetts in the 1630s: what a grand time to be alive if you really loved hearing sermons about the pits of hell. And were a man. And White. And owned land. And were in complete political agreement with the civil and religious authorities (who were basically one and the same). And had already survived smallpox so that you had natural immunity, even though germ theory wasn't really around yet.

Yes, life was a virtual paradise if you fit that bill.

Unfortunately for Anne Hutchinson, a Puritan woman who had recently emigrated to Massachusetts from England with her family, she ticked only a few of those boxes.[1]

Hutchinson began hosting weekly meetings for the colony's women in her home, where they discussed healing and midwifery. They also dissected the sermons they were hearing from their local pulpits and the problematic theology those homilies contained. Before long, men also began to come to these meetings, and attendance sometimes topped eighty. Hutchinson taught that a direct, personal relationship with God was possible without needing clergy as an intermediary. (*The nerve!*) She also criticized the prevailing Puritan theology that promoted works over grace and demanded absolute obedience to church authorities.

Massachusetts Governor John Winthrop and prominent Puritan minister John Cotton were concerned by Hutchinson both as a threat to their own civil power as well as her religious authority as a woman. Together with other clergy, they managed to pass several resolutions designed to stifle her growing influence, including one that specifically banned all meetings in her home.

Hutchinson ignored these orders and continued preaching until, in November 1637, she faced the courts to answer the charges leveled against her of "contempt and sedition"—essentially, daring to express disagreement with the celebrity pastors of the colony and having too much spiritual influence as a woman. Basically, she was charged with preaching without the proper plumbing.

In court, even her accusers admitted that her knowledge of Scripture was above reproach. But on the final day of her trial, when Hutchinson testified that she spoke with God and closed her remarks with a prophecy of divine retribution upon the men of the court and the colony for their action, she was found guilty of heresy and banished from Massachusetts. Her followers were removed from all positions of authority and required to relinquish their firearms. The following spring, as soon as the roads cleared, Hutchinson, her husband, their eleven children, and thirty other families left to move to the colony of Rhode Island at the invitation of Governor Roger Williams. There they established the city of Portsmouth and held to a philosophy of religious tolerance and "liberty of conscience."[2] She was later reported to have maintained a peaceable relationship with the Narragansett people native to the area.

If the story ended there, it would be a shameful chapter in American religious history that at least ended in a "live and let live" arrangement. But it didn't.

In June 1638, Hutchinson gave birth to a stillborn child who suffered from severe birth defects. When word of this reached Massachusetts, John Cotton announced from the pulpit that it was proof God was punishing her. Governor Winthrop, who kept close tabs on Hutchinson even after she left his colony and declared her "American Jezebel" in his almost obsessive journal entries about her, now spread rumors that the deceased infant was actually a demon and that many of her followers had also given birth to tiny, misshapen devil-spawn.[3]

But still the harassment of Hutchinson was not done. After Rhode Island Governor Williams died four years later, clergymen from Massachusetts traveled to Providence and lied to Hutchinson, insisting that Rhode Island was going to be absorbed into the governance of Massachusetts. They demanded that she forswear her teachings and have her followers do the same so that they might be accepted back into society when the takeover happened. Once again, Hutchinson ignored their orders, but she also moved again, this time to Pelham Bay, New York, in what is now the Bronx, to put greater distance between herself and her persecutors. Now a widow, she and her children were settled for barely a year before everyone except her daughter Susannah was killed in an attack by the Siwanoy tribe. When he eventually heard the news about Hutchinson's death, Governor Winthrop praised God for answering his prayers with divine justice against her.

In 1987, exactly 350 years after her expulsion, the state of Massachusetts officially pardoned Hutchinson for her "crimes." It was an important acknowledgment, but ultimately an empty gesture. No symbolic act could give any peace or dignity to Anne Hutchinson, the Kepler family, Galileo, or any other of the countless women and men persecuted over the centuries for daring to fall out of lockstep with the dominant religious powers—Puritan Protestants, Lutherans, Catholics, pick your branch of the faith—in their pursuit of truth.

Easy as it may be to dismiss this example as just something that happened "back then," we all know it isn't just a seventeenth-century phenomenon. What difference is there, really, between John Winthrop reveling in Hutchinson's violent death in 1643 and the crocodile tears of many evangelical leaders who all but crowed on social media at the untimely death of the trailblazing, progressive Christian blogger and author Rachel Held Evans in 2019? Or between the excommunication of Johannes Kepler in 1613 (and the subsequent attacks on his family covered in chapter 5) and the criticism lobbed at Amy Grant by prominent voices in the Southern Baptist Convention for offering to host her gay niece's wedding on her farm in 2022? How many people in your own experience have been shunned or excluded simply for asking questions or challenging certain "sacred cows" of their denomination or faith tradition?

When a religious body becomes obsessed with silencing the challenger, eliminating the competition, crushing the dissenter, or taking out anyone who is a threat to their power, they are teaching a gospel of rejection rather than redemption. Just as in personal relationships, of course, healthy boundaries in church communities are vital; there is a difference, however, between people who are out to cause intentional harm and those who raise questions for the sake of growth, maturity, and self-critique. Unfortunately, we can't know a person's true motives; all we can do is examine our own:

> *When a religious body becomes obsessed with taking out anyone who is a threat to their power, they are teaching a gospel of rejection rather than redemption*

- Why does this challenge feel threatening to me?
- What do I stand to lose here?
- What does it mean if it turns out that this other perspective is true—or even if a firm answer to the question doesn't matter at all in the grand scheme of things?
- If my entire sense of God or salvation is rooted in this one idea being questioned, does that mean my concept of one or both of these things is too small or too limited?

In chapter 5, we looked at the parable of the rich man and his banquet guests, a story that Jesus shares while at a banquet himself. Jesus must have been full of stories that evening, because he shares another parable at that same feast—an object lesson in humility—after watching the other guests jockey for position at the table. The text observes that when Jesus "noticed how the guests chose the places of honor, he told them a parable":

> "When you are invited by someone to a wedding banquet, do not sit down at the place of honor, in case someone more

distinguished than you has been invited by your host, and
the host who invited both of you may come and say to you,
'Give this person your place,' and then in disgrace you would
start to take the lowest place. But when you are invited, go and
sit down at the lowest place, so that when your host comes,
he may say to you, 'Friend, move up higher'; then you will be
honored in the presence of all who sit at the table with you.
For all who exalt themselves will be humbled, and those who
humble themselves will be exalted." (Luke 14:8–11)

Jesus is speaking directly to those whose primary concern
was flaunting their own power by subjugating others. He was at
a literal banquet, speaking about literal behaviors he witnessed.
Understandably, then, this passage is usually applied quite literally in modern-day sermons: Don't be arrogant, and don't hold
yourself above others when you gather together. It's a practical,
solid takeaway.

But the passage is clearly described as a *parable* in verse 7,
which means it has other significance in its *metaphorical* application—the less obvious truth below the surface. Yes, this story
could certainly have social implications, but its moral lesson actually runs much deeper. First, consider who is usually the host
in Jesus's parables about feasting—the ones about inviting people to dine in each other's company, nourish one another, and
celebrate together. Jesus's audience knew very well that he was
talking about God as the host; verse 15 states that "One of the
dinner guests, on hearing this, said to him, 'Blessed is anyone
who will eat bread in the kingdom of God!'"

Notice, too, that there is never any indication that the banquet's host is concerned about running out of food or wine (as
happened at the wedding at Cana in John 2) or that they only
provided a limited number of chairs. This table has a place for
everyone; the host already made sure of that. The job of those
invited is simply to receive the hospitality being offered, not to
police the guest list. It's not their party, after all.

At a lavish banquet like this, the only obligation you have is to honor your host by honoring their guests. Show respect to the other people present by making sure that you are not blocking a space reserved for someone else—and certainly don't do it in the hopes that this gets you nearer to the host. After all, if you think no one could top you in importance—that you're the best your host can do in terms of honored or important acquaintances—you are not only insulting your host's acquaintances and connections, but you are also revealing the inferiority and limitations of your own.

Finally, Jesus closes the parable by speaking directly to his host for the evening, saying: "When you give a luncheon or a dinner, do not invite your friends or your brothers and sisters or your relatives or rich neighbors." Instead, Jesus explains, the host should invite people outside their sphere who have otherwise been rejected and who cannot reinforce the status quo by repaying them and propping up their social position (Luke 14:12–14).

The only obligation you have is to honor your host by honoring their guests

Yet rejection seems to be baked into our modern church culture. I don't know that there is any Christian alive in the Western world who hasn't felt hurt, let down, judged, or excluded by their local congregation at some point. The simple response is usually to point out the obvious—that the church on earth is a perfect vision realized through imperfect people, so it will always have problems and flaws. But what if we stopped entertaining mediocrity in our churches? What if we decided that the body of Christ deserves better than we have done with it? What if we didn't automatically label every dissenting voice as dangerous, but instead considered whether they were offering constructive criticism? What if, instead of ostracizing people for questioning the status quo, we listened to their critiques and actually committed ourselves to the hard work of auditing our own beliefs and practices to separate comfort from commands and tradition from truth?

In Acts 17, the Berean believers are praised for welcoming the message that Paul and Silas brought that challenged old religious ideas, "and examined the scriptures every day to see whether these things were so" (v. 11). The word translated "examined" (*anakrinontes*) means to question or investigate, and can even be translated as being "on trial" in the sense of cross-examining a witness. Rather than getting rankled by the Bereans' questioning, Paul and Silas encourage their curiosity and concern because it shows their genuine engagement and personal investment in pursuing truth, even if it causes them to reexamine their time-honored traditions. The Bereans were praised for their inquisitiveness rather than being told to shut up and fall in line. Truth has nothing to fear from questions.

What if we stopped entertaining mediocrity in our churches? What if we decided that the body of Christ deserves better than we have done with it?

Throughout the ancient world, religion was largely an ethnic designator as much as a belief system. In a world of polytheism, deities were strongly connected to the land their people occupied, and whom you worshipped was largely synonymous with where you lived. Even when a nation was colonized by another, the locals were often allowed to continue worshipping their ancestral gods either in lieu of, or at least alongside, the gods of their conquerors. Judaism, as it had developed by the Second Temple period (516 BCE–70 CE), was unique in its understanding of YHWH as not just the supreme god among a host of divinities, but as the *only* God. One of the hallmarks of Jesus's ministry was his efforts to demonstrate that YHWH was a universal God who wasn't tied to the land and was less concerned with ancient holiness customs than with how people treated one another.

The question, therefore, of who was "in" and who was "out" was of central importance in the early church. Jesus was obviously Jewish, as was the religious tradition from which he emerged, but the movement and its message were not limited to

Jewish people. Despite some archaic usages of the term to mean "European," "Christian" is only a religious designation, not an ethnic one. One does not cease to be Jewish just because one ceases to follow a particular branch of the faith (Orthodox, ultra-Orthodox, Reformed, etc.) or even if one leaves the faith altogether. With Christianity, however, if you leave the fold, you lose that part of your identity entirely. You not only surrender the title of "Baptist" or "Methodist" or "Catholic" but also the overarching term "Christian," which might have kept you tethered, however loosely, to your former faith community. This can make the threat of rejection particularly daunting.

Truth has nothing to fear from questions

Zealous evangelists love to quote Jesus in Matthew 12:30: "Whoever is not with us is against us." Yet they tend to gloss over Mark 9:40, when Jesus is reported as saying the same thing in reverse: "Whoever is not against us is with us." For many denominations, sects, and faith traditions, Christianity has been reduced to an all-or-nothing proposition. Those who fail to fall in line 100 percent are cast "out of the fold and into the cold."

Dan, a historian and political science professor, understands this tension—and the deep anxiety it causes—very well. He grew up primarily in a fundamentalist tradition, then attended and later taught at a denominational college that he described as

> incredibly authoritarian right from the start. . . . There were some good professors and such but underlying it all was the idea that they had their religious views—which were very strict conservative beliefs that go back to some nineteenth-century traditions. And the entire system—the school, the institution, the employment that came after—was built around forcing that view. Even disagreement or questions that might not even have been an attempt to steer in a different direction, just asking for an explanation for certain things, were not only frowned upon but were seen as disloyalty and dis-

sent, and would immediately result in you being marked as a potential problem. And if you didn't at some point make that right somehow, by demonstrating your obedience, you would find yourself on the way out.

Dan explained the extreme lengths the college took toward discipline, citing as an example their policy on movies. "You weren't even permitted to go to a movie theater, and if they caught you buying a DVD—I mean, we're not even talking hard-core stuff. Anything PG or higher, if you tried to buy or rent a DVD and somebody saw you, you could be called in before the administration. As a student, you could be threatened with expulsion, and as an employee, you could be fired." And these were not hollow threats; he recounted seeing people dismissed for challenging even the most basic things, including a senior administrator who was let go for being too disruptive over his suggestions that a campus banquet be organized differently. The result was an atmosphere where leadership went unquestioned—and acted accordingly.

After Dan left that college and began teaching at another Christian institution, however, the same pattern of abuse emerged, but he knew that questioning methods would lead to ostracism. It was a conflict that left him deeply anxious:

> It wasn't even about eternity. It felt like they were using spiritual terms to apply temporal pressure, temporal views, temporal authoritarianism, because ultimately that's what felt like it mattered to most of them anyway: the authority and the power. . . . I saw it at the schools and at subsidiary organizations that I experienced over the years as well. . . . The question for me was always, "Okay, what I do in the face of that power?" Because I didn't want to lose my job; I didn't want to lose friends; I didn't want to lose certain social standing in the community—like anybody would feel. That was an enor-

mous source of anxiety, and it all stemmed from this idea that if I'm not seen as being in the exact same spiritually defined mindset and culture as they are, then I risk that ostracism. I risk danger to my family's emotional and economic welfare. I didn't agree with so much of what they were about, but I got really good at nodding along and saying "Mm-hmm."

Dan and his wife were invited to help rebuild their new institution's associated church, which was struggling in the wake of revelations that the founder and longtime pastor had a series of credible accusations of pedophilia leveled against him. At first, Dan was excited about the process and felt that they were truly helping rehabilitate the organization into something healthy and God-honoring, but, "especially as things became more political in the last several years, as evangelicalism has demonstrated in a lot of ways recently, that soured pretty quickly." He explains:

I'm a professor of history. I teach an American government class. I'm not going to use my position to push my views, but they are certainly a platform for questioning and examining things. We were supposed to be an educational institution, which meant everything should be above board and open for conversation, but I was approached on a number of occasions and told, "You shouldn't be doing that. You're out of step with our message. You're out of step with Christ. You're out of step with the faith."

After expressing concerns in leadership meetings about some of the rhetoric he was hearing in the church, Dan and his family suddenly found themselves labeled as dissenters. Every meeting, Dan said, made him question: "Is this the meeting where I get fired?" Finally, an influential donor at his church called him out for not falling lockstep in line politically with the rest of the leadership at his church:

He said something to the effect of, "Shouldn't you talk to the elders in the church, because they know so much more about this than you do?"

I was a forty-eight-year-old man and a professor of history and political science. I mean, yeah, there are far smarter people than me, but I'm not a novice. Then he followed it up by saying, "Because your position in the institution could be at risk as a result."

I said, "Are you suggesting that A) I'm going to be fired for my views and B) you have something to do with it? Because you don't work for the institution. You don't have a position in the school. You're certainly not in a position of authority over me."

But he was a big donor, and it wasn't much longer before I got called into a meeting and they [the board] told me they were not renewing my contract. I actually felt relieved at that point because what I've shared is just the tip of the iceberg—just the nutshell. It was just a tremendous amount of emotional and psychological abuse coming from a spiritual place as its origin.

The relief Dan felt in parting ways with the institution, as well as with the denomination he'd been a part of most of his life, was not all-encompassing, though. He and his wife were almost fifty years old and suddenly found themselves starting from scratch socially. They were completely and utterly alone, cut off from their former friends, community, and even family. "We left behind just about every adult relationship we had cultivated over twenty to thirty years—all gone, because they saw me as apostate," he explains.

They saw me as somebody who had rejected the faith—their version of the faith—and therefore I was anathema. . . . Even when we left [the first college], I remember the HR director coming up to me at lunch and saying, "You really don't know what you're doing, do you?" . . . Because leaving was automatic rejection. The message was, "You're going to lose everything and you're doing it because you're out of step with us because we're the only arbiters or source of truth."

It is a tremendous load of anxiety, because again you're asking daily, "What if they find out what I really believe? What if they find out what views I have? What if they find out I bought a movie that was PG-13?" All ridiculous things, but they led to a certain degree of terror—a certain degree of uncertainty. That was paralyzing, and it was difficult to try and find a way through that.

If there's one regret I have, it's that we didn't walk away sooner, but I had grown up in it and so had my wife. . . . My mother is one of the relationships I've lost because of this, because in her eyes, and the eyes of a lot of the rest of the family, I'm apostate for leaving. . . . We fell out of favor, and the whole spiritual abuse just felt like a giant sandbag on top of us after a while.

Just as we are wrapping up our conversation, Dan, now an administrator at a state university, steps back into his professorial role; you can see the passion he still has for debating ideas and investigating truth. "There is a monster that is growing within Christian circles," he says sagely:

This is something that has been a problem throughout the entirety of church history: the ability to cope with, let alone manage, power—using the word to act the way you want it to apply. It's a cliché, isn't it? And the church has suffered at its worst when it has done it to itself. It cries persecution a lot, but it has no qualms about allowing it within its own ranks and being the perpetrator of it. Just from a historical perspective, we're seeing it happen again in as ugly a fashion as I think it's ever been seen in church history, and we have to fight it. Somehow, some way.

The experience of Dan and his family is one very real and painful form of control through rejection—or the fear of it. This is a pressure that preachers' kids and the families of church leaders in general understand especially well. It often plays out one of two ways: either as rebellion (à la the proverbially rebellious preacher's kid) or as deeply internalized anxiety.

Marie had the latter experience. Her father was an elder in her church from the time she was in elementary school, "which meant I got to be a fly on the wall for how the elders dealt with different members who came forward," she explains. This insider perspective gave her the added pressure of being extra-scrutinized by church and community members.

We are speaking one autumn evening when her three teenagers are out of the house at their after-school jobs or extracurricular activities. Given her experiences growing up, she is cautious about discussing topics that might give them similar worries and stress about their perception in the church.

"I always felt guilt for not agreeing with what church leaders or my parents told me," Marie says. "When I disagreed with my dad, I would always get a guilt-ridden conversation about how disobedient I was being and how much that went against the will of God. It made me want to shut up and never share my thoughts out loud because I didn't want to be chastised for it."

She struggled with the easy "church answers" that people tossed around as if they were some kind of universal panacea for any and all matters—the be-all and end-all solution for any problem.

"If you were going through something, you were just supposed to stop and pray—just talk to God about it," Marie says. "But what if that doesn't really help much? You can't admit it. Whenever you tried to open up and be honest, people would just say, 'Maybe you just need to pray about that.' Look, I tried that, but nothing is changing. I need something else. But people don't want to hear that. They want prayer to be the simple answer to everything. And if you're a 'good Christian' then you should think so, too."

As she grew up, Marie grew increasingly fearful of speaking up about these apparent shortcomings because she had seen firsthand what happened to people who stepped outside the accepted behavioral model. "I remember when I was in fifth or sixth grade," she begins,

> and there was a woman who got pregnant out of wedlock, and the elders—who were all men, of course—had this whole meeting trying to figure out how to deal with that "situation."
>
> I was like, "What situation? She is having a baby and she's by herself. She didn't have an abortion, because that's something you say is wrong, so you should be happy with her, right? Because now that she's keeping the baby, why is this even something that needs some behind-the-curtain discussion?"
>
> But they concluded that they had to ask her to step down from her teaching roles and would probably have to ask her to leave the church, too. I was eleven years old, and I thought, "Is that really the right thing?"
>
> But because I had been raised to feel so much shame around questioning, I wondered, "Am I wrong in my thoughts or am I allowed to have my own opinions?" I honestly didn't know, and I doubted myself, because I was raised to be concerned about what everyone else was thinking. *How was this going to affect my parents' roles in the church? Am I doing what is right for other people or for the reputation of my congregation?* I was under a constant microscope because of my dad's leadership position. The message was always, "Your actions reflect on me." Every move, every mistake I made I was afraid was going to lead to one of those elder meetings where the men would discuss what had happened and decide if we had to be asked to leave the church, too.

The anxiety stemming from this intense pressure followed Marie her entire life. Even as an adult, when she told her parents she was planning to divorce her abusive spouse: "Their first reaction was, 'How will this impact Dad's eldership? Oh, okay, it's scriptural so he'll be fine.' I was just like, 'At this point in time, I don't need Scriptures, I need my parents.'"

Despite several moves and trying out different denominations over the years, Marie confesses:

> I still have a lot of anxiety in church as an adult because any time I ask something that maybe questions or goes against the church party line, I feel like everyone is looking at me like I'm a troublemaker, even if it's an innocent question or something I'm really actually wondering about. I'm getting better; I've grown a lot and gotten better at prioritizing my children's needs over other people's opinions. But I still worry I'm going to get excluded or rejected and whether my opinions aren't even worth voicing. So a lot of times, I just shut down and don't say anything at all.

The threat of social rejection or the perceived loss of group identity can be major contributors to spiritual anxiety. When your overall identity is fundamentally rooted in your religious beliefs, what do you do when your religious body rejects you? If they are the sole mediators of God and of God's truth (as many present themselves to be), the idea of being outside the fold also implies that you are outside of the will or love of God.

The rejection doesn't even have to be a complete casting out, however. Sometimes, people become isolated *within* a church because of the anxiety brought on by one of the most basic and stereotypical Christian sins: gossip.

Does this sound familiar? You are going through a difficult time and struggling with feelings of isolation until someone in your church reaches out and says, "You don't seem like yourself right now. Is everything all right? Please know I'm here if you ever need to talk." It feels like a lifeline. You're not invisible after all;

someone sees you and cares enough to reach out. Surely God sent this person into your life at just the right moment to come beside you and be a friend you can trust to help you unburden your heart and maybe even offer you some wise counsel. So you do, and you feel a profound sense of gratefulness and acceptance.

And then, a few weeks or months later, someone else says something that seems a little too pointed, perhaps a bit too on-the-nose. Maybe it's a raised eyebrow or knowing look—little hints that they might know more about you than you realized. Sometimes it even becomes a passive-aggressive form of condemnation, with seemingly innocent comments tossed out like grenades wrapped in plausible deniability and punctuated with a shrug and "I'm not speaking to anyone directly, but if the shoe fits . . ." Suddenly, you're caught in a deluge of nervousness bordering on paranoia. *Who knows what? Did someone tell them, or do they just suspect? And what do they think of me now?*

Or maybe someone even reaches out to you directly to ask whether a rumor they've heard is true and, as you pull the thread backward, you quickly realize that the "trusted friend" who seemed like a godsend at the time has actually been less-than-respectful of your confidence. It turns out they've shared your story—maybe even with embellishments—and you once again find yourself feeling alienated and on edge. *Who did they tell? Who knows my deepest, darkest secrets—and what are they thinking about me?*

Now that you need community more than ever to help walk you through this betrayal (on top of your original struggles), you feel alone, ashamed, and always on the alert. Who is safe? Sure, the guiltiest party is the person who violated your confidence, but what about the people who willingly listened to secrets that were clearly not something meant for public consumption? Is there *anyone* you can trust?

I imagine that nearly everyone reading this has experienced something similar at one point or another. Churches are notorious gossip mills, and we are all familiar with the old "gossip disguised as a prayer request" move. It can be intriguing or even entertaining to be on the receiving end of spicy insider information, but it is a painful and isolating experience to be the person whose personal struggles have been turned into a form of entertainment or social capital—especially in a place that is supposed to be safe, welcoming, and free of harsh judgment.

Let me be clear: *This is absolutely not advocating for hushing up potentially dangerous or dire situations.* We all know the horrific damage and abuses that have been swept under the rug and allowed to persist because of deliberate silence. But we all also know that it is one thing to speak in confidence with church leaders or other trusted individuals who have the authority to investigate matters and it is something else to either whisper about someone's secrets at a social gathering, embellish a story to make yourself seem "in the know," or spread stories to deflect from one's own problems or dysfunction.

Unfortunately, churches are a breeding ground for gossip because they are places where people can unburden their souls (as indeed they should)—and also because we enjoy demonstrating that we've been entrusted with confidential information to "prove" we are trustworthy enough to have been confided in in the first place. We're also just really good at rationalizing our actions and disguising our motives in the name of God.

This is not news to you, nor am I so naive as to think I am writing anything groundbreaking or particularly illuminating here. Church gossip is, sadly, so common as to be cliché. And that's all the more reason why we need to address it as a potential contributor to spiritual anxiety. When people feel unsafe in their local congregation because of rumors that have been shared irresponsibly, they are likely to withdraw or disengage from the church—and for good reason. The anxiety of feeling like your pain might be a topic of entertainment to others is enough to drive anyone away.

It is essential that we recognize church gossip as a form of spiritual abuse. Among the qualifications for church leadership in 1 Timothy are the requirements that candidates not be "double-tongued" (3:8) or "slanderers" (3:11), yet how often is gossip a part of the very fabric of our churches? It is a behavior that can be weaponized for the sake of executing control over someone else or self-elevation at the cost of another person's emotional well-being, and it leads to rejection either by the gossipers or by the subject choosing to remove themselves from the community. Again, *this is entirely different from bringing legitimate concerns about safety to the proper authorities*; this is the careless, immature, or reckless sharing of someone else's personal business with unconcerned parties.

If we are going to demand that we no longer accept mediocrity from our churches, we must ask ourselves what we have done to contribute to this kind of culture. How often have we violated someone's trust either because it didn't seem that significant to us or because doing so made us feel more important? Maybe we don't spread stories, but how often have we willingly listened to them rather than shutting the conversation down, calling out the behavior, or at least walking away when it was clear that the information had originally been shared in confidence?

In fact, walking away may lie at the heart of easing spiritual anxiety. For people who remain in unhealthy environments—whether abusive to themselves or to others—the anxiety is only going to get worse. For those who live in fear of loss of community, loss of identity, loss of relationships, loss of livelihood, or loss of belonging, the unease will only increase as the disconnect grows between what you *actually* believe and the role you have to play to stay "in the fold." It can be excruciatingly painful and deeply terrifying to separate from a religious family (and sometimes from a real one, too, as a result)—but this is exactly what Jesus told us to anticipate when he warned:

> "For I have come to set a man against his father,
> and a daughter against her mother,
> and a daughter-in-law against her mother-in-law,
> and one's foes will be members of one's own
>   household. . . .
> Those who find their life will lose it, and those who
>   lose their life for my sake will find it." (Matthew
>   10:35–36, 39)

He repeats this message again, this time to Peter, in Matthew 19: "And everyone who has left houses or brothers or sisters or father or mother or wife or children or fields for my name's sake will receive a hundredfold and will inherit eternal life" (v. 29). Jesus knew that his followers would face rejection for pursuing him and the message of radical love he taught. Nothing about rejection—either the anticipation of it or the actual realization of it—is easy. Neither is the decision to leave (that is, provided that the decision has not already been made for you). Jesus understood that the path of faith he was teaching was going to divide groups, dissolve relationships, and uproot people from the places they call home. But he promised even greater abundance of relationships and belonging for those who were willing to step out in faith to look for him elsewhere. Of course, maybe the alienation from family, tradition, and community is not worth the trade-off to you right now. Maybe you would rather choke down the cognitive dissonance, disagreement, or anxiety in order to maintain certain relationships. Maybe IIL makes the act of seeking God elsewhere feel too daunting or too daring (and perhaps it helps explain why loved ones stay enmeshed in toxic religious systems, as well). No judgment—you need to do what sits best with your soul, and that may change with time and circumstances. Only you can decide when and if the cost of staying outweighs the burden of leaving.

Just know there is nothing wrong with walking away from a place where God *isn't* in order to reach a place where God *is*. If you struggle to feel the Holy Spirit in your church, ask yourself why. Has Jesus been abandoned for the sake of power, tradition, comfort, or control? If Christ feels absent, maybe he is. If the old mantra is true that "a person is known by the company they keep," perhaps those who have been rejected by manipulative or abusive religious groups are in good company after all.

When we combat spiritual anxiety by breaking the hold that threats of exclusion, shunning, excommunication, disfellow-shipping, or alienation have over us—when we choose to walk away when Christ no longer seems present—we are following a direct command from Jesus to actively "seek" the kingdom of God, rather than to passively receive it at the hands of our friends and family. In fact, Matthew 6 contains one of the great "clob-ber passages" often weaponized against people with spiritual anxiety. After all, right there in the Sermon on the Mount, Jesus preaches his famous words on worry:

> "Therefore I tell you, do not worry about your life, what you will eat or what you will drink, or about your body, what you will wear. Is not life more than food and the body more than clothing? Look at the birds of the air: they neither sow nor reap nor gather into barns, and yet your heavenly Father feeds them. Are you not of more value than they? And which of you by worrying can add a single hour to your span of life? . . . But if God so clothes the grass of the field, which is alive today and tomorrow is thrown into the oven, will he not much more clothe you—you of little faith? Therefore do not worry, saying, 'What will we eat?' or 'What will we drink?' or 'What will we wear?' . . . But seek first the kingdom of God and his righ-teousness, and all these things will be given to you as well." (Matthew 6:27–33)

Please note that when Jesus says not to worry, it's not a blanket statement condemning all worry ever; he is saying not to get caught up in matters of personal luxury or ease. The more important thing is that you dedicate your energy to seeking out God—and sometimes that means seeking God *away* from a place where God seems to be absent. Leaving a church doesn't have to mean leaving your faith; it simply means you are following

We are following a direct command from Jesus to actively "seek" the kingdom of God, rather than to passively receive it at the hands of our friends and family

where God is leading, pursuing Christ at the cost of your own comfort. As Anne Hutchinson reportedly declared in her 1637 trial: "Better to be cast out of the church than to deny Christ."

Or, put another way, it's the same question the angel asked the women at the empty tomb in Luke 24:5: "Why do you look for the living among the dead?"

DEGRADATION—
CONTROL THROUGH SHAME

Content warning: discussions of self-harm, body image, homophobia, and child sexual abuse

If you were to ask, "Who is the villain of *The Sound of Music*?" most people would promptly reply, "The Baroness."

Elsa Schraeder, referred to more often by her peerage title, is a widowed bombshell socialite with her sights set on Captain Von Trapp. Oozing style, sexuality, and scathing snark, she is confident, self-possessed, and always ready with a witty remark or biting commentary delivered with a sardonic smile. Under different circumstances, the Baroness's cleverness and conviction would make her a good ally for Maria, the buoyant and indefatigable novitiate-turned-governess with headstrong ideals and a song for every occasion.

To that point, "I've Got Confidence," Maria's anthem of determined (if performative) self-assuredness, brings girl power anthem vibes to 1930s Austria. Whereas Maria belts out the lyrics in an effort to convince herself of their veracity, one can almost imagine the Baroness carelessly humming the song as a daily affirmation of what she already knows to be true as she affixes an unlit Gitanes in her cigarette holder and descends the stairs to preside as *Grande Dame* over Vienna's social scene. The two women are both bold, fearless souls who unapologetically speak their minds and win over hearts with a combination of charm and force of will.

So what, exactly, makes the Baroness the villain of the story? She seems genuinely in love with Captain Von Trapp, and while she clearly lacks Maria's maternal inclinations, she is not unkind to the children. She laughs along with them when they gleefully tumble out of the boat to greet their faither. She even seems approving of their musical performances and marionette skills. True, she alludes to "a delightful little thing called boarding school," but boarding school was the norm for wealthy European children of the time; this hardly makes her the evil stepmother of fairy tales. Most importantly, unlike many other characters in the Von Trapps' orbit, Baroness Schraeder expresses no sympathy for the Third Reich. All told, her only apparent sin is the fact that she is positioned as the antagonist to the cheerful, lovable Maria. Set against the backdrop of rising fascism, the Baroness seems comparatively saintly.

And yet, we inherently recognize the Baroness as someone we dislike, distrust, and actively root against. But *why*? Is it really as simple as the fact that she is the romantic rival to the beloved protagonist? That doesn't seem fair. Who hasn't tried to pull strings to maintain the favor of a love interest whose attentions appear distracted? That hardly qualifies her as a "bad guy." And yet, she certainly isn't one of the "good guys"; so what is it that places her so clearly in the "villain" column?

I think the answer is that we dislike the Baroness not so much because of what she does but because of *how* she goes about trying to achieve her aims. The world-wise socialite recognizes something Maria does not: they are rivals in a contest only one of them even realizes exists, and she exploits this knowledge to come out ahead.

Despite the Baroness typifying a modern woman radiating sexual confidence and freedom while Maria is the singing, frolicking domestic ideal of a virginial mother-figure, the two actually fulfill the opposite roles. Elsa Schraeder, for all her performative independence, represents the status quo. Tradition. Convention. The time-honored order that undergirds society once you peel away a few glittering new trends. The way things have always been and as they will go on unless some major social upheaval occurs.

Maria, on the other hand, is an interloper. She has essentially gate-crashed the comfortable social structures that elevate people like Captain Von Trapp and Baroness Schraeder comfortably into a higher caste. As an interruption to the established, accepted order of things, Maria's mere presence as an energetic outsider who has won the loyalty of a large swath of the Von Trapp family threatens the carefully maintained social order of her environment.

As soon as the Baroness realizes that Maria is operating outside of the conventional rules of the cultural power structure, she purposely makes Maria aware of her natural feelings of attraction—and then smoothly shames her for them until Maria retreats entirely. It is a deliberate, calculated strategy to control someone else's behavior in order to achieve a desired outcome.

This is the exact same technique used in shame-based cultures, including many Christian movements built around certain themes of purity or prescriptive behavior. The people at the top promoting these messages as gospel may not act in an overtly insidious manner, but just like Baroness Schraeder, their primary motivation is holding onto power. When the other person is shamed into a posture of humiliation or disgrace, there is no longer a threat to the objectives, goals, agendas, loyalties, and well-worn traditions that have kept them in control.

Maria's feelings for Captain Von Trapp are natural—predictable, even. But when the Baroness realizes that they threaten to displace her from her position of primacy, she exploits Maria's religious background and inherent moral earnestness for her own ends. She manipulates Maria with shame in order to bring the young woman's potential deviation from the traditional script back under control.

If we inherently detect Baroness Schraeder's duplicity and devious motives of control, why have so many of us languished under similar circumstances of self-serving religious manipulation that caused us to cower, retreat, or try to shut down our natural but "problematic" feelings altogether?

Probably because it's usually easier to spot the villain from outside the story than inside it. Manipulators aren't usually obvious about their agenda or techniques; if they were, they would be far less effective at orchestrating the outcome they desire. Instead, they are subtle, smooth—dropping a kind word here and a two-sided compliment there, winning allegiances and power struggles with a calculated smile. If they can achieve their objectives by leveraging the power of shame to subdue challengers, they can claim to hold the moral high ground. After all, shame only works because it feeds on a sense of guilt in the accused party. The person, in essence, convicts themselves, even if no crime has been committed. And the manipulator emerges from it all with clean hands.

This is what makes shame-based control so effective.

In order to understand how shame functions in a religious environment, we need to first consider how religious guilt is different from run-of-the-mill guilt. The common distinction between guilt and shame is that guilt means you acted wrong and shame means that you *are* wrong—that something is fundamentally bad about you as a person. Current pop psychology makes a big deal about this difference in an effort to help people overcome debilitating feelings of shame, and that is certainly a valuable tool.

That differentiation does not always work in faith-settings or for people raised in strictly religious environments, however, because we are taught that our actions stem from our character: "Thus you will know them by their fruits" (Matthew 7:20). Our actions proceed directly from who we are; they are not independent from our most fundamental being: "No good tree bears bad fruit, nor again does a bad tree bear good fruit; for each tree is known by its own fruit. For people do not gather figs from thorns, nor do they pick grapes from a bramble bush. The good person out of the good treasure of the heart produces good, and the evil person out of evil treasure produces evil" (Luke 6:43–45).

With this in mind, we can recognize that the common linguistic nuance between guilt and shame doesn't carry the same sharp division of concepts that it might to a more secular audience. It also helps to explain why shame is such an effective tool for manipulation and abuse within religious settings; if what you do is simply the visible manifestation of who you are, then guilt and shame are essentially the same thing and point to the same inevitable conclusion: something is wrong with *you*.

Please keep in mind that this discussion should not be taken to imply that sin and its consequences are not real, nor that a person who has sinned should not practice penitence. Some degree of guilt can be a good thing; it is a sign that your conscience is calibrated properly ("I did wrong = I feel bad"). If you feel bad after causing someone harm or acting against the dictates of your conscience—*congratulations! You're probably not a full-blown sociopath.* But that's not the type of shame we are discussing in this chapter.

Abusive shame is designed to take agency away from a person for the sake of controlling their behavior or allegiance. It is mental manipulation with an eye toward triggering self-reproach and stifling independence by causing the victim to doubt, distrust, or despise themselves.

So how are shame and guilt leveraged in the church? (I am going to be using the terms interchangeably, since they function in virtually identical ways in religious settings.) For starters, we often point out that Jesus cancelled our debt while still insisting we must always be mindful of what we "owe" or "deserve." The results of this kind of mixed message can be far more damaging than we realize. One person I spoke with said that the glorification of blood in the Christian faith in songs, prayers, and metaphors like celebration over being "washed in the blood" triggered their desire for self-harm through cutting: "If Jesus shed his blood for our sins, why shouldn't I want to shed my own when I feel guilty for my sins?"

What's more, shame is often quantified; we make judgments on whether a person has shown *enough* shame to warrant their current behavior. Yes, the blood of Jesus washes away all sins . . . but was the person penitent enough in their apology? Did they act humble enough for long enough afterward to have sufficiently communicated their ownership of wrongdoing? What if they go back to acting "normal" or even (God forbid) *happy* too soon after their transgression? What do we do when someone does not exhibit what we would consider sufficient shame to warrant full acceptance back into the community?

In Betty Smith's semiautobiographical coming-of-age novel, *A Tree Grows in Brooklyn*, first published in 1943, the young protagonist Francie watches from her apartment window in a poverty-stricken portion of 1913 Brooklyn as a young woman named Joanna steps outside to take her baby for a walk in his carriage:

> A gasp came up from some housewives who had stopped to gossip on the sidewalk while going to and fro about their shopping. You see, Joanna was not married. She was a girl who had gotten into trouble. Her baby was illegitimate—bastard was the word they used in the neighborhood—and these good women felt that Joanna had no right to act like a proud

mother and bring her baby out into the light of day. They felt that she should have kept it hidden in some dark place.

In the past, when Francie has asked her mother about Joanna, who she has seen through the window lovingly playing with her exceptionally clean and well-cared-for son, her mother answers, "If she's a good girl at heart, she'll learn from the pain and the shame and she won't do it again. If she's naturally bad, it won't bother her the way people treat her. . . . Let Joanna be a lesson to you."

This afternoon, as Francie watches, she notices that even though Joanna smiles at her neighbors as she walks the carriage up and down the street, no one smiles back—especially not the housewives, some of whom were shotgun-wedding brides themselves. In fact, the scowls grow more pronounced each time Joanna passes, straightens the baby's blanket, or shows him any kind of tender affection:

She maddened the women by touching the baby's cheek and smiling tenderly at it. How dare she! How dare she, they thought, act as though she had a right to all that? . . .

Joanna recognized their hate but wouldn't cringe before it. She would not give in and take the baby indoors. Something had to give. The women broke first. They couldn't endure it any longer. They had to do something about it. The next time Joanna passed, a stringy woman called out:

"Ain't you ashamed of yourself?"

"What for?" Joanna wanted to know.

This infuriated the woman. "What for, she asks," she reported to the other women. "I'll tell you what for. Because you're a disgrace and a bum. You got no right to parade the streets with your bastard where innocent children can see you."

"I guess this is a free country," said Joanna.

"Not free for the likes of you. Get off the street, get off the street."

"Try and make me!"

"Get off the street, you whore," ordered the stringy woman.

The girl's voice trembled when she answered. "Be careful what you're saying."

"We don't have to be careful what we say to no street walker," chipped in another woman. . . .

"Bitch! You bitch!" screamed the stringy one hysterically. Then, acting on an instinct which was strong even in Christ's day, she picked a stone out of the gutter and threw it at Joanna. (chapter 30)

The women continue throwing stones and horse dung until one rock misses Joanna and hits the baby in the forehead. He begins to cry and reach for his mother, an act that seems to snap the women out of their righteous fury. Without a word of apology, they turn and walk away. They hadn't meant to hurt the baby, but they had certainly meant to harm the mother—to extract some kind of payment or penitence from Joanna for refusing to cower in front of them and daring to find joy in her life after committing such a taboo.

Francie watches the scene in agony, struggling to reconcile the warnings she has heard about Joanna and the blatant cruelty she observes. She holes herself up in the cellar of her tenement building for hours, sobbing not just at the awfulness of it all, but also at her own complicity. She, too, had refused to smile back when Joanna had greeted her. Francie can't seem to reconcile who is the worse sinner, nor what lesson it was that her mother wanted her to learn from Joanna's life, but she is certain of one thing:

Now she would suffer—she would suffer all the rest of her life every time that she remembered that she had not smiled back. . . . From that time on, remembering the stoning women, she hated women. She feared them for their devious ways, she mistrusted their instincts. She began to hate them for this disloyalty and their cruelty to each other. Of all the stone-throwers, not one had dared to speak a word for the girl for fear that she would be tarred with Joanna's brush. . . . They stuck together for only one thing: to trample on some other woman, whether it was by throwing stones or by mean gossip.

Sometimes, as in Joanna's case, performative shame is the price we must pay for admission to a community. Other times, as in Francie's case, secret shame is the very thing that keeps us outside of it—a painful position that can be deeply harmful or (possibly) healthier for us in the long run if the community itself is toxic.

And sometimes, shame and guilt are leveraged in religious environments when they are applied to situations that do not even merit such responses. We have a tendency, as Christians, to make ethically neutral matters into referendums on morality, and then shame those who do not perform according to our artificial standards. Rather than recognizing things for what they actually are, we often attach much greater significance to them based on cultural values we have decided are external indicators of a person's character.

We have a tendency, as Christians, to make ethically neutral matters into referendums on morality, and then shame those who do not perform according to our artificial standards

As an undergrad at the evangelical college I attended, I was once fined ten dollars during the weekly housekeeping check for having "a dusty toilet." The portion of the commode that attaches to the floor had dust around the bolts that I had not cleaned to the dorm mother's satisfaction. When I appealed this decision by pointing out that I had made time in the midst of preparing for my senior honors capstone presentation the following week to scrub the rest of the toilet and that the dusty base was a minor oversight, I was told (and I will never forget this): "But if you have a dusty toilet, how will your family know you love them? It shows you aren't prioritizing taking care of your home and the people you live with."

Did I fail to do the job as thoroughly as I could have? Yup. I can absolutely own that. Did I fail in my walk with Jesus because of that toilet? I mean . . . *really?*

At the time, as a broke student, I was furious. Now, as a grown woman with a dangerously enlarged sarcasm gland, I laugh about it. When I prioritize playing or snuggling with my daughter over some minor household chore, I sometimes jokingly ask myself, *"How will she know that I love her?"* But, sometimes, attaching these kinds of character judgments to morally neutral actions can be far more damaging.

I spoke with Maya, who has struggled with body-image issues her entire life, about how her body size led to judgment in her church. "I was told things like, 'You know, gluttony is a sin,'" she says. "Like skinny people can't be gluttons? I'm lectured on self-control being a fruit of the Spirit, but nobody thinks twice about the guy who's addicted to the gym or ruins his knees jogging for hours and hours. Maybe there are some obsession or self-control issues going on there, too, but nobody judges *him*."

Maya and I talk about how the story of "fat King Eglon" in Judges 3 is always played to comic effect, as if his physical size were somehow evidence of his evilness, and how numerous passages that equate weight with morality get taken literally rather than metaphorically to symbolize people who live in luxury while others suffer. I point out that Daniel 1:15 considers it a point of celebration that, when Daniel and his companions protest the ceremonially unclean food of the king of Persia and eat only vegetables and water, the text says that "At the end of ten days it was observed that they appeared better and fatter than all the young men who had been eating the royal rations." Yet I've never heard Daniel, Meshack, Shadrack, and Abednego celebrated as models of "good fatness" in the Bible. Maya laughs ruefully. "Yeah, we don't like fat heroes."

The body-shaming Maya has endured her whole life—both within her church and in society at large—greatly impacted the way she saw her own spiritual worth for a long time:

Church should be the one place where you're safe from judgmental comments like that. It's bad enough to hear it from kids at school, but then to get it from the adults at church, too, is just, well, it's crushing. It's devastating. They watch your plate at potlucks to see what you put on it, and they say stuff like, "The body is the temple of the Holy Spirit." I want to say, "Maybe I'm just giving the Holy Spirit a little more living space." But, really, what they're saying is my body makes God mad and how I carry weight is really just reflection of how bad of a sinner I am. Think about what that does to a kid—to anyone. You feel ashamed just to be in your body in church. Just to be in your body before God.

People say, "I just want you to be healthy." I'm like, "Trust me, I know I'm fat without you pointing it out. But if you really want me to be healthy, maybe stop trying to make me feel guilty about the way I look, like being big is a sin."

Artificial standards of perfection are actually just expressions of preference. Just because something differs from an arbitrary cultural value does not mean it is "wrong." Having a messy desk is not a sin any more than having a room painted blue is a sin. A spotless countertop is no more virtuous than one spread with newspaper soaked by the fallout from a papier-mâché volcano. Yes, responsible stewardship of our blessings matters, but as we discussed in chapter 5, *anything* to which we attach moral imperatives where none actually exist is idolatry. People make idols out of thin bodies, muscular bodies, spotless homes, organized workspaces, report cards, GPAs, sales numbers, social media hits, number of sermons preached, the count of people who come forward in a revival meeting . . . There is nothing to be ashamed of in a misalignment with someone else's preferences—especially if they have confused and conflated their preferences with eternal truth.

When we apply cultural lenses—like judgments about body size and shape, the way our home looks, how our children perform, whether we are the "cool" church in town, or even just how we understand the world to work—as absolute markers for universal morality, we run the risk not only of placing eternal significance on deeply temporal things, but also of missing the point altogether.

In John 4, we read of a Samaritan woman who meets Jesus at a well around noon. He asks her for a drink of water—a move that shocks her, since Jews and Samaritans were closely related people who fostered deep distrust of and prejudice against one another. After she tells him so, Jesus answers: "If you knew the gift of God and who it is that is saying to you, 'Give me a drink,' you would have asked him, and he would have given you living water" (v. 10).[1]

This response astounds the unnamed woman who immediately challenges Jesus:

> "Sir, you have no bucket, and the well is deep. Where do you get that living water? Are you greater than our ancestor Jacob, who gave us the well and with his sons and his flocks drank from it?"
>
> Jesus said to her, "Everyone who drinks of this water will be thirsty again, but those who drink of the water that I will give them will never be thirsty. The water that I will give will become in them a spring of water gushing up to eternal life." The woman said to him, "Sir, give me this water, so that I may never be thirsty or have to keep coming here to draw water."
>
> Jesus said to her, "Go, call your husband, and come back." The woman answered him, "I have no husband." Jesus said to her, "You are right in saying, 'I have no husband,' for you have had five husbands, and the one you have now is not your husband. What you have said is true!" The woman said to him, "Sir, I see that you are a prophet. Our ancestors worshiped on this mountain, but you say that the place where people must worship is in Jerusalem." Jesus said to her, "Woman, believe me, the hour is coming when you will worship the Father neither on this mountain nor in Jerusalem. You worship

what you do not know; we worship what we know, for salvation is from the Jews. But the hour is coming and is now here when the true worshipers will worship the Father in spirit and truth, for the Father seeks such as these to worship him. God is spirit, and those who worship him must worship in spirit and truth." The woman said to him, "I know that Messiah is coming" (who is called Christ). "When he comes, he will proclaim all things to us." Jesus said to her, "I am he, the one who is speaking to you."

Just then his disciples came. They were astonished that he was speaking with a woman, but no one said, "What do you want?" or, "Why are you speaking with her?" Then the woman left her water jar and went back to the city. She said to the people, "Come and see a man who told me everything I have ever done! He cannot be the Messiah, can he?" (vv. 11–29)

If you were raised in Western Christianity, you probably encountered the passage above as a story of a woman whom Jesus called out for her sexually loose morals as exhibited by her five divorces, her current co-habitation, and her subsequent forgiveness as she calls to the people of the town to "come and see a man who told me everything I have ever done!"

But what if we've been understanding her character all wrong simply because we were reading it through a cultural lens that prioritizes stories of sexual shame—especially against women? And what if an alternate interpretation seems not only possible but actually far more likely when we consider a few very basic facts we probably already knew about her context but have been conditioned to disregard?

Many of us were taught to read this unnamed woman as some kind of ancient Elizabeth Taylor who tore through a string of husbands and lovers until Jesus finally called her (the Samaritan, not Elizabeth Taylor) out as a wild woman. This reading is convenient if you exist in a culture where women are routinely shamed for sexualized behavior, but it takes quite a few assumptions for granted.

First, marriages in first-century Palestine were not the affairs we think of in modern terms. No matter the social class, unions were almost always arranged between families. Therefore, this woman likely did not have much, if any, agency in selecting her five previous husbands.

Second, divorces were hardly a casual affair. While records and accounts from the era vary about the ease by which women could obtain a divorce in the Jewish and Samaritan cultures, the fact remains that a religious court would need to be involved in order to deem the validity of the request. So if the Samaritan woman initiated each divorce (as is often the way the story is presented in modern churches), there must have been a reason that each was unfit as a spouse—which means her family was repeatedly failing her in the partners they were selecting. The same is true if the divorces were sought by her previous husbands. If something was so drastically wrong with her that five men would deem her an unacceptable mate, it should have fallen upon her family to help care for her.

But where in the text does it ever mention the word "divorce"? (*Hint: It doesn't.*) The woman may have been widowed a number of times or was possibly involved in a series of levirate marriages, wherein a woman married to one brother who died without a son would then automatically become the wife of the next brother in line (Deuteronomy 25:56). While Samaritans enforced a version of this law "only when the woman was betrothed and the marriage had not been consummated,"[2] the fact remains that unless this woman was secretly killing off her husbands in some kind of "Black Widow" situation, she likely suffered a tremendous amount of trauma whether from the multiple divorces, deaths, or some combination of the two.

Let us also consider that nothing in the text tells us if the man with whom she was connected at the time of her conversation with Jesus was a consensual lover. Nowhere are we told that she is living with (or, as I have heard more than one preacher put it, "shacking up with") the current man in her life. Jesus simply points out that she is not married to "the one you have now"— meaning the man currently acting in the role of a husband, whether that means sexually or simply as a protector. This is an assumption we read into the text based on our own modern Christian anxieties about cohabitation before marriage. It could be that she is living with this man in the role of a wife, but not necessarily; she might simply be a domestic worker under the shelter of his household. If she is, in fact, residing with him without being married to him, that indicates she either had no family to take her in after her last marriage ended or else that her family was failing in their duty in finding her a capable spouse.

Whatever the case, the Samaritan woman at the well must have felt rejected, abandoned, confused, and alone. Yet when is she ever spoken of with compassion in churches? When is her story explored from a trauma-informed perspective? This was a failure of her support system, not her morals. Here is a woman who, in all likelihood, was given to (at least) six different men and had been widowed or divorced five times and whose family of origin now seems to be entirely absent—and the modern Western church has written her a backstory as a wild woman of loose morals. In this version, Jesus's conversation with the woman is a condemnation of her life, even though the topic is actually about comfort, fulfillment, and acceptance. This story is not about Jesus deigning to speak to a sexually depraved woman but about the Son of God seeing and acknowledging the experiences of a broken, hurting person.

In condemning the Samaritan woman's behavior on the basis of our own cultural assumptions, we are bearing false witness against her

It is an interpretation that has been hiding in plain sight; it seems so obvious once we remove our cultural blinders and presuppositions that project onto the text assumptions that aren't really there and make us oblivious to truths we probably already know—like how marriage worked in first-century Palestine. But because we have been culturally conditioned to understand the woman's story through the lens of shame, this is the message that most of us take from the story. The disparaging reading of this woman whose "crimes" are merely assumed rather than confirmed is more of a statement about the values of the modern church than about the life of the person we are judging. In condemning the Samaritan woman's behavior on the basis of our own cultural assumptions, we are bearing false witness against her.

It's easier said than done, of course, to shed our cultural biases—and we can never fully divest ourselves of them, no matter how hard we try. We will always be coming at faith having been indelibly shaped by the history that preceded us in terms not only of theological understanding but also of the evolution of social, economic, and intellectual philosophies and histories that have primed our minds for the way we receive and process information. This is in addition to the various demographics that shape our lived experiences in the world that we bring to our encounters with Scripture and with God as well as our questions, struggles, and possibly even doubt.

Maybe *especially* doubt.

Let's talk about doubt, and let's do it without soft-pedaling or hushed tones. Doubt is treated so often as a shameful thing in churches rather than as a natural part of the development of an authentic life—whatever that may look like.

Because so many people fear that questions are the first step on the slippery slope of doubt—doubt inevitably leads to disbelief (or so goes the fear)—it is often cast as a moral failing, as if a person who questions is somehow rebelling. How many lessons have you heard about "doubting Thomas," casting him as frustrating to Jesus or somehow an inferior apostle simply for saying, essentially, "I'd like to see some proof of this highly unlikely thing before I believe the rumors"? Isn't that the same kind of discernment we try to instill in ourselves, our children, and internet trolls who spout "facts" with no evidence to back up their claims? Why does the standard for responsible inquiry suddenly change when we talk about religious faith?

True, John 20:28 tells us that Thomas did change his mind once he was presented with the evidence he asked for, but how many among us have ever been physically visited by the resurrected Christ? In that light, is it really fair to cast someone as hard-hearted or willfully disobedient to God when they have earnestly entertained questions of faith and still find themselves struggling to believe?

Julia, whom we first met in chapter 5, spent years wrestling with this very question. Despite being raised in a highly religious family and attending parochial schools for much of her childhood, Julia always struggled with the leaps of faith required by the church. When she asked her priest about certain questions that troubled her that the Bible didn't seem to answer, she was always brushed off, told not to worry about it, or treated like she was trying to make trouble. She explains:

> All around me I saw people who have faith go there for answers, but I'm asking questions and there are no answers, so what's the point of it for me? . . . Look at Jesus. Jesus is God's Son, but aren't we all God's children? Why is this one guy special? It just wasn't making sense to me. Hell never made sense to me, either. God will punish me for not believing in him, even though he made my mind this way? I mean, if there is a God, I would think that the point would be to look at creation and go, "Hey! Good job!" versus having to go and sit in church and listen to someone talk for an hour every Sunday to show my faith or devotion.

Julia never felt antagonism toward Christianity, but she struggled to reconcile what she was being taught with what she actually believed. "My spiritual anxiety came from coping with the not knowing," she explains:

> There's no way to test. There's no proving godliness; there's no way to check and see that you know that there's something divine—to try it out, see, learn. It always requires that leap of faith to something that you can't test. So you have to have blind faith. And I've seen so many people be manipulated in other ways, like by politicians, because they trusted whatever they were fed because they were primed through blind faith. I've always been curious, but I'm just not really good at leaps of faith—which left me wondering, "What's wrong with me?"

In an environment where no one was willing to have open discussions about these issues or admit that there might be a valid viewpoint beyond biblical literalism, Julia felt alienated. "Why did faith seem to come so easily to some but not to others? I didn't understand that." She finally settled on considering herself agnostic. "I like the classic definition of the word as 'not knowing.' I'm certainly open to the idea of a God," she says. "I'm open to the idea of there being something. But the only people who know for sure are the ones who are dead."

Doubt, Julia found, was usually seen within the church as a kind of willful disobedience. In trying to be honest about her beliefs, she was regarded as someone intentionally rejecting truth:

> I had a college roommate who was very, very smart and had a very strong faith—I loved her to death—and she and I used to argue religion back and forth all the time. It was always super respectful, but one time she expressed her frustration with me. She said if someone is dying and you have something that will save them and you say, "All you have to do is drink it," and they go, "No, I don't believe it's going to work"—that's how I feel about you.

I know that her arguing faith with me respectfully was a very caring and loving thing for her to do, but it was never going to sink into my head. But I've wondered that so often—what is it that made me different from her that she could believe, that she could have this faith, and I couldn't?

When these types of conversations happen in ways that *both* sides recognize as loving, they can be an important means of planting the seeds of faith for someone who might feel called to God later in life or who may feel willing to try religion again because of the kindness shown by people of faith.

Too often, however, one side believes they are acting in a loving way because they are attempting to save someone else's soul, but the other person simply feels browbeaten, looked down upon, or deeply—even purposely—misunderstood.

Too often, churches and "church people" try to shame the doubt out of someone, as if that somehow builds a stronger case for belief in a loving, merciful God.

Too often, this is passed off as evangelism.

Where we have failed as a religious body is in our belief that the presence of or capacity for faith—that "God-shaped vacuum" in the human heart that Blaise Pascal wrote about almost five centuries ago—is present in everyone in equal amounts . . . and that it is *always* a choice.

In 1 Corinthians 12:8–10, Paul outlines a number of spiritual gifts, noting:

> To one there is given through the Spirit a message of wisdom, to another a message of knowledge by means of the same Spirit, to another faith by the same Spirit, to another gifts of healing by that one Spirit, to another miraculous powers, to another prophecy, to another distinguishing between spirits, to another speaking in different kinds of tongues, and to still another the interpretation of tongues.

Did you catch that? Nestled in there among a list of other spiritual gifts that some people have but others don't—gifts like wisdom, advanced understanding, healing, and tongues—is faith. Faith is a spiritual gift. It is not an automatic condition; it is not even necessarily a decision. It is a spiritual gift, and spiritual gifts are not apportioned evenly among everyone. Some people—many people, even—have the gift of easy belief. That's not to say that their life or experiences are easy, but that the ability to believe in God and put their trust in God's workings and ultimate plan comes naturally. But it's a *gift*, not a guarantee—and not everyone has been blessed in that way.

We don't generally shame people for their inability to perform healing acts or exhibit miraculous powers, so why do we shame them when faith is a struggle? Why are we so afraid of doubt—both in others and ourselves—that we feel the need to hush it up, deny it, or "cure" it? What if churches allowed people to explore doubt honestly, asking questions and accepting that not every one of them will likely be answered in a satisfactory way? Isn't the ability to say "I don't know" about some things more honest to the concept of *faith* (rather than objective knowledge) than performing mental or ethical gymnastics in order to have a response to everything?

When we *act* as if every single credal question or doctrinal doubt inevitably leads to a collapse or abandonment of faith, *people will believe us.* When doubts arise, such thinking can automatically put a person into a state of crisis—especially if they struggle with Involuntary Internalized Legalism. Suddenly, one internal check-in of "Do I really believe what the preacher just said?" leads to an avalanche of guilty feelings and self-reproach when, in all actuality, this is exactly what every believer should be doing all the time: asking, "Is what I am being taught consistent with what I know about the character of Jesus or the heart of God?"

Protestant theology is deeply rooted in Martin Luther's principle of *sola fide*, "by faith alone." But faith is nuanced. It's not something you either have or don't; it's the way we approach the world, the way we treat others, the way we respond to injustice, the way we understand our responsibility to the world around us, the way (like Julia observed) we see the divine in creation. In an effort to make the path to God simpler, we have stripped faith of its deep and beautiful complexities. Rather than allowing doubt to be part of the richness of faith, we have cheapened faith by reducing it to a simple "yes-no" answer—a box to tick with only one right answer upon which all of eternity hinges.

What is so scary about making our churches safe places for wrestling with belief rather than places where questions must be hidden in order to be accepted? Is our faith so fragile that we are threatened by someone else's doubt? If church is supposed to be a place of truth and integrity, no wonder people leave when they feel they have to lie in order to stay there.

And no wonder so many members of the LGBTQ+ community have struggled with shame several times over—both because of their sexual orientation as well as for the lie they are expected to live.

A common argument in Christian circles when discussing the place of LGBTQ+ believers in the church body goes something along the lines of: "It's okay if they 'feel gay' as long as they don't act on it. Just because someone has homosexual feelings doesn't mean they have to carry them out. I mean, just because a person might have a predisposition for alcoholism doesn't mean we say, 'That's just how God made them.'" Another version is the pithy, popular adage, "Love the sinner, hate the sin."

People may genuinely believe that they are adopting an open and welcoming stance when they make such statements, despite the fact that they are equating a destructive addictive disorder like alcoholism with what could very well be a loving, committed relationship between two consenting adults. Baked into the idea is the assumption that any sexuality besides heterosexuality is automatically a sin.

This is actually a type of rhetorical fallacy called "begging the question"—that is, an assumed conclusion is presented as if its veracity has already been established. A classic example is a politician asking their opponent, "So, have you stopped cheating on your taxes?" There is no way to answer the question without convicting oneself, even if the statement isn't true, because it presents the charge of tax fraud as already proven. If the answer is yes it implies that criminal activity was, in fact, taking place at one point. If the answer is no it implies that it is still going on. The statement establishes tax fraud on the part of one's opponent as accepted fact, just as summing up one's philosophy of "Love the sinner, hate the sin" assumes that being gay is a sin.

It is not the goal of this book, nor is it my place as a cis, hetero woman to present myself as an authority on this point. There are resources, such as the 1946 Project, that do a far more thorough and far better researched job than I could possibly offer. My point is simply that agenda-driven language has been used to shape beliefs and stances (and the conversations around them) for millennia. When we better understand how that kind of linguistic manipulation works, we may have a better chance of breaking its power over us. Many churches and politicians warn about a vague threat they call "the gay agenda," as if their own actions, beliefs, and even their language itself does not carry an agenda—in this case, an evangelical one. We all have agendas. My own language in writing this book is steered by my agenda of exploring spiritual anxiety and exposing ways it can be exploited. Your language at work and at home has an agenda (sell the product, appease the customer, encourage children into better behavior, convince your partner to see things your way, etc.). The question is not whether a specific point of view, stance, or philosophy has an agenda; the question is whether that agenda is to shame, exclude, or control people or whether it is to welcome, nourish, and love.

In translation studies, one of the major concerns is how to interpret words that carry situational nuance or change meaning depending on their context. For example, consider all the questions a translator might be forced to consider when faced with the line, "The journalist scribbled furiously on his pad." If you have a strong grasp of the English language, you probably have a pretty clear mental picture of what that line means and, if asked to translate it using different words, might say something like "The reporter quickly took notes in his notebook."

The thing is, the sentence could also be translated like this: "The diary-keeper made nonsensical marks angrily on soft material he owned for cushioning or absorption." The *words* are the same, but the meaning of the sentence has now changed entirely. Throw in differing grammatical structures and syntax from another language, and this seemingly simple sentence might suddenly become completely unreadable.

That's why accurate translations require much more consideration than a simple, word-for-word substitution; they require an overall understanding of the passage being moved from one language to another. When faced with words that have different connotations or ideas associated with them, which one best matches the overarching point of the work? And who determines what the ultimate meaning of a work is? Is *Field of Dreams* primarily a movie about baseball or about the fractured relationship between a father and son? Of course, the answer could be "both/and," but which takes precedence when trying to determine how to translate a complicated word or phrase that might feed into either theme—say, "he ran home"? That's why context matters and, once again, the question of agenda comes into play.

These are the same questions we should be asking ourselves as we read the Bible in translation, as most of us do. What other meanings might the original Greek, Hebrew, or Aramaic have carried? How might the cultural lenses or agendas of the translators—or our own—cause us to elevate, consciously or unconsciously, one meaning over another? Are there any alternative meanings that might be more in harmony with the overarching theme of this section of Scripture, book of the Bible, or the gospel itself?

Similarly, it is worth asking whether the traditional "clobber passages" about homosexuality assigned to Jesus are actually in line with some of his primary themes like protecting the powerless. Tiberius, the second emperor of Rome from 14 to 37 CE—in other words, exactly when Jesus was living and teaching—had a well-known proclivity for sexually abusing children. Graphic records exist of Tiberius hosting orgies of children for his own amusement, training toddlers and infants to gratify him sexually in especially horrific ways, and ordering that the legs of two young brothers who worked in a temple and accused the emperor of rape be broken.[3]

In fact, this is exactly the behavior forbidden in the *Didache*, the first-century church manual we looked at in chapter 5. In chapter 2, verse 2, the book lists behaviors explicitly forbidden in the Christian life, including "pederasty"—translated literally "child sex." Yet nowhere does the *Didache* name sexual relationships between same-sex adults as forbidden.

Does it not seem likely, or at least possible, that in light of what we know about the character of Jesus—the man who said, in Matthew 18:6, that anyone who engages a child in immorality would be better off in the middle of the ocean with a massive stone tied around his neck—might have been more concerned with stopping the pedophilia and child exploitation that was common under the colonizing government of his land than he was concerned about the bedroom habits of committed, consenting adults?

But when passages from the Bible are applied broadly and without care for contextualization, historical-cultural positioning, nuanced meaning, and translator agenda, they become easy weapons in the hands of people who want to feel powerful, chosen, and (above all) *right.* What does that do to anyone who falls outside of whatever that narrow, exacting definition of "right" may be? What does that communicate to them about their place in the church and the broader kingdom of God?

Spiritual anxiety has driven countless members of the queer community out of churches because of the shame heaped upon them for their lack of conformity to culturally acceptable definitions of gender and sexuality. "I wasn't your typical rough and tumble boy. I liked the arts and I hated getting dirty," one man told me:

> Growing up when I did, that wasn't okay. It wasn't okay to cry or to be sensitive. People in my church told me I need to be more manly, but I wasn't ever going to be their idea of it with the hunting and football and all. Whatever "Christian manhood" means, I wasn't it, and that meant I was a disappointment to God, I guess. They said that being too "soft" meant you were gay, and I could do the math: Being soft means you're gay, and gay is an abomination. Therefore, I am an abomination.

"There are so many of us who grew up in the church and love Jesus," another man told me. "But we are afraid to come back because so many of us have heard all our lives that we are just sinners who choose to keep sinning by being gay. Being gay cost me my parents, relationships with my siblings, friendships—the whole community I grew up with. I lost them all when I came out. Who would choose that? Especially not fifty years ago when there weren't many support groups or queer communities in small towns."

Despite all the talk about honesty, integrity, and character in the church, he experienced the opposite. "Sometimes you ended up in situations that were unhealthy or dangerous because it was the only place that accepted you, and then that only added to the shame because now *everything* about you was sinful. Jesus is supposed to wash the shame away, but if you were gay and wanted to be honest, you had to leave the church because Jesus didn't want you."

The woman across from me has silver hair and a joyful smile. It's a few weeks before Christmas, and she is a singer nursing a sore throat ahead of a whirlwind of holiday choir concerts, but she is eager to share her story.

"What name would you like me to use for you in the book?" I ask.

She pauses a moment, staring into the middle distance while she thinks. "Lucy," she says, finally. "Yes, I would like to be Lucy. She's the brave girl from *The Lion, the Witch and the Wardrobe*." As she shares her story, I understand why a character full of courage and tenacity resonates so strongly.

Lucy grew up Pennsylvania Dutch, enjoying a loving church community and being outdoors. "I was really close to God when I was a kid," she recalls. "I especially liked being out in nature. I always could just feel that there was something more there."

Still, despite her wonderful religious background, somehow, she always knew she was different from what was expected. Then, when she was fourteen,

> I was reading a *Seventeen* magazine, and Farrah Fawcett was doing shampoo ads at that time. I took one look at those beautiful green eyes, and I thought "Oh my God!—*Oh my God*." . . . But I kept it to myself. My church didn't preach a lot about homosexuality and maybe it was because it was pre-AIDS, since that seemed to bring out the righteous anger in a lot of people; but anyway, I went to college, then I went into the Army, where it wasn't "Don't ask, don't tell" yet, it was just *don't*. Just flat out don't.
>
> I kind of drifted away from church, you know, as one does, but I would go from time to time if I needed comfort. That was where I would go sit and just think and meditate, and still when I was out in nature, I'd still feel that connection. I'd still feel God.

During this time, Lucy tried to make herself attracted to men, chasing any opportunity to prove to herself and to the world that she was what she had been taught she was "supposed" to be. "I had probably fifty or sixty male partners by that point because I was trying so hard to be straight," she says. "I thought if I just met the right man, it would 'take.' I didn't want to be what society said wasn't okay, and I am a rule follower, not a rebel, so I just kept trying."

It didn't work. She finally decided to embrace the truth, but when Lucy tried coming out to her mother, her mother stopped speaking to her:

> She said, "It's a sin. You better learn to like men." Well, Lord knows I had tried. So I had stayed out of the closet for about nine months, which was just long enough to bury a friend of mine who had been in the Army with me. He had AIDS and was medically retired and then passed away. But I just couldn't take all the pressure . . .
>
> And then I met a very charismatic man, who was about my age and had a very similar background, a lot of sexual experimentation—a lot of what conservatives would consider pretty appalling behavior, you know—and he was just so charming. He absolutely convinced me that maybe I was bisexual but he would help me, and I could work through that, because he had once been attracted to men and had been "cured."

They married and were living in California at the time, attending a very conservative church, when Lucy's husband wanted to pursue a law degree at a prominent evangelical college in the Southeast. She desperately did not want to go, worried about the oppressive culture of the school, but "he was the head of the house, and this was what he said we were going to do, so I put him through law school and finished my master's degree in psychology at the same time at night."

When the couple returned to California and the same church after completing school, Lucy learned that her husband had

been carrying on a number of extramarital affairs. "When I finally found out, I asked how many women there had been," she
says, "and he told me 'about twelve.'" At a time when she needed
support most, the church that had once felt like home suddenly
changed its tune. Suddenly, it was all about her deficiencies as
a woman:

> They blamed me. They said I must not have been good
> enough. I must not have been a good enough wife. It was my
> fault, not his.
>
> They didn't see how he would tell me I was too fat, tell
> me I was ugly. He kept trying to make it about me. He would
> even say, "In the Old Testament, David had lots of wives and
> Solomon had lots of wives. So I didn't do anything wrong." It
> was miserable, but the church kept saying it wasn't his fault.
>
> We tried to reconcile. We tried dating for a year while we
> were separated, but he would never break up with the other
> woman he was seeing then. He was with her the whole time.
> And then we were at a church picnic as part of the little fel-
> lowship group we were with, and I got called out in public for
> being "unforgiving." And at that point, I just walked away.
> I walked away from the marriage. I walked away from a beau-
> tiful house. From my whole life. It was really painful.
>
> But when I left him, I didn't know where God was. I didn't
> know who God was. Because he had been my interpreter of
> God for the past ten years.

After her marriage ended, Lucy started getting anxiety attacks
at unpredictable times, triggered by the most seemingly innocu-
ous things. When she tried to buy a dining room set for her new
apartment, "I realized I could tell you everything in that store *he*
would have liked or not liked but I couldn't tell you what *I* wanted.
I walked out of the store, and I just sat in my car, and I cried.
I thought, 'This is crazy. I don't have any idea who I am or where
God is. I don't know anything outside of my ex-husband.'"

She did remember what the pastor at her old church had said: "When all else fails, just keep doing the stuff: keep reading your Bible, keep praying, keep going to church." Lucy laughs, "Well, the going to church part wasn't in the equation just then, but I was trying the rest. I was just in a dry spell. I would read devotions that would all sound empty to me. I wasn't hiking to find God in nature."

As she worked to try to rebuild her shattered faith and redis-cover God again on her own terms instead of filtered through the manipulative agendas of her emotionally abusive ex-husband or church, she also struggled to be honest with herself. She wasn't out about her sexuality, but that was because she was still not able to reconcile with that side of herself yet after her early pain. Finally, Lucy came upon a small church near her favorite coffee shop. She admits that it was "a little intimidating" her first Sun-day in the small chapel with a much more diverse congregation than she was used to. And it was there, in a room full of strangers, faces she knew from the neighborhood, plus "homeless people, coffee, and Costco Danish, the pastor came out and talked, and he was so soft-spoken, and so full of love—"

Here, Lucy pauses for a moment to wipe tears from her eyes before she continues:

And it was like, "That's the Jesus I remember. That's the Jesus that I was brought up with." They have this window in the front, and it's a stained-glass window. It's illuminated from behind and it's a picture of Jesus with the little children. It says, "Suffer the little children to come unto me," and every time I look at that, I think "That's the God I follow—the God who's full of grace. The God who listens. The God who says ev-erybody's welcome." That was about eight years ago, and now I'm on the church council and I'm taking classes to become a certified lay speaker so that I can substitute in pulpits. I hike every weekend, and every weekend I get to be in nature, and I get to be with God and God is becoming real again for me. It's the best. But I'm also so angry right now about all those years, you know. But I'm working through it. So, yeah, my story has a happy ending. I know not everyone's does; but mine does. And I'm grateful for that.

What does an authentic life look like—a life that acknowledges the guilt it has accrued and then releases it back to God in the name of freedom? A life that is free from the unnecessary shame that others want us to shoulder because of their own big image of themselves and small image of God?

Many of us have been punished by our communities for embracing the gifts of life and grace rather than groveling for acceptance.

Many of us have spent our lives chasing the wrong forgiveness—looking for God to pardon us for things that were never crimes at all.

Many of us hid our questions because someone told us asking them was wrong.

Many of us have spent years begging Jesus to cure us when it turns out we were never sick to begin with.

Many of us were taught to read Scripture through a lens clouded by culture and predisposed toward shame. How might defogging that lens shift the way we understand not only many familiar Bible stories but also our own? Alternately, how might a modern perspective on how we understand human psychology and trauma responses add meaning and significance in Scripture that is far more relevant to the spiritual needs of readers in our current context than what someone in a vastly different cultural context decided it meant fifty, five hundred, or 2,500 years ago?

> *Many of us have spent our lives chasing the wrong forgiveness—looking for God to pardon us for things that were never crimes at all*

In Genesis 2:25, we are told that Adam and Eve, newly created in the Garden "were both naked and were not ashamed." Perfect creation has no place for shame, so how do we pivot from a shame-based theology to a grace-filled one? We hear plenty about it in sermons, but what does that actually look like in practice?

First, we must acknowledge that spiritual abusers are not likely to stop leveraging shame, because it gives them power—or at least the illusion of it. The only way to combat this is to learn how to reframe internalized shame.

One of the simplest ways to combat the effects of IIL and stop a descent into self-condemnation is to focus on your second thought. By this I mean when you have an unkind, judgmental, problematic, or sinful thought about someone, instead of immediately condemning yourself for having an evil heart that produces bad fruit, take a breath and recognize that the part of your brain you just heard from is the side designed to make snap judgments—the immediate, split-second evaluations that take stock of situations to try to keep you alive: "That hole seems pretty deep, maybe I should go around it" or "This food looks rancid" or "I bet I would cut my feet if I tried to climb on those rocks." That's what psychologists often casually refer to as the "lizard brain." It's the part of your neurological wiring that makes automatic judgments without complex or conscious thought; in other words, it's not a reflection of your heart.

It's your second thought that you should be focusing on. What do you think when you have a moment to override the hardwiring of your brain and have a chance to respond with intentionality and deliberateness? This is a much more accurate picture of where your mind is focused. So you looked at someone and immediately felt judgment or lust—that doesn't mean your heart is inherently godless, and it certainly doesn't mean you need to question whether the Holy Spirit still resides in you. Just try to channel your knee-jerk reaction into a more positive secondary response: "That is the stupidest-looking haircut I've ever seen

. . . but they sure seem happy with it" or "but it doesn't change the fact that they're going to help me fix my computer" or "but remember how dumb my hair looked with mall bangs and a crimping iron?" Or, alternatively: "That is the sexiest human being I have seen in real life . . . and they seem to be enjoying a nice lunch with some friends" or "and they really seem to be good at their job" or "and I hope they have a really nice day." It sounds so silly—even pedantic—to describe, but it can be a helpful way to reframe and stop a spiritual shame–spiral before it begins. What you do with your second thought—the one you *choose*—reveals far more about where you've focused your mind and the kind of fruit you are actively cultivating. Even something as simple as purposefully pausing to rescript your thoughts—to pull them out of a place of automatic self-condemnation—can help break the stranglehold of shame that IIL can bring.

I experienced an important lesson on this very topic in a different way when a friend invited my family to partake in an *iftar* dinner at her mosque as part of a community event to share about Ramadan as well as for building interfaith relationships and understanding. About a dozen Christian female clergy and friends sat in the women's side of the building while we prepared for the sun to go down so that we could eat together with our hosts. As we waited, women from the local Islamic community shared some of their personal and cultural customs around keeping the fast, preparing the meal, and observing the special prayers. Describing the challenge of cooking a meal in the midst of a daylong fast, one older woman laughed as she explained that sometimes you get caught up in the habits of regular cooking and forget it is Ramadan; as a result, you might taste a spoonful of something for flavor before remembering that you are supposed to be abstaining from all food and water.

I cringed, imagining the frustration the cook must feel as she realizes she has just undone an entire day of fasting right at the end and will have to make up the day later as part of her fasting requirements. "Oh, no! You offer thanks, not worry for it," the woman said. "We see that as a gift from Allah. You didn't do it consciously. Allah saw your need and supplied you with that bite to help you get through the final hours of the fast while you prepare the meal. It is a blessing of provision, not a sin."

What a beautiful and grace-filled perspective. Rather than an unintentional error instantly invalidating all their efforts at respect and obedience to their religious mandates, these women saw it as a *blessing*—the loving hand of God giving them a little boost to demonstrate the care of God's presence. This honest mistake, which causes no damage except for internal reprimand, does not require the fast to be started over or deep penitential prayer. It certainly does not require worry, anxiety, or self-condemnation. You acknowledge the mistake, thank God for making provisions, *and you move on*. Imagine the freedom if, the next time you find yourself obsessing over a slip-up that caused no harm except for inner shame, you instead thanked God for recognizing your need and meeting it rather than panicking that you set back your entire faith journey simply by being human? God expects effort, not perfection.

You fell asleep while trying to do your nightly Bible study one evening? *Thank you, God, for helping my body get the rest it needed!* You gave up social media for Lent but a week later caught yourself accidentally flipping through your feed? *Oops. I'm putting my phone back down now, but thank you for recognizing that I was feeling lonely and giving me a way to feel connected to my broader community for a moment.* You find yourself wrestling with doubt? *Thank you, God, for blessing me with critical thinking.*

Why not, instead of punishing or berating ourselves, we take a moment to marvel at the fact that we are loved by a God who became a human and therefore knows it's *really freaking hard* to be a human sometimes and, like any loving parent, cuts us little breaks here and there? Why not, instead of punishing ourselves for acting out of habit, we instead thanked God for providing us with a little reprieve from strict obedience in that moment?

And what about shedding the guilt that was never ours to carry in the first place? This can be especially hard when shame is an essential part of the soup in which we live, touching and influencing everything about the way we see ourselves, the world, and God. It takes a lot of time and intentionality to shift our thinking; you're probably going to fall back into old patterns. A lot. But when you do, remind yourself of Romans 12:21: "Do not be overcome by evil, but overcome evil with good."

This is not some pie-in-the-sky, Pollyanna theology. In fact, Romans 12 is a beautiful picture of what it should be like to live in Christian community. Paul urges his readers not to fall into cultural traps and easy patterns of behavior but to actively grow, explore, and expand their understanding to draw closer to God and God's heart for humanity rather than expecting everyone to conform to the same design. He writes: "For as in one body we have many members and not all the members have the same function" (Romans 12:4).

You do not have to be controlled by the manipulative agenda of people who seek to sacrifice you to the gods of their own ideals

You do not have to be controlled by the manipulative agenda of people who seek to sacrifice you to the gods of their own ideals. You do not have to continue to carry shame Christ has already freed you from just because someone else says so. Instead, fight back by embracing what is good: love, beauty, compassion, joy, celebration, community, hospitality, fullness, and living your very best life in light of the goodness to which God has called you.

9

DIMINISHMENT— CONTROL THROUGH DEHUMANIZING

The ending of Mark Twain's seminal but highly controversial 1884 novel *The Adventures of Huckleberry Finn* has long been debated among literary scholars. Most of the book focuses on the shared journey of a boy (Huck) running away from his abusive father with an enslaved man (Jim), who is attempting to escape north to freedom.

In 2012, the pioneering Christian deconstructionist Rachel Held Evans published a blog post in which she discusses Huckleberry Finn's act of defiance at the end of *The Adventures of Huckleberry Finn*, when he decides that he doesn't care if people tell him that helping an enslaved man run away is a sin.[1] "All right, then, I'll go to hell!" Huck declares as he tears up a letter he wrote revealing where Jim is hiding. Evans pointed out to her readers that this is the same stance we should all take on the side of marginalized and powerless people, despite what popular church teachings tell us: if Christians insist the morally right option is a sin, then we accept the sin.

Interestingly, there is *another* lesson about abusive theology embedded in the ending of the book, as well. Although it is written with a heavy dose of Twain's signature dry humor and irregular spellings that capture the local color of regional accents, the overall tone is serious as the characters grapple with the inherent dangers posed to them in rural, Southern, antebellum American society. Jim's position is especially tenuous, since, as a Black man, he is threatened with recapture, corporal punishment, and reenslavement at any moment. The final section of the book takes a sharp turn away from serious themes, however, when Twain's high-spirited, troublemaking protagonist from an earlier novel, Tom Sawyer, comes into the story.

While visiting family in Arkansas, Tom encounters Huck and Jim, who have been slowly drifting south along the Mississippi for several months but are now in a bad situation. Jim has been sold as a runaway by some unscrupulous men and is currently being held captive in a shed by Tom's aunt and uncle while they try to contact his enslavers to come and retrieve him—and pay a reward.

Tom relishes the idea of helping Jim escape, but he gets angry whenever Huck suggests a straightforward or simple solution to release Jim from his bondage. The thing is, Tom Sawyer actually knows that Jim is already free; the woman who enslaved him manumitted him in her will when she passed away weeks ago. But Tom keeps this information to himself and instead vastly overcomplicates the plan, insisting (for example) that Jim must be tunneled out through solid rock; releasing snakes, rats, and spiders to make Jim's shed feel more like a castle dungeon; and demanding that they saw off the leg of the iron bedstead to which Jim is chained (or even saw off Jim's own leg), despite the fact that the three of them could simply lift the heavy bed and slide out the chain if they worked together. Tom also insists that Jim keep a diary written on a shirt, carve messages into pie pans with spoons-turned-shivs, develop a coat of arms, and jump through any number of increasingly ridiculous hoops, all of which Tom insists are the only correct way to free a prisoner: "It don't make no difference how foolish it is, it's the *right* way—and it's the regular way. And there ain't no *other* way, that *I* ever heard of, and I've read all the books that gives any information about these things" (chapter 35).

The result, of course, is Jim's prolonged misery and captivity, despite the fact that he is already legally free. To Tom's credit, he does genuinely want Jim to escape, just not until Tom is finished enjoying himself with the pageantry. At one point, Huck even asks Tom what his goal is in all of the scheming:

> And he said, what he had planned in his head from the start, if we got Jim out all safe, was for us to run him down the river on the raft, and have adventures plumb to the mouth of the river, and then tell him about his being free, and take him back up home on a steamboat, in style, and pay him for his lost time, and write word ahead and get out all the [enslaved people] around, and have them waltz him into town with a torchlight procession and a brass-band, and then he would be a hero, and so would we. (chapter 43)

Tom's heart *appears* to be in the right place (at least, *he* thinks so) in helping an enslaved person to freedom, but his philosophy is problematic, to say the least, because he insists on directing the entire scenario in a manner that satisfies his own desires and agenda. He wants to create a spectacle, putting all of his grand, flashy ideas into play for the sake of his own gratification. Jim's rescue is not really about a rescue at all, but about Tom's enjoyment of the drama of saving someone. The story in Tom's head is clearly centered on himself as the protagonist with everyone else around him merely the supporting cast. Huck observes that Tom "was so proud and joyful, he just *couldn't* hold it in" when thinking about the elaborate plot he concocted. When his aunt questions afterwards why he would go to so much trouble when he knew Jim was already free, Tom replies, "Well, that *is* a question, I must say; and *just* like women! Why, I wanted the *adventure* of it; and I'd a waded neck-deep in blood" (chapter 42).

Tom's endgame may have had an ethical outcome (Jim's freedom), but his motivations and methods are nothing short of immoral. He treated another human being as merely a prop to further his own schemes and ambitions, using someone else's oppression to serve his own ends. He intentionally prolonged the enslavement of another human being, vastly increased that person's suffering, and utilized his social privilege for his own comfort and amusement at the cost of others—all while only paying lip service to opposing an unjust system. In the end, Tom assumes he can simply throw some money at the situation by paying Jim for his trouble, as if that makes everything all right—and then sink back into his daydream of being celebrated as a hero.

In order to carry out his own agenda, Tom dehumanizes Jim, as does just about every White person in the story—even Uncle Silas, who Jim says visits "every day or two to pray with him" (chapter 36). Uncle Silas expresses concern for Jim's soul while he keeps the man shackled to a bed, holding him captive as he waits to turn Jim over to his enslavers for a reward. Even after Jim gives up his own chance at freedom in order to save Tom's life when Tom is shot in the leg during an escape attempt, the doctor announces that a Black man like Jim "is worth a thousand dollars—and kind treatment, too" (chapter 42). Like all enslaved people, Jim is reduced to a mere commodity with his worth measured only by how well he serves the people in power—even to the point of sacrificing himself for one of the very people orchestrating his captivity.

It should be noted that, despite being a White male member of a landowning family, Tom does not hold a tremendous amount of social or civic influence; he is not a community leader or officer of the law. He is only a child. He doesn't have much real power to wield himself at that point—and yet he still finds a way to oppress someone else. And Huck, despite his occasional misgivings and objections, goes along with it, too. Tom's charisma and energy override Huck's anxieties and scruples.

This is what we must remember as we critique the misuse of power within our churches and the social structures our churches prop up: spiritual abuse is not confined to celebrity pastors or authoritative leaders. Anyone—even someone relatively powerless like Tom—is capable of dehumanizing someone else. Even someone like Huck, the character through whose eyes we have received the narration of the book and thus who is positioned to align most closely with ourselves. Any of us is capable of casting aside everything we know or believe about someone else for the sake of conforming to social pressures or simply because it doesn't impact us directly. Even if we don't actively diminish someone's humanity intentionally or deliberately, if we do so from habit, ignorance, or convenience, we are still accomplices to their oppression. We are still denying the *imago Dei*—the image of God—in which they were created.

((●))

What does it mean to be human? A scientist might point to a specific sequence of DNA; an anthropologist to the formation of complex social systems; a linguist to advanced languages with grammatical systems; a psychologist to complex emotions and awareness; a theologian to the idea of a soul; and an artist to an inherent aesthetic appreciation for beauty. There isn't one simple answer to the question.

What, then, does it mean to *de*humanize someone? That is even less straightforward, but it might be worth evaluating by these same metrics. It could mean insisting that someone's biology makes them innately inferior; it could mean excluding an individual or group from the community; it could mean taking away a person's voice or expression; it could mean reducing an individual to one characteristic of their being rather than allowing them to be a whole person; it could mean threatening or disparaging their soul; it could mean viewing them as flawed, broken, or inherently monstrous. In the book of James, we read about the immense power of the human tongue; it is compared to fire that can completely consume and destroy, and it is compared to the rudder of a ship that can steer the direction of the entire vessel. "With it," the Scriptures say, "we bless the Lord and Father, and with it we curse people, made in the likeness of God" (James 3:9).

The ways that people dehumanize or "other" their fellow humans are innumerable, but of all communities, surely people of faith who believe that we are created in the very image of God should be one group that bucks this trend, right?

(*Sigh.*)

This chapter is not a detailed breakdown of all the different ways that Christianity has historically failed to emulate Christ in its treatment of others. We can all think of examples, from the scriptural justification of slavery to cultural genocide of indigenous people groups to overtly religious movements like the Crusades or the Spanish Inquisition. These are shameful chapters in the history of our faith that none of us should want to see repeated. But this book is not a takedown of Christianity; it is an exploration of the roots of spiritual anxiety—its causes and forms, and the ways it can be manipulated by unscrupulous leaders. We may reference some of these specific incidents in the discussion, but I want to focus on how toxic theology can dehumanize others, especially on the grounds of gender, race, ethnicity, disability, sexuality, and socioeconomic status—anything that differs from the White, hetero, cis male perspective that has steered and shaped Western Christian theology for so long. These are hot-button topics in many of our churches right now as well as in the culture at large, but this is not a discussion of political perspectives or party agendas; I think we've all had enough of the church embedding or wrapping itself in politics. This discussion is about how attitudes and actions designed to diminish another human being's personhood can foster spiritual anxiety.

Let's begin by exploring the way that some of these methods of diminishment are baked into the Bible as we have it today, beginning with the character of Vashti.

CHAPTER 9

In case that name doesn't ring a bell, Vashti is the queen at the opening of the book of Esther—the one who refuses to appear before her drunken husband and his drunken guests, "in order to show the peoples and the officials her beauty, for she was fair to behold" (Esther 1:11). The king is humiliated, so he consults his royal advisors and experts on the law, and one sage named Memucan cautions the king that he must banish the queen forever:

> "For this deed of the queen will be made known to all women, causing them to look with contempt on their husbands, since they will say, 'King Ahasuerus commanded Queen Vashti to be brought before him, and she did not come.' This very day the noble ladies of Persia and Media who have heard of the queen's behavior will rebel against the king's officials, and there will be no end of contempt and wrath!" (1:17–18)

That's right, *the text literally says that the king casts his wife out of her home to make an example of her to all the other women of the empire, lest they rise up and disobey their husbands.*

Let the implications of that sink in a minute.

How many of us ever spent more than a few seconds on Vashti's story when we study the book of Esther? In my own experience, even when preachers or teachers point out that the request for Vashti to appear at the party likely involved nudity or at least suggestive dancing ("So you can't really blame her for not wanting to do it"), they skim past her story in a rush to get on to the Esther part of the book—you know, the part where a dutiful woman is required to make herself sexually available to a powerful politician to save her own life and, eventually, that of her people.

But Vashti's story should concern us. Did she really deserve to lose her marriage and home for refusing to dance for a bunch of drunk bros? Is that the message we want to be teaching when we have book studies on Esther as part of a "Women of the Bible" series? Vashti is a woman of the Bible, too; what are the implications of a book that seems to approve of a woman being cast out simply for refusing consent and that elevates a woman whose every action is directed by men? And how much might many divorced women see themselves in Vashti—a woman cast aside for a "newer model"—while the lion's share of the book is then in praise of the second wife?

Although one ultimate takeaway from the book of Esther seems to be that a woman who honors her husband is a woman who trusts God, there are some other interesting messages in it, as well. For example, Esther can hardly be considered a "loud and proud" believer given that the king does not even know about her ethnic and religious identity until she specifically tells him. What does that reveal to us about how much she had assimilated into Persian culture as a Jewish woman—and how discreetly she wore her religious beliefs?

For those of us raised hearing over and over how we should never hide our Christian lights "under a bushel" or who were challenged repeatedly with the zinger "If being a Christian were a crime, would there be enough evidence to convict you?" Esther hardly seems to be a hero who is leading by example in wearing her own faith on her sleeve.

It is interesting to consider how differently our faith might have taken shape if characters like Vashti had not been relegated to the margins but were held up as figures worth considering rather than as mere plot-points to get us to the moral we were "supposed" to take away from the text (and a rather problematic moral at that). Questions like these aren't disrespecting Scripture; they are inviting us to consider ways that we can approach our faith with a bigger lens.

We like our predictable, comfortable narratives both in terms of how we view Scripture and our Christian community. But people who challenge those ideas—not through any direct defiance but simply by their existence in the Bible or in our churches—are often pushed aside or forced into a more conventional mold so that they don't upset the established order of things. This can result in deep spiritual anxiety and self-loathing when an individual is taught that this facade of acceptability is the only way to be tolerable to God. By imparting a sense of IIL onto them, manipulative leaders can try to force "spiritual outliers" into a more convenient framework—and then control or even condemn them by it.

Sometimes people find themselves wrestling with their sense of identity in the church because they are expected to serve as a kind of mascot based on the story that makes the overall congregation feel good. This is especially true for those who are part of traditionally marginalized communities; even well-intentioned people who are trying to be inclusive and welcoming by embracing diversity often end up reducing individuals to a single trait and either patronizing them or getting upset when that person fails to conform to a certain "church-approved" script.

Stan, who shared about his spiritual anxiety in *Gaslighted by God*, spoke more about his internal spiritual wrestling as he tried to find his place in the church as a member of the disabled community.

Stan's tics began in high school, and at first he thought they were just tied to his anxiety around the possibility of the Rapture occurring at any moment: "I was the class of 2000, and with Y2K and everything, I grew up thinking either Jesus was going to come back or I was going to have died a horrible martyr's death because the world had gone so wrong, so I didn't expect to make it to my high school graduation." As the tics continued to worsen, he wasn't sure what to think, but he was afraid to talk to a medical professional:

> I didn't come from churches that said you shouldn't go to the doctor if you get sick or that it's because you don't have faith. I'd heard of them, but that wasn't us. But, at the same

time, if it was something like a mental health situation, it was different. If you have cancer, then it was one thing you could go to the doctor for, and of course it's a struggle and it's a battle and we pray for the chemo and radiation treatments to work. But if it was someone who was having depression or something like that, then the church was very quick to start off with, "Here are seven different Bible verses and four different devotional books about being in the storm." And if all that doesn't work for you magically, then people either get painted as if they don't want help—they don't want to get better—or else they're not really believing. They're not really putting their faith in God.

It's so transactional that if you don't have some sort of positive outcome, we can't make God look bad, so it's got to be you. And we may not say that to you, but Lord knows we're real comfortable saying that to everybody in our prayer group and everybody in Sunday school, and that's when you start becoming a prayer request. And God help you if you become that kind of prayer request, because on top of all of that we're not going to forget that this is where you were. And so now you are irreparably broken because God might save you and fix you from being a drug addict . . . but something like a mental illness, you are never going to be asked to share your testimony or lead in church. There are just some things that if God didn't wave a magic wand, then it's you and it's your fault and you're broken. . . . You're not someone that's going to be asked to lead, you're not going to be welcome in the choir, you're not going to be treated like a full member because we can't have you be visible because people are going ask the questions about why you aren't healed.

So I knew better than to speak up, because I was praying but my situation wasn't getting fixed, and I knew I wanted to serve in a pastoral role, but if I was that broken or that stained, I knew I couldn't do that. I couldn't be in ministry.

One summer in college, while in a ministerial training program, Stan's tics grew worse, but this time, his circle of Christian support was incredibly uplifting. One man, who had experienced a miraculous healing from a brain tumor a few years earlier, told him, "God sometimes works that way—but not always. You need to see a doctor when you get home. Please take care of yourself." Stan explains, "The concept of someone telling me to take care of myself was foreign because I'd been praying to God make all this go away, and it wasn't going away. So maybe there was something physiological here, not just a matter of faith."

After a medical evaluation, Stan was diagnosed with Tourette's syndrome, and suddenly, his entire identity changed in the church. Since it wasn't a "mental illness," he wasn't dismissed as he had feared; instead, however, he found that he was suddenly thrust into a new role of "overcomer." This was his new identity; everything about him was now defined by his Tourette's. By this point, he was working as a worship minister in a large congregation, and when someone observed that his tics didn't seem to affect him while he was translating the service into sign language for Deaf members, people asked:

"What is this miraculous thing that 'cures' Tourette's Boy? Isn't it just wonderful that God lets you have control of your body while you are serving others?" I wanted to say "Brain chemistry. The 'miraculous thing' is brain chemistry." . . . But I felt I had to lean into it because that was what was expected of me from my church community. You know, this is my identity now and . . . this is the only way to do this thing I feel called to in the church. I've got this thing and I don't know why God gave it to me, but just like Paul had his thorn, if I lean on Jesus every day, I am an overcomer.

If I wanted to stay in ministry, that was the identity I had to take on. And I was getting mixed messages from the church. I would hear, "We are praying so hard that God takes your

Tourette's away," but at the same time, "God gave you this as a gift to help you minister to people."

. . . On the one hand, God was "supposed" to cure me because of my tremendous faith. Well, I had prayed for the Tourette's to go away and it didn't, so this meant that there was that problem with me inherently. On the other hand, God had given me this "gift" to use for his glory. But it got to be where if I felt bad, if I had a bad Tourette's day—because it physically hurts sometimes and I can't drive—then I felt guilty because then I was wallowing. I'm not being appreciative enough for this gift or how can I feel that way when there are so many other people who have things worse than I do?

When a reorganization changed some of Stan's responsibilities at church, he found himself working in a much higher-stress situation with an authoritarian boss, and his tics began to worsen. "I thought, this isn't the area where I felt called, but maybe I just misread God, so I need to go with this . . . but I remember going into sanctuary and lying, full-body prostrate down on the ground cruciform and praying about how to get my heart right so God would fix everything." Eventually, Stan's doctor advised him to speak to the church about adapting some of his duties to accommodate his Tourette's. When Stan went to speak to the pastor, however:

He just looks at me and goes, "Okay, so you've turned in your two weeks' notice." This was 2006; I was just two years out of college; I didn't know my legal rights—and besides, how do you fight a pastor? I know what I've always been taught; I'm supposed to submit to authority. It was like I wasn't the overcomer fighting through everything, which was what they wanted, so I couldn't be visible anymore.

Even building a life outside of ministry, Stan has found that many Christians handle disabilities and neurodivergence poorly.

He has dealt with cashiers in stores "rebuking Satan in me: 'Demon, get out!'" and even beloved family members trying to perform faith healings on him. "I remember actively trying to make something happen," Stan recalls, "and basically dry-heaving and thinking 'Is this spiritual?' There I am, retching, wondering if this is the Holy Spirit (and [the family member] taking it that way) but it was me just wanting something so much. I was so desperate for some sort of validation. I wanted to believe that God loved me more than my Tourette's—that I had value in the church outside of my condition."

One day, in the middle of an ordinary week at his ordinary job teaching historical crafts to schoolchildren, Stan noticed that he had not had any tics for a week. When he shared that with his mother, she responded, "Well, maybe you're going to wake up one day and it will be gone. Maybe God is going to bless you with that." Stan realized in that moment how wholly his identity had become tied up in his Tourette's, even to himself. "I remember looking at her and saying, 'I don't know what to do if that happens. It's been a part of me for so long, and it's what I define myself by and what everybody else defines me by. I don't know what I would do or who I would be anymore without it.'"

That was several years ago; now, Stan has released much of his anxiety around how he is supposed to make sense of his condition in light of his relationship with God. "That's not where my spiritual anxiety is anymore," he says:

> I've reached the point where I've decided that if God's my co-pilot, then the Tourette's is in the back seat—*and it ain't getting out*, so I better take some time to get okay with that. Because my relationship with God may be weird and full of anxiety, but as unpredictable as Tourette's can be, it's predictable in some ways. More predictable than God, sometimes. And it's even funny sometimes; it can lead to some funny situations, and I'm totally okay with that. . . . People will ask,

"Can I pray for you?" and I say "Please don't. I've already had a lot of people try that." Now, there are *other* things that may need prayer, so I might say "Can I tell you something that I *do* want prayer for right now?" But, of course, some people don't ask at all; they just lay on hands or start praying for God to heal you. Consent matters, people. Jesus asked so many people, "Do you want to be healed?" If God incarnate asks for consent, surely you can do the same.

I remember there was one time someone was getting really insistent about it, and they were like, "Why are you fighting me asking for God's blessing on you?" And I was like, "I'm not fighting you; I just don't need that right now. That's not the blessing I need."

People say, "Do you think this is a generational curse?" No, I think it's genetics. . . . If my back is thrown out, then maybe I'll ask you to pray for that, but this is *my* body . . . and my faith in God tells me that I am loved exactly as I am. We are who we are, and that's what God can use, if we're okay with it. But we are whole people. Disabilities are a part of us, but they aren't who we are.

One of the easiest ways to dehumanize someone is to create a narrative for them and then expect them to fulfill it, as if they are nothing more than a supporting character in a reality centered on ourselves.

We may struggle sometimes to accept that the main focus of the current conversation isn't actually about us at the moment. That is one of the biggest obstacles many of us need to overcome in the church: the belief that those of us who are White, middle class, cisgendered, heterosexual adults are the protagonists of reality. Not every message is going to be for or about us. And we (myself included) have to learn to be okay with that. Those of us in the majority must remember that the church has always been a safe place for some people, but not for everyone.

Perhaps our primary concern right now should not be making things easier for people who have always been comfortable in the church. That is not shutting down conversation; that is opening the door for people who don't feel that they have a voice or a place to speak up to say, "I felt alienated, too" or "I felt dehumanized by what was said here." Let us invite people back into conversation who have been pushed away by toxic theology and harmful traditions. People who have left the faith don't want to come back unless they know that they are entering a system that affirms their inherent worth and personhood.

Perhaps our primary concern right now should not be making things easier for people who have always been comfortable in the church

I can't speak for other branches of Christianity, but I know that in White evangelicalism, every sermon on forgiveness inevitably seems to include at least one story about a Black person forgiving a White person for some horrible, violent, racially motivated act.

These are certainly humbling and praiseworthy stories of incredible human beings performing superhuman feats of Christian forgiveness, and we *should* be honoring those remarkable souls capable of such obedience. But those of us in the White evangelical tradition should also be willing to examine our motives for sharing them. Are we telling these stories only to illustrate the Christian principle of radical forgiveness? Or do we consistently rely on them to carry the point because we like stories of radical forgiveness *when they are directed toward people who look like us*? By consistently including such stories in our sermons, we can virtuously signal that we believe racism is wrong while also appreciating that stories of profound reconciliation after deep injustice maybe somehow let us off the hook by proxy.

Think of the message we are sending when we reduce an entire group of people's lived experience to a sermon illustration: "The civil rights movement teaches us so much about forgiveness" or "Divorced people still have value" or "Members of the LGBTQ+ community show us that God can love *anyone*" or "People with disabilities can make us thankful for our own lives." Consider the inherent diminishment of those statements. They communicate that the central significance of the fight for human rights is about the parties in the wrong having their bad behavior excused, that there was ever any question as to whether divorced people retain their inherent worth when their marriage ends, that God can scrounge up some care "even for 'those people,'" or that the primary purpose of someone else's physical existence is to be a measuring stick for our own blessings. Not only do these attitudes reinforce the common lens many Christians unwittingly carry—that anything that differs from a White, male, heterosexual norm is a deviation from the original, God-ordained model—they also transmit a message to anyone outside those categories that they are an exception, a concession, an allowance, a compromise.

Think of the message we are sending when we reduce an entire group of people's lived experience to a sermon illustration

What do you think that does to the inner spiritual life of someone who knows they are more than the church has permitted them to be, but who meets resistance when they try to live that out? As Stan said, "Respect me as the individual that you say that I am. Get to know me. Get to know my story, and we can talk. Let me be who I am, not who you want me to be."

Of course, there are other ways that people are dehumanized in the church that can cause them to question their own worth. Sometimes, verses we hold up as celebratory or honoring of certain people actually just set impossibly high standards and reduce their personhood to a checklist.

Consider first a scene from chapter 8 of Jane Austen's classic 1813 novel *Pride and Prejudice* in which a group of acquaintances debate what makes a young woman "accomplished" by the standards of upper-class Regency England. After Mr. Bingley comments on the universality of certain talents like painting, embroidery, and working with silk, his friend counters that these skills are hardly enough to merit use of the word "accomplished." Mr. Darcy, who (at this point) the text is still taking great pains to portray as snobbish and condescending, remarks:

> "I am very far from agreeing with you in your estimation of ladies in general. I cannot boast of knowing more than half a dozen, in the whole range of my acquaintance, that are really accomplished." . . .
>
> "Then," observed Elizabeth, "you must comprehend a great deal in your idea of an accomplished woman."
>
> "Yes, I do comprehend a great deal in it."
>
> "Oh! certainly," cried his faithful assistant, "no one can be really esteemed accomplished who does not greatly surpass what is usually met with. A woman must have a thorough knowledge of music, singing, drawing, dancing, all the modern languages, to deserve the word; and besides all this, she must possess a certain something in her air and manner of walking, the tone of her voice, her address and expressions, or the word will be but half deserved."
>
> "All this she must possess," added Darcy, "and to all this she must yet add something more substantial, in the improvement of her mind by extensive reading."

Elizabeth, the protagonist, marvels at this impossible standard, and wryly observes, "I am no longer surprised at your knowing *only* six accomplished women. I rather wonder now at your knowing *any*."

This conversation, intended to satirize impossible standards of womanhood in the Regency period, could have easily been applied to one of the most anxiety-inducing passages in all of Scripture: Proverbs 31.

In recent years, social media has been crowded with various "takedowns" of this mythical figure, which is testimony to how widely this passage of Scripture has been used in oppressive or abusive ways. Show me a Christian woman who has never felt stressed out by or resentful of this impossible combination of Stepford wife, Fortune 500 CEO, Oprah, the professor from *Gilligan's Island*, and Daniel Tiger's mom. She runs a perfect home, has a keen business sense, is well known for her philanthropy and good works, can create or repair anything, and always has exactly the right response of calm wisdom for any circumstance.

Proverbs 31:10 calls her *eschet chavil* ("woman of valor")—a wonderful term that honors a woman who lives into her own fullness—but just like the comic book heroine of male fantasies, the woman described here isn't real. Proverbs 31 isn't describing a person, just a list of idealized attributes—which is exactly how many women feel when it is celebrated, encouraged, or weaponized.

As we discussed in chapter 6, a person's value is rooted in more than simply what they produce, but this verse has been co-opted by many Christian leaders as a prescription for female behavior. Conveniently, they seem to ignore that the *only command* the passage contains is aimed toward a man: "Give her a share in the fruit of her hands, / and let her works praise her in the city gates" (Proverbs 31:31). He is instructed to treat the woman with dignity and respect both in terms of allowing her control over her own work as well as public recognition. (And, for the record, I think it's safe to assume that "praising her at the city gates" means much more than a pastor referring to his wife as "smokin' hot" in sermons.)

But why is men's conduct rarely addressed from the pulpit in such biblically prescriptive terms? While many women wrestle with anxiety over their failure to measure up to an artificial and misapplied scriptural standard of both excellence and submission, men are often only chastised for how poorly they are fulfilling their roles of "masculine leadership." Women's behavior is delineated in every sphere, but men's behavior is prescriptive only in how they are supposed to act in their role of authority over women. At least, that is the way it is presented in many churches and Christian media.

Of course there is a whole section of hypermasculine, evangibro literature in every Christian bookstore, but it doesn't carry quite the same authority as a divinely ordained checklist like Proverbs 31. This is actually one way that men, too, are dehumanized in churches. Conveniently ignoring centuries of Christian music, art, and scholarship that built cathedrals, composed symphonies of praise, and promoted biblical understanding, it is usually only the alpha male, carnivorous, warrior-type standard that popular evangelicalism seems to consider worthwhile. *Sure, Michelangelo painted the Sistine Chapel . . . but could he grill a steak?* Imagine the anxiety that invokes in boys and men who don't fall into that mold. "You tell a boy he isn't supposed to cry, and he's going to think it's wrong to have a gentle heart or a sensitive conscience," one man told me.

Yet there actually *is* a biblical blueprint for the ideal man—and nowhere does it indicate he must be a chest-beating "man's man." Nor is this text trotted out every Father's Day to sink men deep into a shame-spiral or imposter syndrome because they don't measure up despite their best efforts. Let us consider the qualifications for elders and deacons as outlined in 1 Timothy 3 and Titus 1. If a leader insists that these positions of leadership can only apply to men (conveniently ignoring 1 Timothy 3:11, which mentions the qualifications of "the women," which could mean the wives of candidates but could also mean women candidates themselves), then according to these passages, the ideal man of God must:

- have a solid reputation and be above reproach in the broader community outside the church
- be faithful to his wife

- be self-controlled
- be wise and cautious
- exhibit good, orderly, and respectable behavior
- be hospitable
- be able to teach about righteous living
- not be a heavy drinker
- not be violent
- be patient and gentle
- not be quick-tempered
- not be obsessed with money
- run his household well, including the behavior of his children
- not be a new convert
- not be stubborn
- be a lover of goodness and righteousness
- be just and fair, not prejudiced or biased
- be devout in his faith
- hold firmly to truth as the heart of the gospel

How many men do you know who hit every single one of these out of the park every time? Are the men who insist that women embody the whole of Proverbs 31 womanhood themselves consistently self-controlled, not violent, orderly, patient, gentle, not stubborn, and so on?

And how many of these qualifications of male leaders are often passed along to women to take care of? As one former pastor told me, "There is a reason why churches want their preachers to be married. It's not because they are worried about him being distracted by girls in the youth group, but because the wife is a freebie. A married preacher gives them a two-for-one deal; they hire one person but get the work of two because that is what we expect from preacher's wives."

Consider, for example, the charge to be hospitable. Notice that this does not say the man's *wife* needs to be a good hostess; this is a characteristic the man *himself* ought to possess. Notice also the well-run household and children who are "not wild." This does not say that the man needs to have a wife who can look after these things; it says that *he* bears responsibility for them. And what about the requirement of self-control? How often is *that* buck passed on to the women and girls in the congregation to watch their clothing and behavior "lest they cause a brother to stumble"? Is the onus for this behavior not on the righteous man himself, according to this passage, as well as twice from Jesus in the Gospel of Matthew (5:29; 18:9)? We will explore the spiritual anxiety brought on by Purity Culture in chapter 10, but it could certainly fit in here just as well. Women are not only reduced to their own checklist but they have to pick up some of the men's responsibilities, too—often with none of the authority.

Women are not only reduced to their own checklist but they also have to pick up some of the men's responsibilities, too—often with none of the authority

In fact, while we are on the subject of dehumanizing people, let's explore this issue of authority. If women are not meant to lead, then why are some women given the spiritual gift of leadership? If women are not meant to preach, then why are some women given the spiritual gift of preaching? If women are not meant to be full members in the body of Christ, why does God place that desire on the hearts of so many—and why have those women been accused of being sinful, dangerous, and displeasing to God as a result?

A common counterargument to this is to say, "Some people have the desire to murder, too; that doesn't mean that desire is from God." This is what is called a "false equivalency." In this case, the speaker is equating the behaviors (e.g., women preaching and murder) so that the listener receives the information as if the connection between them has already been proven. The two behaviors are now associated, and the moral implications of the one are shared with the other.

If that's getting confusing, just think of it as the idea behind the colloquialism, "comparing apples and oranges." True, both are fruit, but they are fundamentally different types with different taste, structures, and chemical components. The speaker is drawing a connection between two unrelated things in an effort to apply the same argument to both circumstances. So common is this type of rhetorical fallacy, in fact, that languages from all over the globe have expressions that capture a similar sentiment.

But this kind of false equivalency, which is usually used to shut down conversation on the topic without any further discussion, does not allow us to ask the necessary follow-up questions, such as: Is murder a spiritual gift? Is pedophilia? Is megalomania? Is ecologic destruction? Is the subordination of indigenous people? Is greed? Is gossip? Of course not. The world is full of urges that run contrary to the heart of God and full of people who carry them out. But to compare those traits to ones that Scripture specifically says are a result of the indwelling of the Holy Spirit—traits that are driven by a desire to serve and edify God's people, traits that cause no harm to others, traits that are rooted in love for Christ—is to create a false equivalency that erroneously equates a woman behind the pulpit with violent crime. No wonder so many women struggle with feelings of guilt and anxiety over internal spiritual calls to speak with authority; they've been taught it's on par with crimes against humanity.

Unfortunately, many churches continue in this tradition because of another rhetorical fallacy, that of "appeal to tradition." This is essentially the idea that "the way we do it is correct because it's the way it's always been done." Appeals to tradition have been used to justify all kinds of sin in the church: racism, segregation, discrimination, sexism, antisemitism, colonialism, oppression, slavery, and so on. Those who hold this position rarely stop to consider that maybe it *hasn't* always been done this way . . . or maybe we've always been wrong.

Yet appeals to tradition tend to be very selectively applied only to things that don't upset the established order and those who sit at the top of it. With the exception of certain groups like some Mennonites, "We've always done it this way" usually does not apply

Sure, we love people; we just love our traditions more

when it comes to things like automobiles, deodorant, or penicillin. But letting someone in the pulpit who has a uterus? Worshipping next to someone with brown skin? Welcoming a lesbian couple and their three kids? That's usually when we start throwing walls back up faster than an Amish barn-raising: "Sure, we love people; we just love our traditions more."

In our determination to defend the comfortable way we've always done things, churches often lose sight of the difference between political preferences and religious imperatives, mingling the two ideas until they become indistinguishable. Sometimes, this can be a good thing, such as when orphaned children are protected and cared for. Far too often, however, this can lead to seeing people as little more than talking points or easy clichés that reduce them to an issue rather than a life. How does that communicate worth and value to people in our churches who fall outside the neat and tidy cultural boxes we have decided are the "right way" to be?

Nileen was raised in the Midwest attending Catholic and Episcopalian churches growing up. Her father carried unresolved religious anxiety for most of his life, due (Nileen believes) to some unresolved trauma connected with growing up in an immigrant family in an otherwise homogenous area. "He was the only non-White kid growing up, and I think that impacted him," she explains. "I know it was on his mind a lot. He would come with us to Mass sometimes, but never go forward to take the host. I would say, 'Why don't you come with us?' and he would say, 'No, no, no. It's a long story.'"

Unfortunately, some of the same ideas and attitudes that affected her father's religious experience as a child persist today in

Nileen's parish. She has found herself sitting through sermons where, rather than focusing on how churches could fulfill the charge of James 1:27 ("Religion that is pure and undefiled before God the Father is this: to care for orphans and widows in their distress and to keep oneself unstained by the world"), the priest decided to call out various groups of people who he felt were responsible for the moral decay of the country. "We were at the feast of the Holy Family of all things," Nileen says,

> and there was a priest from the diocese who had no recent experience with the art of the homily. Basically he'd been kind of doing a lot of like clerical ecumenical stuff, so he's pretty out of touch, and during the homily, he started going off about homosexuals and single mothers. And I was really insulted by that. My husband was raised by a single mother. Her husband died and she was raising three kids on her own. I thought his comments were really insulting to people like her—and she was with us that Sunday—who had to be very resourceful and have a lot of resolve to grieve their husbands and also have children to raise as well.

((((●))))

We haven't specifically discussed anxiety as much in this chapter because I want to be careful about how I speak about something as deeply personal as identity. In this book, you have read accounts from people are Black, White, Hispanic, multiracial, gay, straight, male, female, nonbinary, neurodivergent, members of the disabled community, or any combination of these or various other categories. Many of them spoke, as Stan did, of feeling as if they were diminished until they were reduced to a single thing or having significance only as a prop in someone else's narrative. Rather than highlighting every experience that touched on this topic, I decided to avoid any further dehumanization that could occur by me boiling down their spiritual anxiety to being caused by that one thing. I wanted to make sure their stories were woven throughout the book to acknowledge the complexities and depth of their experiences. That doesn't mean that the spiritual anxiety dehumanized people experience in this area is any less intense or debilitating than in others; it simply means that all the swirling doubts, questions, concerns, worries, and struggles with self-worth they face in the church can show up in multiple ways. Maybe those complex feelings impact you, too.

Conversations around issues of diminishment and dehumanization often center around the need for more and greater empathy—we need to be able to look past our differences and recognize how alike we truly are deep down. While this solution sounds good in theory, it also kind of misses the point. I shouldn't feel bad about harming someone because I suddenly recognize that we have some shared bonds; their worth as human beings is not dependent on the fact that they are like me. I shouldn't have to compare others to myself to be able to recognize their value. Their worth is inherent because they are beloved children of God and part of the crown of creation. Empathy is deeply important, but it ultimately should not be necessary.

I shouldn't have to compare others to myself to be able to recognize their value

In Luke 10, when Jesus is asked the key to salvation, he affirms that the answer is to "love the Lord your God with all your heart and with all your soul and with all your strength and with all your mind and your neighbor as yourself" (v. 27). But when the questioner then poses a follow-up question: "And who is my neighbor?" (v. 29), Jesus responds not by saying, "Look around you!" or even "Everyone is." Instead, Jesus answers by telling the parable of the good Samaritan; in other words, he went out of his way to demonstrate that the man who acts most like a neighbor to the injured victim is the outsider in the story—the one who was most different from everyone else. He wasn't inspired to act because of some shared sameness but simply because he "was moved with compassion"

(v. 33). Empathy is, perhaps, the starting point, but the ultimate goal should be to look beyond it. Christ calls us to treat others with love and respect regardless of whether we share similarities. Communication and mutual understanding are good things, but the worth of another human life is in no way dependent on whether or not we "get" the way they are in the world because of their race, gender, marital status, sexual orientation, socioeconomic standing, or any other demographic characteristic.

This point may be best illustrated by a nameless character who appears in both Mark 14:13–15 and Luke 22:7–13. Jesus tells Peter and John to enter the city and look for a man carrying water who would meet them. They were to follow him to a specific house where they should ask the owner about a large room where they could celebrate Pass-

Empathy is, perhaps, the starting point, but the ultimate goal should be to look beyond it

over. The room would be ready for them, as it appears Jesus had already made these arrangements in advance. The Scriptures tell us that things played out exactly in this manner.

As preachers like to point out when sharing this story, toting water was women's work, so a man with a jar would have been easily spotted. What sermons *don't* usually linger on is this: If this job was so strongly coded as women's work, what does that say about this mysterious figure who crossed gender barriers and helped make the Lord's Supper happen?

Maybe this was a man who was willing to do whatever needed to be done for the sake of his household—like the husband who is willing to buy his wife menstrual products. Or maybe he was a man who had taken on a female role in society. Either way, there was a place for this person in Jesus's vision for the Last Supper.

Jesus didn't command his disciples to ask the man why he was doing a woman's job; he simply told them to meet the man, follow him, and then ask the owner of the house for a room they could use. What's more, if this man was an enslaved person in that home, as it seems may have been the case, then he likely would have been involved in hosting and serving Jesus and his disciples at the table. In other words, it's not our place to demand that someone explain themselves to us; we should simply be willing to include, listen, and break bread in their company.

Jesus's orders were, essentially: "Everybody be cool. Peter and John, just let this person do their thing. We have our own understanding." So that's what they did. They didn't automatically start toting water just because they saw this guy do it, nor did he try to convert them into being water carriers themselves; the disciples simply met this man on his own terms and interacted with him respectfully. In the end, it came down to a basic agreement: "You like Jesus? Me too! Awesome. Let's have supper."

If you struggle with questions of self-doubt or self-loathing due to feeling dehumanized in the church, remember that the anxiety you feel is coming from the outside—from the narratives, roles, or even the silence that other people are asking you to shoulder in order to have a place at the table. But that's not the example of Christ. When Jesus sends his followers out into the world as well as when he invites them into his presence, we should be mindful of his intentionality about whom he included and how. Whether we are meeting people out and about in the marketplace or meeting together to celebrate Communion—a reenactment of the same Last Supper the water carrier helped bring about—let us remember that our job is not to police who gets a part in the story or what that role should look like, but instead to humbly recognize that we are mere players in it, too. And the story isn't ours to dictate.

10

DOMINATION—CONTROL
THROUGH POWER IMBALANCE

Content warning: discussions of child sexual assault

First published in 1891, Thomas Hardy's *Tess of the D'Urbervilles* is widely considered a classic work of late Victorian England. The novel tells the story of Tess, a beautiful and innocent young woman born to a rural farming family who is preyed upon by a distant, wealthy relative named Alec. By offering her impoverished family financial gifts, Alec sexually exploits Tess and then casts her off, sending her back to her family pregnant and "ruined" in the eyes of society. The baby dies, and Tess later marries a pious young man named Angel who abandons her mere hours after their wedding when he learns of her past.

Destitute, but with a growing sense of her own strength and inherent worth, Tess supports herself, her siblings, and her alcoholic parents as a manual farm laborer. Eventually, she has a chance encounter with Alec, who has renounced his past sins and is now living as an itinerate preacher.

After Alec tries to be friendly with Tess, she challenges his supposed conversion, telling him:

"I feel indignant with you for talking to me like this, when you know—when you know what harm you've done me! You, and those like you, take your fill of pleasure on earth by making the life of such as me bitter and black with sorrow; and then it is a fine thing, when you have had enough of that, to think of securing your pleasure in heaven by becoming converted. Out upon such—I don't believe in you—I hate it!"

"Tess," he insisted; "don't speak so! It came to me like a jolly new idea. And you don't believe me? What don't you believe?"

"Your conversion. Your scheme of religion."

. . . "Don't look at me like that!" he said abruptly.

Tess, who had been quite unconscious of her action and mien, instantly withdrew the large dark gaze of her eyes, stammering with a flush, "I beg your pardon." And there was revived in her the wretched sentiment which had often come to her before, that in inhabiting the fleshly tabernacle with which Nature had endowed her, she was somehow doing wrong.[1]

Despite her objections to his company, Alec accompanies Tess down a country road during this exchange, and they come upon a place where two roads meet called "Cross-in-Hand," marked by a small monument. Here, Alec pauses and makes a demand of Tess:

"Well—you will see me again."

"No," she answered. "Do not come near me!"

"I will think. But before we part, come here." He stepped up to the pillar. "This was once a Holy Cross. Relics are not in my creed; but I fear you at moments—far more than you need fear me at present; and to lessen my fear, put your hand upon that stone hand, and swear that you will never tempt me—by your charms or ways."

"Good God—how can you ask what is so unnecessary! All that is furthest from my thought."

"Yes—but swear it."

Tess, half-frightened, gave way to his importunity, placed her hand upon the stone, and swore.

"I am sorry you are not a believer," he continued; "that some unbeliever should have got ahold of you, and unsettled your mind. But no more now. At home at least I can pray for you; and I will; and who knows what may not happen?"

A short time later, finally alone, Tess encounters a shepherd in the road and asks about the old stone at the crossroads. She learns that it was never a Christian relic at all, but a marker to warn travelers that the bones buried beneath it belong to a man who sold his soul to the devil.

Alec eventually leaves preaching to pursue Tess, even though she repeatedly rebuffs him, begging him to leave: "Go, in the name of your own Christianity!" He insists that he cannot, as she has "been the means—the innocent means—of my backsliding, as they call it."

When her father dies suddenly and the family is cast out of their home, Alec once again steps in and plies the family with gifts of money in order to create an obligation that places Tess in his debt. She finally assents from exhaustion and desperation, but due to her traumatic past, has reached a point of total detachment from her physical body: "Tess had spiritually ceased to recognize the body before him as hers—allowing it to drift, like a corpse upon the current, in a direction disassociated from its living will." In fact, when her estranged husband finally returns only to discover she is once again living with Alec as his mistress, Tess explains to Angel, "[Alec] was very kind to me, and to mother, and to all of us after father's death." She then adds a significant line that was eventually cut from subsequent publications of the book after 1892: "He bought me."

Alec's social and economic power over Tess seems inescapable. He blames her for his own lustful thoughts and makes her feel shame for the mere existence of her God-given body. Despite her repeated resistance to his attentions, Alec manipulates Tess for his own gratification without regard for her willingness or consent because he knows he holds the upper hand as a man of political standing, as a man of financial means, as a purported man of God, and simply as a man in a patriarchal system. She is trapped in a society where sexual availability is a means of survival. The dynamics that define Tess's world hinge entirely upon her ability to be exploited, and the power imbalances embedded in her community not only favor her abuser but also protect him.

((●))

Arguably one of the Bibles verses most ripe for abuse, Hebrews 13:17 exhorts readers: "Obey your leaders and submit to them, for they are keeping watch over your souls as those who will give an account. Let them do this with joy and not with sighing, for that would be harmful to you."

Obey. Submit. These are strong words without much wiggle room, and abusers know this. With one verse, they can prooftext their way out of responsibility, accountability, and sometimes even liability. It is such a convenient verse both for justifying and covering up abuse. Whether the manipulation is through financial control, enforced dependence on an authority figure, behavioral manipulation, or exploitation within a system designed to protect the perpetrators, control through power imbalances within religious systems has been a cornerstone of toxic theology for millennia.

Within contemporary Western Christianity, this has been one of the primary ways that those in power have remained in power. Through a variety of efforts, people who wish to retain control have had easy access to any number of tools to shape and manipulate the beliefs and anxieties of those they seek to subjugate by means of exploiting their earnest desire to please God by honoring their leaders. The results can range from cultural genocide to an epidemic of system-wide abuse with little accountability—all in the name of controlling the message and (supposedly) protecting God's chosen leaders.

Some authoritarian leaders rely on trauma bonds—a milder form of Stockholm syndrome—to generate allegiance to their message. The abuser may not even be consciously aware of their methods because they are focused solely on the results, which is a loyal following. Trauma-bonding is a natural human response. According to a 2021 *Psychology Today* article, in the midst of traumatic circumstances

> we are chemically wired to focus on getting to the "other side." When the abuser is the person that brings us relief, the brain associates them with safety.
>
> *The brain latches on to the positive experience of relief rather than the negative impact of the abuser.*
>
> This happens because the body's threat response (fight, flight, freeze, fawn) turns off the part of the brain that can think long-term when we are in crisis. This creates the feeling that we need the abuser to survive, and is often mistaken for "love."
>
> Trauma-bonding is a hormonal attachment created by repeated abuse, sprinkled with being "saved" every now and then.[2]

Several people I spoke to talked about experiences with authoritarian leaders who denigrated them until they had no self-worth left to even consider that they might deserve to be treated with more respect. Several others described charismatic leaders who cultivated devoted followings by paradoxically insulting people as a way of "keeping it real," and ended up kingdom-building under the guise of Kingdom-building. One person summarized it this way:

They say no one else is willing to speak the truth like they are, and you believe them because that's what you've been conditioned to do for religious leaders. You actually feel grateful for their attention—like, "Wow! The pastor noticed me! I matter enough for him to point out my failings. I need that kind of leadership to do better." It becomes a vicious circle, and all the while, the pastor is just building up his own reputation and his own following for his own ego.

As we saw in our discussion of control through rejection in chapter 7, often when someone steps up who challenges these methods or jeopardizes the face of the "brand" of a popular or powerful leader, they are disciplined or removed. That is not just true in our churches, however; it also happened in the Bible.

Last chapter, we looked at Vashti; now, let's consider another character who was erased from Scripture not by the plot of their story but by translators who changed their identity because it threatened the external narrative of the church.

If you've done much research into the role of women in the early church, you are probably familiar with Junia. If not, you're in for a treat—the kind of treat that makes you feel excited, intrigued, affirmed, saddened, and angry all at once and stays with you for a long time.[3] In Romans 16:7, as Paul is sending his thanks and acknowledgment to the various believers who have aided and encouraged his work, he writes, "Greet Andronicus and Junia, my fellow Israelites who were in prison with me; they are prominent among the apostles, and they were in Christ before I was." What can we learn about these faithful friends from this short passage? They were Jewish, like Paul; they were imprisoned for their faith alongside him; they are well-known and respected leaders "among the apostles"; and they were early converts to Christianity, possibly serving as spiritual mentors for Paul because of the special care he takes to point out the fact that they preceded him in the faith. Before we go any farther, let's take a quick look at this word "apostles." While "the apostles" (often capitalized in English) has traditionally been used to refer to the eleven men (that exclusion is 100 percent on you, Judas) closest to Jesus during his ministry, the same word, *apostolos,* is used throughout the New Testament to refer to the key members in authority within the church. It does not necessarily mean the eleven themselves in an exclusive sense. Acts 15:22 speaks of "the apostles and elders" who oversaw the church in Jerusalem; Ephesians 3:4–5 talks about "the mystery of Christ, which was not made known to people in other generations as it has now been revealed by the Spirit to God's holy apostles and prophets." In other words, it was not a word used lightly; it implied a position of leadership, headship, and governance.

Whoever Andronicus and Junia were, they were "prominent" among this group of esteemed leaders in the early church. Oh yeah—*and Junia was a woman.*

As wildly inconvenient as this is for those who want to prop up a complementarian model of church authority, Romans 16:7 clearly demonstrates that women held not just positions of leadership but "prominent" (literally "conspicuous") leadership among the highest levels of ecclesiastical hierarchy from the earliest days of the faith.[4]

So what do you do when the Bible that you insist must be taken literally *literally shows a woman in a position of authority?* As the quote commonly misattributed to Einstein says: "If the facts don't fit the theory, change the facts." And that appears to be exactly what some scribes did. The female name Junia, which appears in the earliest known manuscripts, began to appear in later copies as Junias, the male form of the name. But history attests to the fact that Junia was recognized as a woman by even

> *The stroke of a pen undid a huge portion of the great equalizing work central to Christ's message and subjugated more than sixty generations of women to subservience in the church*

the most prominent voices in the first few centuries of the faith. John Chrysostom, in his thirty-first *Homily on Romans* (late fourth century), explicitly praises Junia as a "woman" of extraordinary devotion. Even so, the more convenient (albeit less authoritative) rendering of Junia's name caught on, and so she became Junias, the decidedly male church leader who poses no threat to the patriarchal order that had assumed control of the Christian church by late antiquity. The stroke of a pen undid a huge portion of the great equalizing work central to Christ's message and subjugated more than sixty generations of women to subservience in the church and condemned countless souls to wrestle with anxiety, fear, and self-loathing if they presumed to think differently.

I include the example of Junia not only to illustrate how the church literally stripped someone of part of their humanity for the sake of promoting a specific narrative agenda but also to demonstrate a point we discussed in chapter 5, which is that spiritual anxiety can work two ways. When people within a system act in dishonest or manipulative ways in order to bolster their own position or protect the system itself at the cost of justice, authenticity, or truth, they are highlighting their own anxieties. They are working to protect what they feel is being threatened—and they justify it by convincing themselves (and others) that it is right. What makes this especially insidious in a faith context is that these alterations and falsifications then become baked into the structure of the broader system that few people think—or dare—to challenge.

Unfortunately, the history of Christian theology is rife with examples like this. In *Gaslighted by God*, for example, we examined a translation bias present in the story of Mary and Martha in Luke 10, where a word that is translated every other place in the New Testament as "ministry" or in a manner that implies "service" or "preparation" is, in this story about a busy woman, rendered as "tasks" in almost every major translation. Martha's efforts are traditionally portrayed as simple household chores tied to cooking or cleaning—even though Luke uses a different word for similar basic tasks just a few verses later. This reduction of "women's work" to something distinct from true "ministry" has been a backbone of Western Christianity and Western culture for centuries.

Beyond mere translation issues, however, the text of the Bible has been manipulated in other even more blatant ways that reveal the anxieties of the powers that be and their efforts to preserve the established order by convincing people that they were inferior or undeserving of dignity in the eyes of God.

In 1807, the first copy of what has come to be known as the "Slave Bible" was published in London by the Society for the Conversion of Negro Slaves, an organization staffed by missionaries who aimed to convert Africans enslaved in the Caribbean to Christianity by teaching them how to read the Bible . . . sort of. *Parts of the Holy Bible, selected for the use of the Negro Slaves, in the British West-India Islands* was a freely redacted version of the Bible that eliminated verses like some passages from Exodus that it was feared might incite an uprising or rebellion among the enslaved people. Also removed were verses that are condemnatory toward the act of enslavement, such as Jeremiah 22:13: "Woe unto him that buildeth his house by unrighteousness, and his chambers by wrong; that useth his neighbour's service without wages and giveth him not for his work" (KJV).[5] Missionaries instead focused on passages that normalized slavery and promoted submission toward enslavers.

Through propaganda like the Slave Bible and other agenda-driven teachings, European and American Christians actively dehumanized millions of people not only through the support and tolerance of slavery as an institution but also by trying to brainwash the very people entrapped by it into believing their enslavement was divinely ordained and that any thoughts to the contrary were sinful. In the name of Jesus and through the word of God, they built a self-propagating system of condemnation, conversion, and control. It's almost like a spiritual case of factitious disorder imposed on another (FDIA, also called Munchausen syndrome by proxy), a recognized psychological condition in which a person solicits pity or praise for taking care of someone else—even though they caused that person's injuries or illness in the first place. The behavior is as pathological in religious systems as it is in individuals. People in power created a problem, perpetuated it, and then promoted a self-serving theology as the only acceptable response to it. And the repercussions of such heinous abuses are still with us today. Of course many of the most ardent abolitionists were Christians as well—but they were working to undo harms that were originally justified under the banner of their common faith. Their efforts were only necessary because of the exploitation of power in the name of God that came first.

Unfortunately, oppression via selective theology is not a thing of the past.[6] Even today, many of us are taught a view of God that highlights only the portions of the Bible that steer us toward obedience and control—a theology promoted by the very people who benefit most from it. Consider, for example, the way that male headship and dominance over women is often taught as a punishment for what happened between Adam, Eve, and the serpent in Genesis.

Yet do those same complementarians ever point out that if pre-fall Eden is the way the world is supposed to be and Eve is *cursed* with subservience, then egalitarianism is God's ideal? Genesis 3:16 tells us that the curse for woman was that childbirth would be painful, yet she would have desire for her husband and he would "rule over" her. Gender inequality is a punishment; it's evidence of a broken world. The subjugation of women is directly tied to sin.

But if Jesus supposedly broke the curse, as Romans 5 clearly argues that he did, then male headship was broken as well. This explains Galatians 3:26–28 ("for in Christ Jesus you are all children of God through faith. As many of you as were baptized into Christ have clothed yourselves with Christ. There is no longer Jew or Greek; there is no longer slave or free; there is no longer male and female, for all of you are one in Christ Jesus") *because the gospel obliterated gender divisions.* If we allow ourselves ways to push back against or contend with the other curses of Genesis 3—we invent labor-saving devices like plows and tractors to make working the land eas-

If pre-fall Eden is the way the world is supposed to be and Eve is cursed with subservience, then egalitarianism is God's ideal

ier; we have epidurals, Lamaze-technique breathing, and advances in medicine and hygiene to help make childbirth a little easier and safer—then why can we not push back against the curse of female submission, too? Are women supposed to simply shut up and accept their fate as the God-ordained way of the world? Either Jesus broke the curse or he didn't. He didn't resolve just a part of it. He didn't tell his followers: "Okay, you can have eternal life with God, *but that women-are-subordinate-to-men thing has got to stay.*"

Yet only a certain, selective theology has been promoted in many churches because people in power tend to interpret Scripture through a lens that keeps them in power—and not just in the church. This kind of self-insulation can happen in all aspects of society if systems are in place that allow abusers to dominate through whatever means suit their aims. Armed and emboldened by such knowledge, this allows some abusers to also become predators, as we see is the case with Alec in *Tess of the D'Urbervilles.* They absolve themselves of responsibility by pinning the blame on someone who does not share the same protections, position, or privilege under the system, forcing their victims to endure both the physical impact of the sin as well as the mental load that comes with it. This is, perhaps, most commonly seen in attitudes toward young people's bodies in the church.

That's right—we have finally come to the moment I know many of you have been waiting for. Let's talk about spiritual anxiety and Purity Culture.

This topic certainly could have been covered in almost any of the other chapters; heaven knows there is enough fear, indoctrination, misguided praise, threats of rejection, shame, and dehumanizing that fill these conversations. Ultimately, however, I chose to cover it in the chapter on power imbalances because asserting control over the bodies of people with less power is one of the most insidious ways that spiritual anxiety has been exploited in the church.

There is not nearly enough room here to cover even a fraction of the issues and anxieties that people have struggled with as a result of the manipulative and problematic ideas and methods of Purity Culture. Social media is rife with people sharing stories of bizarre and shocking ways that Purity Culture was promoted within their churches: passing around a licked cookie or chewed gum and asking if anyone would want it, then comparing that to a person with a sexual past; girls being forced to wear T-shirts over their swimsuits or even remain fully dressed at pool parties while boys walked around in just shorts; heavily supervised "courting" so that the couple is never allowed to be alone together because they can't be trusted to control their passions; couples not being allowed to kiss until the wedding. The list goes on and on, but it all comes back to the same fundamental idea: people are not to be trusted to make decisions for themselves. Fixed and immutable standards of behavior must be dictated by authority figures because men can't control themselves and a woman's worth is tied directly to the condition of her hymen.

One friend of mine shared a painful conversation she had with her eighteen-year-old daughter following a breakup with her high school boyfriend. "She said, 'I am so glad I didn't sleep with him because I know if I wasn't a virgin, I would want to kill myself.'" This was a young woman with no mental health issues or behavioral challenges that would prompt such a strong emotional response. What's more, she was raised in a stable, loving home with parents trained in ministry and active in their local church. Knowing some of the pitfalls of Purity Culture, they had actively worked to instill healthy attitudes toward sexuality in their children, encouraging them to honor God with their choices but not leaning on shame or fear to frame conversations. Even so, after several years at an evangelical high school, the toxic rhetoric of Purity Culture still found a way into this young woman's perceptions of God and herself.

But Purity Culture isn't just about overt sexual activity; it also has to do with the way bodies are inherently sexualized by a church culture obsessed with, well, not being obsessed with sex (supposedly). Many of the women I interviewed shared stories of going to see Christian counselors or trusted pastors about their spiritual anxiety around other matters, only to be criticized during the conversation for their appearance—shirts too low cut, jeans too tight, dresses too short, too much makeup. Most of these meetings had little or nothing at all to do with questions about sex, yet these leaders still found ways to work it in. The comments came from male and female leaders alike—men who warned against causing others to lust and women who warned about "protecting men from sin." When seeking help for feelings of unworthiness, distance from God, religious self-loathing, IIL, or generally unwelcome and intrusive religious thoughts, these young women were dismissed not with helpful advice but with a new cause for anxiety and more reasons to fear divine judgment and disapproval.

Never did any of these counselors invoke Jesus's commands to men to remove the eye or hand that causes them to sin (Matthew 5:29–30) or the fact that Paul writes about avoiding putting temptations in the way of the "weak" (1 Corinthians 8:7–12), implying that those who struggle are the ones who are not as strong in their faith as they could be. The emphasis in discussions about dress codes seems not to be on encouraging the weak to grow stronger by viewing other people as something more than sexual objects, but instead only on women not being "stumbling blocks" for men—even though it is women, not men, who are supposedly the "weaker vessels" (1 Peter 3:7). Just as external legalism places the burden of one's personal preferences on others, Purity Culture places the weight of artificial cultural burdens primarily on women's shoulders—both the physical and mental responsibility for maintaining the state of someone else's soul. It is one more way of passing the buck of sin onto someone else—usually someone who has been taught that their place is one of submission and acceptance.

Yet while most of the current discussion around Purity Culture focuses on women, it absolutely affects men, as well. Boys indoctrinated with this rhetoric generally receive one of two ideas: either they are not responsible for controlling their own sexual urges or else they are monsters whose biological inclinations disgust God. Neither one sets up a young man for a healthy understanding of his own sense of self as a person divinely created with sexual feelings.

In cultures like these, it is no wonder that the church is rife with accusations of abuse of children and adults alike. When conversations around sexuality are clouded with shaming the vulnerable or blaming the victim, victims are reluctant to come forward. As we have seen in numerous sexual misconduct charges brought against leaders in prominent ministries and popular preachers in recent years, accusers are often defamed and their claims denounced as "baseless attacks designed to hurt their gospel work."[7] Staff at Ravi Zacharias International Ministries (RZIM), for example, found that when they questioned the organization's dismissal of sexual misconduct allegations, "Sometimes leaders would invoke Zacharias's reputation, saying, 'But that's Ravi,' suggesting he was above reproach." Katelyn Beaty, an editor-at-large at *Christianity Today*, explained the problem succinctly in an interview for *Vox* about the charges brought against evangelical megachurch pastor Bill Hybels: "Many evangelical institutions are beholden to the power of celebrity and of charismatic men, and have staked too much of their future on the 'success' of those men, regardless of potential wrongdoing. There can be a fear that if 'bad news' comes out about those men or the church, it will harm the spread of the gospel."[8]

Under the guise of playing public relations agent for God so that the reputation of Christ is untarnished, many organizations have chosen to extend protection to the face of the organization rather than to the vulnerable. The thing is, Christ will always be untarnished. It's the people who claim to follow him who perpetuate the damage. But too many organizations find it more convenient to shrug off ac-

> *Many organizations have chosen to extend protection to the face of the organization rather than to the vulnerable*

cusations of abuse than to investigate them with any rigor because an unfavorable result would be devastating to the "brand" upon which so many people have staked their livelihoods.

It should be noted, however, that on February 23, 2021, Vince Vitale, the director of RZIM, and his wife, Jo (who also held a prominent role in the organization), published a "personal confession" video on Vince's Facebook page in which they made the startling move of accepting responsibility for "believing Ravi's lies and then passing on his false narratives," by which they "deeply hurt people—the very people most in need of our care—and we added to their pain. We are sorry. We are so very, very sorry." Later in the message, they admit that their actions "not only lengthened but also intensified the pain of Lori Anne and Brad Thompson [two of the accusers], as they were then slandered for years. The suffering they and their family have experienced over the last four years has been horrendous. It must also have been wrenching for survivors to watch as Ravi continued to be praised while Lori Anne was maligned."

The Vitales also made the rare and somewhat shocking move of deciding not to continue operating RZIM as the multi-million-dollar business it once was because we serve a God who is infinitely more concerned about the cries of victims than about our reputations, and far more interested in repentant hearts than rebranded ministries. In light of the severity of what has occurred, it may be right for this organization, at least in its current form, to come to an end. We are at peace with that. We have absolutely no interest in getting back to business as usual.[9]

This response sent shock waves through the evangelical world because it demonstrated something that had rarely before been seen: a faith-based organization accepting blame for covering up the abuses committed by its leadership and prioritizing the voices of victims. But some felt it did not go far enough; the Vitales confessed their willingness to believe Ravi's claims of innocence for so long based on their experience with him, not because they were on the receiving end of extremely well-paying salaries from his organization. The RZIM case is a fascinating study in organizational collapse because of how it both followed and defied so many predictable patterns. Ultimately, though, it was just one more example of the type of abuse that can run rampant in systems of unchecked power.

What if we stopped excusing harm with indifference masquerading as forgiveness?

What if we decided, as a faith, that easy answers aren't enough anymore, and glib responses aren't doing anyone any favors except for those who are let off the hook too easily without accountability for their actions? What if we stopped excusing harm with indifference masquerading as forgiveness?

Compulsory forgiveness is one of the most dangerous practices within Christianity. Many Christians insist that it is necessary for the individual who has been wronged to forgive the person who harmed them in order to move on with their life—a life that has, in some cases, been forever altered. But we all know that forgiveness doesn't erase impact. It may release the injuring party of their guilt, but it does not lift the weight of the sin from the person who is forced to live with the consequences. Individuals who struggle with spiritual anxiety often find forgiveness one of the most difficult issues to contend with because of the cultural pressures that surround it. If you do not forgive fast enough you are "living in the past"; if you keep your distance from the person who harmed you, you are accused of not truly forgiving at all; if you raise concerns about their involvement with other vulnerable parties, you are "holding a grudge." All these questions can lead to deep psychological wrestling and self-doubt, which ultimately adds to the burden of spiritual anxiety already heightened by the initial injury. Who hasn't heard the warning that "a lack of forgiveness is a sign that your heart isn't right with God"? But what does this communicate to someone who is still sorting through the fallout of someone else's sin that they have been forced to carry?

I spoke with people involved with an advocacy group for children and teens who attended Kanakuk, the largest evangelical sports camp in the world. Over the past decade, accusations of sexual abuse by employees and subsequent cover-ups by the organization's administration have surfaced, with more than a hundred people sharing their own accounts of mistreatment over a span of several decades.

Survivors have voiced stories about the mental health struggles, deep feelings of shame and guilt, addictions, and other forms of self-harm all stemming from the abuses they endured. A family member of one victim told me that despite visiting close to a dozen therapists and inpatient treatment centers, "he was never really able to reconcile the God of his youth with his spiritual mentor raping him and people not caring—especially Christians. So he died by suicide.... I used to call him a survivor, but he didn't survive. It is life and death. So I refer to him as a victim again."

According to one victim advocate who operates on a grassroots level, the entire process of trying to pursue legal action has been a series of power plays where the organization covers its tracks or avoids responsibility by leveraging its size, scope, and financial resources to protect the perpetrators rather than to seek justice for the people it harmed. In their view, it is made worse by being wrapped in toxic Christian theology. "The rush to forgiveness over justice and accountability is sickening," this individual told me:

That's not my Jesus, and it's probably the biggest form of abuse that I've seen consistently in all of the church environments where it existed—a rush to forgiveness: "God will do the accountability thing later." But I just see God as more of a God of justice, and that we are the hands and feet now on this earth to deliver that accountability and justice *now*, and pursue truth *now*, and to walk in light *now*, and use our voices *now* and the voices of these victims. The voices of truth in this situation have just been completely squashed—first by the spiritual guilt of "You need to forgive" and "If you speak up, you're bitter, and that's not having a heart for Christ"; and then with legal tools, such as NDAs.

Affected families describe being stonewalled when trying to access their camp records or being told that the statute of limitations has expired. Many signed nondisclosure agreements (NDAs) in an effort to secure some form of recompense to cover extensive counseling costs that can run tens of thousands of dollars. "The system is rigged against victims, certainly against children and their trauma and parents who have been brainwashed by the evangelical cult of forgiveness and reconciliation," the advocate explained. They added that the same pattern seems to repeat itself every time a major Christian organization or ministry finds itself up against allegations of misconduct. The goal appears to be "isolating victims, controlling the conversation, and controlling the message with fancy PR firms and intimidating attorneys."

Such a view is often cast as rooted in cynicism or bitterness—the result of a heart hardened against forgiveness rather than one torn to pieces by trauma. We see an example of this in the books of 1 and 2 Samuel, where we meet Michal. The younger daughter of King Saul, she married David, her father's protégé, and helped him escape one of her father's murderous rages by lying to the guards after she allowed David to climb out of a palace window (1 Samuel 19:11–17). Then, in 1 Samuel 25:44, we learn that Michal was inexplicably married off by her father again to another nobleman named Palti (or Paltiel), perhaps on the basis of David's absence. After Saul is killed by the Philistines, David demands that Michal be returned to him before he will take the throne. She is escorted to him under force, "but her husband went with her, weeping as he walked behind her all the way to Bahurim" before Palti is finally sent away (2 Samuel 3:13–16).

Michal's final appearance in the Bible is a short time later, in 2 Samuel 6, when David famously dances before the Lord in jubilant ecstasy, spinning in such a way that his robes fly up and he exposes himself to the crowd, including the maidservants of the royal household. Michal watches this display and later confronts David on his behavior:

> David said to Michal, "It was before the LORD, who chose me in place of your father and all his household, to appoint me as prince over Israel, the people of the LORD—I will dance before the LORD. I will make myself yet more contemptible than this, and I will be humbled in my own eyes, but by the maids of whom you have spoken, by them I shall be held in honor." And Michal the daughter of Saul had no child to the day of her death. (2 Samuel 6:21–23)

This scripture has been invoked in many an object lesson against criticizing "God's chosen leaders" as well as a warning against bitterness, holding up Michal's barrenness as either divine punishment or David refusing to sleep with her for her shrewish behavior.

It doesn't take a trauma counselor to recognize a number of inherent problems in these interpretations of Michal's story. She is used as a political tool by both her father and first husband; she is then remarried and subsequently torn away from a spouse who appears to cherish her dearly; then, when her husband flashes his genitals at crowds of young women, *Michal* is the one accused of being a hardhearted troublemaker simply for expressing reasonable displeasure at the situation and refusing to offer instant forgiveness.

Let's take a closer look at what the text actually says, which isn't very much. It doesn't actually directly state that her barrenness was related to her conflict with David (and, in fact, 2 Samuel 21:8 states that she bore five children to her brother-in-law, though that is suspected to be a scribal error). But even assuming that her childless condition *was* connected to the conflict, is Michal really the one being petty and bitter if *David* is the person refusing intimacy for the rest of their lives simply because she admonished his behavior? Yet all sorts of assumptions—almost always in judgment against Michal rather than David—have been read into this story. And why is Michal the one put under the microscope? Why do we so quickly dismiss her emotional turmoil with all she has endured and been left to make sense of? Because the text reminds us again and again that David was chosen by God; the implication, therefore, is that he is above reproach—at least by a woman. (The prophet Nathan, after all, holds David accountable for his sexual exploitation of Bathsheba and subsequent murder-by-proxy of Uriah when Nathan visits David with a divine rebuke in 2 Samuel 12.) No wonder so many leaders express such a strong association with David; his story comes with an astounding lack of accountability and a convenient warning against anyone with less power who might dare question his actions, no matter how political, selfish, or abusive they might be.

But David's story comes with another warning, too—one whose implications seem to go largely unheeded by abusers who exploit from and hide behind their positions. To find that story, we have to go back to the anointing of David's predecessor and father-in-law, Saul, by the prophet Samuel:

> Now the day before Saul came, the LORD had revealed to Samuel: "Tomorrow about this time I will send to you a man from the land of Benjamin, and you shall anoint him to be ruler over my people Israel. He shall save my people from the hand of the Philistines, for I have seen the suffering of my people, because their outcry has come to me." When Samuel saw Saul, the LORD told him, "Here is the man of whom I spoke to you. He it is who shall rule over my people." (1 Samuel 9:15–17)

In this passage, we see that, just like David, Saul was also a leader chosen by God. Authority is not a be-all-end-all assignment for life nor a guarantee of God's unwavering favor. Those who are quick to claim privileged status on account of being "chosen by God" to lead would do well to remember Saul's legacy: a despised despot who died at the hands of the very people he was

Those who are quick to claim privileged status on account of being "chosen by God" to lead would do well to remember Saul's legacy

appointed to defeat, but not before he was overshadowed by a charismatic new leader who could claim an anointing from the Lord as well.

Romans 13:1–5 declares:

> Let every person be subject to the governing authorities, for there is no authority except from God, and those authorities that exist have been instituted by God. Therefore whoever resists authority resists what God has appointed, and those who resist will incur judgment. For rulers are not a terror to

good conduct but to bad. Do you wish to have no fear of the authority? Then do what is good, and you will receive its approval, for it is God's agent for your good. But if you do what is wrong, you should be afraid, for the authority does not bear the sword in vain! It is the agent of God to execute wrath on the wrongdoer. Therefore one must be subject, not only because of wrath but also because of conscience.

This is often taught as an outward-facing text—a message from the pulpit to the people, a top-down lesson. But the words could just as well be read as a bottom-up pronouncement, calling on earthly leaders to remind them of the responsibility they assume along with the mantle of power. Those who resist authority put in place by God—not necessarily the individuals but the divinely appointed moral laws that govern human behavior—are the ones who face punishment. And what authority should we follow? "He has told you, O mortal, what is good, / and what does the LORD require of you, / but to do justice and to love kindness / and to walk humbly with your God?" (Micah 6:8).

Abuses of verses like the passage from Romans that are wielded to subjugate others into compliance "because of conscience" (Romans 13:5) are exploiting spiritual anxiety by giving leaders God-sanctioned immunity no matter the state of their heart, soul, mind, or strength. They are counting on people to be too fearful of incurring divine wrath to resist; they have taken God's authority as their own. Even the act of reading the Bible from a posture of power and pride can reinforce this artificial conflation of God and self. In his treatise on Christian community, *Life Together*, the great theologian and Nazi resister Dietrich Bonhoeffer urges Christians to maintain an intentional space between themselves and the Bible in order to avoid falling into this trap. He writes, "It may be taken as a rule for the right reading of the Scriptures that the reader should never identify himself with the person who is speaking in the Bible. It is not I that am angered, but God; it is not I giving consolation, but God; it is not I admonishing but God admonishing in the Scriptures." It is essential, Bonhoeffer insists, that the reader does not align themselves with the voice of God but "as one who knows that he himself is being addressed."[10] What a powerful reminder of humility this is; when we read Scripture, where do we see ourselves in the story—as the audience receiving the message, or as the voice of God transmitting it? That question alone, if answered honestly, may be enough to convict many a self-proclaimed "mouthpiece for Christ."

Jesus never traded on his authority; if anything, he used it to his own *dis*advantage. Even when it was dangled in front of him as a temptation (Matthew 4; Mark 1; Luke 4), Jesus refused to exploit his power; he used it only to protect and empower others—so much so, in fact, that Philippians 2:5-6 exhorts us:

> Let the same mind be in you that was in Christ Jesus,
> who, though he existed in the form of God,
> > *did not regard equality with God*
> > *as something to be grasped*,
> but emptied himself,
> > taking the form of a slave,
> > assuming human likeness. (emphasis added)

Jesus was careful to deflect praise and power. As he says in John 12:44, "Whoever believes in me does not believe in me but in the one who sent me." Many modern translations insert "alone" or "only" so the verse reads, "whoever believes in me does not believe in me *alone/only* . . ." but that word does not actually appear in the text. It has been added to the English as an "implied" word so the translation better aligns with orthodox understandings of the unity of God. But Jesus is actually making an intentional effort to redirect honor away from his incarnate form and toward the transcendent truth of God. How often do we consciously do the same? And what messages are we telegraphing to future generations about what Christ actually taught about power and privilege when we see it run rampant in our own religious bodies?

Laura, whom we met in chapter 4 when her pastor told her suicide would send her straight to hell, explains that she and her husband want a faith community that is more focused on loving people as Jesus did than on doubling down on some combination of dogma and politics. As a new mother, this issue feels especially heavy. "As we move through this process of what's next for our family," she says,

> I really love the church we go to now, but when I look at it closely enough, I can see there are things that are probably potentially problematic. When it's just us as adults, a few minor differences aren't that big of a deal. But I've realized I have to be really thoughtful and diligent about the community where we choose to raise our child—and, unfortunately, there just aren't a lot of options.

She explains how spiritual anxiety looks in her life now, as an adult, and how she wants to model something better as a parent than the rigidity and inflexibility in which she was raised:

> You have a set of beliefs, you have faith, and you're trying to find an answer for something. But when you're going about it, you don't feel like you're getting clear direction or clear answers. And there are a lot of things in life that come up in this category. The Bible talks a lot about really specific situations, like adultery, for example, which we can all agree is clearly something we're not supposed to do. But there are a lot of gray areas in life, too, and having answers without nuance ... creates a lot of confusion, especially for young believers who are trying to figure out what's right and what's wrong.
>
> As a millennial, I think a lot of that has to do with the experiences I've had growing up where you feel like you trust

someone or you put your faith in someone—a spiritual teacher, a pastor—and then they abuse that, or they maybe don't quite abuse it, but they kind of use their power in a way that just doesn't seem right. Of course we're all human and everyone makes mistakes, pastors included. But I think that a lot of that "old thinking"—the black and whiteness of it—can contribute to a lot of that spiritual anxiety where you feel like, "Maybe I'm not doing the right thing. Maybe this is my fault." You feel like the systems you have used your whole life maybe aren't working, or don't work for that specific problem, and you're worried you're going about it wrong.

Carlos, an engineer turned high school math teacher in Arizona, was raised devoutly Catholic and still holds his beliefs very dear, but he and his wife struggle with many of the same issues that Laura and her husband do, like how to raise their young children in a faith community where the abuse of power—and the abuse of others—has been so rampant. This, he explains, is a source of "real and deep spiritual anxiety." Already deeply disenfranchised by the numerous scandals and controversies that rocked the church over the past twenty years, Carlos and his wife stopped attending services in person when they found they could no longer contend with the apparent disconnect between power and the message of Christ. "Look at the people Jesus spent his time with," he says. "It wasn't the powerful people."

By Carlos's reckoning, it seems like every branch of Christian culture is caught up in the misuse of political, social, and religious power. He points out several prominent evangelical Christian celebrities who "are bold enough to come out and say what they say, and basically hide their bigotry behind God. . . . Those in power use power because they can, even if they're not conscious of it. I feel like I see that everywhere, and maybe I have a little confirmation bias because of my experiences, but I know that's not totally unsound."

To Carlos, the entire faith seems deeply rooted in abusive power and completely unaware (or completely unconcerned) about it:

> You can't fix a problem if you're not looking at it, and you won't look at it if you don't think you *need* to look.... Most of my reaction, especially before I had kids, was just anger and frustration, just like, "Why are so many people in church like this?" But now, as a dad, I have actual anxiety because it's too close to home. What are we going to do about them? ... [I]t is important to my wife and me that we introduce them to Jesus, but we don't have fellowship. How do I integrate faith and Jesus into their lives in a meaningful way without that?
>
> ... A lot of the values that Christians have are not actually Christian values, but that's what my kids will see in church. What do I do when my four-year-old says, "We're Christian. Why are we right and other people are wrong?" when Christians she sees are living or talking about those views. Honestly, I don't know. I don't have a good answer for that. We're trying to figure out how to navigate all of that—how to expose our daughters to the Christ in Christianity as opposed to the other side—the ulterior motive of things....
>
> So much has been swallowed up by what Christianity has become in this country. If this was just me and my wife, I wouldn't be as concerned because we're grown and can figure it out as we can walk the line of what we believe and what we know is wrong. But our kids are too little; they don't get it. I'm definitely still a Christian ... but it's just hard to want to interact with my faith, to stay close to my faith and stay close to God, but keep a distance from all of that.

If the old saying is true that "power corrupts; absolute power corrupts absolutely," then perhaps the church as an institution and the people within it should be more mindful of the fact that Christianity is *literally rooted* in the voluntary sacrifice of power. When we, as a body of believers, look toward an uncertain future where Christianity holds less cultural power in the West than at any time in the last 1,500 years, we *should* feel spiritually anxious. We *should* have fear for what this signals for the future. What we are seeing now is the collateral damage of the collective sins of our religious past. A lip-service faith is not going to win people back to a faith devoid of the Spirit; neither is doubling down on what got us here in the first place. Sacrificial love is not taking power from others; it means using your own power to make room for the vulnerable and silenced. This is what the godly use of authority looks like and what it means to be "subject to one another out of reverence for Christ" (Ephesians 5:21): those with more power are willing to sacrifice so that those with less can have justice. It is the heart of God's call for "true fasting" in Isaiah 58 in the face of economic and social injustice; God's wrath is fueled not by the lack of effort but by *too much* effort channeled in the wrong direction—notably, toward the self in the form of self-enrichment, self-aggrandizement, and self-sanctification. We give up our own power rather than using it to control or exploit others for our own benefit.

‹‹◆›››

On December 10, 1869, the territorial legislature of Wyoming passed a bill entitled "An Act to Grant to the Women of Wyoming Territory the Right of Suffrage, and to Hold Office." For twenty years, this act protected the rights of women—including the ten Black women who appear in the census records during that time (though it did not extend its protection to women from indigenous populations). It was one of the most radical examples of political equality in history at that point.

Then in 1889, Wyoming had an opportunity to obtain statehood, but its policy of near-universal suffrage was an impediment to its acceptance into the union, as many lawmakers elsewhere in the country felt it set a dangerous precedent. A group of powerful women in Wyoming made it clear that they were willing to give up their right to vote and hold office in order for the territory to officially be incorporated into the United States.

The all-male group of representatives from Wyoming, however, sent a telegram to Washington, DC, informing Congress: "We will remain out of the Union 100 years rather than come in without the women."

Wyoming was granted statehood, its women retained their rights, and almost exactly thirty years later, the Nineteenth Amendment granted universal suffrage to adult citizens of the United States.

If secular institutions can grasp the essence of mutually sacrificial love, surely the church can do the same. If we shift our anxieties from the dominion of Christ losing supremacy in the future to empowering the love of Christ by meeting the needs of the present, we might end up a lot closer to mirroring the wholeness and abundance of heaven on earth. And one of the first steps in dismantling this misplaced understanding of power is demanding accountability from corrupt systems that have used it for evil. In this way, our spiritual anxiety becomes a blessing for ourselves and others as a source of wisdom, discernment, bravery, and empowerment that gives us the ability to recognize and call out

> those who call evil good
>> and good evil,
> who put darkness for light
>> and light for darkness,
> who put bitter for sweet
>> and sweet for bitter! . . .
> who acquit the guilty for a bribe
>> and deprive the innocent of their rights!
>
> (Isaiah 5:20, 23)

Conclusion

PREACH, WRITE, ACT

The bane of English classes for generations, *The Scarlet Letter* has been parsed, prodded, praised, and panned from every imaginable angle. It is the story of a woman, Hester Prynne, who is forced to wear a bright red "A" on her chest for the rest of her life to designate her as an adulteress after she gives birth to a child out of wedlock in 1640s Massachusetts. Shunned by her strict Puritan community first for her pregnancy and then for her refusal to reveal the name of her lover, Hester lives with her daughter Pearl as an outsider.

As the years pass, Hester's acts of benevolence, generosity, and kindness to the same people who cast her out prove her more morally sound than the "good church people" who initially condemned her. Hester's empathy and strength of spirit raise complicated questions like "Who is a sinner?" and "What is sin?" as well as issues of guilt, penance, punishment, identity, belonging, and female independence.

It is also the story of different responses to spiritual trauma.

The local preacher, the beloved and celebrated Arthur Dimmesdale, is revealed to the reader to be Pearl's father, though no one in the community is aware. Though Hester and Dimmesdale both carry equal weight of their shared sin, Hester bears the public shame of it alone.

As they move forward in their lives after Pearl's birth, it is Hester who is able to foster a healthy spiritual life in spite of her neighbors' past judgment. Dimmesdale is consigned to constant spiritual torture due, on one hand, to his own guilty conscience and on the other to the intentional baiting of the man who claims to be a doctor named Roger Chillingworth but is actually Hester's estranged husband (who she thought was dead) maliciously seeking revenge on her erstwhile lover.

When Hester and Dimmesdale meet by chance in the forest after seven years of separation, the preacher reveals the burden of his sin that has been his constant companion this whole time. In anguish, he confesses that the extreme piety for which his parishioners praise him is due entirely to his overwhelming awareness of his moral failings for the very same offenses that Hester has borne openly and gracefully.

The Scarlet Letter is, ultimately, about two people plagued by sin and the impact of their suffering on their souls. One does her penance and comes to reject the systems that would shame her by keeping her locked in her guilt. The other person is hailed and celebrated for his piety, but he is privately tortured by his secret sin and by the scheming of someone who exercises control and exploitative power for self-serving purposes. The parallels are not perfect, nor is the book itself without problems, but it is a fascinating study of the impact of trauma—and specifically abuse—within a faith community.

Hester finds that, despite the admiration she has won for her redeeming virtues, her public humiliation and social rejection have left her heart no longer seeking justification within an authoritarian church, nor does the arc of her life bend toward the religiosity of her past. If fact, her experiences have purged her of any lingering loyalty to the Puritan faith:

> For years past she had looked from this estranged point of
> view at human institutions, and whatever priests or legisla-

tors had established; criticizing all with hardly more reverence than the [Indigenous People of America] would feel for
the clerical band, the judicial robe, the pillory, the gallows,
the fireside, or the church. The tendency of her fate and
fortunes had been to set her free. The scarlet letter was her
passport into regions where other women dared not tread.
*Shame, Despair, Solitude! These had been her teachers,—stern
and wild ones,—and they had made her strong, but taught her
much amiss.* (chapter 18, emphasis added)

Dimmesdale, by contrast, has responded to his secret trauma
by entrenching himself even deeper in church culture in an attempt to both acknowledge and purge his guilt:

The minister, on the other hand, had never gone through an
experience calculated to lead him beyond the scope of generally received laws; although, in a single instance, he had so
fearfully transgressed one of the most sacred of them. But this
had been a sin of passion, not of principle, nor even of purpose. Since that wretched epoch, he had watched, with morbid
zeal and minuteness, not his acts,—for those it was easy to arrange,—but each breath of emotion, and his every thought. . . .
as *a man who had once sinned, but who kept his conscience all
alive and painfully sensitive by the fretting of an unhealed wound,*
he might have been supposed safer within the line of virtue
than if he had never sinned at all. . . . *[H]e was broken down by
long and exquisite suffering; his mind was darkened and confused
by the very remorse which harrowed it; that between feeling as an
avowed criminal, and remaining as a hypocrite, conscience might
find it had to strike the balance.* (chapter 18, emphasis added)

In fact, Hester can see firsthand the devastating effects that
Chillingworth's abusive techniques have had on Dimmesdale.
She observes that

his authorized interference . . . with the minister's physical and spiritual infirmities,—that these bad opportunities had been turned into a cruel purpose. By means of them, *the sufferer's conscience had been kept in an irritated state, the tendency of which was, not to cure by wholesome pain, but to disorganize and corrupt his spiritual being.* Its result, on earth, could hardly fail to be insanity and hereafter, that eternal alienation from the Good and True, of which madness is perhaps the earthly type. (chapter 17, emphasis added)

In other words, Dimmesdale is literally being driven to madness by the manipulations of someone who purports to help him but secretly relishes the power he holds over the struggling man. By constantly pricking and agitating the preacher's already tender conscience, Chillingworth is able to control and manipulate the people around him until he has reduced Dimmesdale into a nervous, exhausted shell of himself.

For those of us who live with spiritual anxiety, whatever form(s) it takes, we know how exhausting the struggle is to sort out the promptings of the Holy Spirit from the analytical spiral of Involuntary Internalized Legalism, and how taxing every decision can be when it feels like everything has a religious component. We may grow tired of hearing verses like John 8:32, "You will know the truth, and the truth will make you free" when the truth is that our religious devotion actually makes us feel imprisoned by our own mind.

Spiritual anxiety may be a burden, but it is not a sin

Spiritual anxiety may be a burden, but it is not a sin. Philippians 2:12 instructs believers to "work out your own salvation with fear and trembling"—two things people with spiritual anxiety know quite a bit about. In this case, "fear and trembling" are even a command, not something of which to be ashamed. As Jesus tells his followers, "Come to me, all you who are weary and are carrying heavy burdens, and I will give you rest. Take my yoke upon you, and learn from me, for I am gentle and humble in heart, and you will find rest for your souls. For my yoke is easy, and my burden is light" (Matthew 11:28–30). He does not condemn them for the weight of the loads they are carrying. He does not demand that they set those burdens down before they can come into his presence. He welcomes them as they are, acknowledging their weariness with compassion and encouraging them to experience comfort, not trepidation, as they encounter him.

We opened this book by looking at the term "ghosting," in which someone withdraws their presence suddenly and without warning, and how people with spiritual anxiety often feel as if God's presence or pleasure has been taken from them. Throughout the chapters that followed, we read excerpts from a number of classical literary works that highlight various ways circumstances can be manipulated in order to control someone else to create this kind of internal disquiet. In that spirit, I want to ask you to consider one last literary scene:

Two brothers sit in a café while one expounds to the other all the reasons that he feels he cannot believe in God—a central conflict faced by his character. This is the setting of chapter 4, book 5 of *The Brothers Karamazov*, Fyodor Dostoyevsky's literary masterpiece about free will, morality, and the nature of God.

Ivan, the elder of the two brothers present, shares with his younger brother Alyosha, an aspiring monk, a series of horrific examples of child abuse. In one story, Ivan describes a five-year-old girl who is forced to endure unimaginable torture from her parents. After they have subjected her to beatings and shoved filth into her mouth, Ivan observes that despite the child not knowing any other way of life and not even realizing that her treatment is not normal or that her parents are monsters, she still cries out to God in her agony. "Can you understand why a little creature," he challenges Alyosha, "who can't even understand what's done to her, should beat her little aching heart with her tiny fist in the dark and the cold, and weep her meek unresentful tears to dear, kind God to protect her?"

While Ivan intends to demonstrate that this example proves a godless world, it actually highlights the fact that there *is* a fundamental moral law that governs the universe. At the most basic level, the soul of this deeply injured child knows that something is not right. Without being taught, her mind, body, and spirit reject the treatment she has endured. Her "unresentful tears" do not convict her parents of these crimes; she does not even realize that they are the perpetrators of profound evil because they are all she knows. They are the arbitrators of her reality. And yet, she still cries out to God to save her—even if she has no idea what that salvation or liberation might look like—because the very essence of her being inherently understands that what she is experiencing is wrong.

The human soul (provided it has not been desensitized to morality) knows when something is "off." It may or may not recognize the issue as abuse—a sad truth that is far too common— but it certainly recognizes the resulting misery. It recognizes ill treatment and manipulation. It recognizes the misuse of power and control. It recognizes fundamental injustice. It recognizes when intervention by a loving God seems overdue.

People besieged by spiritual anxiety rooted in exploitation by authorities may struggle to name exactly what is dissonant about their experience, but they know inherently that *something* about their circumstances does not align with the heart of God. Their heart cries out, perhaps wondering what they did wrong to deserve such treatment, but their view of their own power has been shrunk to such an infinitesimal degree that even the act of silent, internal protest feels like dan-

Spiritual anxiety is a natural result of abuse—it is the soul crying out for deliverance from a place where God's divine presence seems to be lacking

gerous rebellion. If they dare to speak those concerns aloud, the response is usually swift and devastating: "You're willfully disobedient"; "You shouldn't question God's anointed leaders"; "You clearly don't understand how salvation works"; "If you prayed and read your Bible more, you wouldn't have these questions"; "If you were truly saved, you wouldn't have these thoughts"; "This happened because *you* are inherently sinful."

Spiritual anxiety is a natural result of abuse—it is the soul crying out for deliverance from a place where God's divine presence seems to be lacking. Romans 8:26 even describes this state of anguish and longing that transcends language and comprehension when "we do not know how to pray as we ought, but that very Spirit intercedes with groanings too deep for words."

Perhaps the issue at hand is more than just an anxious response to spiritual abuse; maybe spiritual anxiety is

There is no need for shame, self-punishment, or struggle against these feelings; they are evidence that the Holy Spirit is alive within you, fighting on your side

the Holy Spirit interceding with God on your behalf, communicating the fears, worries, shame, loneliness, emptiness, disconnection, and aching that your soul has been wrestling with long before you were even aware of it. Spiritual anxiety may be an indication that something is wrong with your outer circumstances, not your inner life. It is a sign of wisdom, perception, discernment, and closeness with God—not distance *from* God. It may even mean that you understand right and wrong better than the people around you.

If you become increasingly aware of abuse in your environment, your soul will likely struggle because it recognizes disharmony with divine truth and love. The trauma of abuse through power cuts deeply because it can be so all-consuming—so seemingly impossible to overcome. But according to 1 Corinthians 6:19, your body is a "temple" or "sanctuary" for the Holy Spirit, which means that anyone who sins against you also sins against the Holy Spirit. There is no need for shame, self-punishment, or struggle against these feelings; they are evidence that the Holy Spirit is alive within you, fighting on your side against people and systems that abuse, manipulate, and debase God through their sinful, selfish, and exploitative actions.

((((((((()))))))))

Let us conclude by returning to *The Scarlet Letter*. As Hester and Dimmesdale speak in the forest on the afternoon of their chance encounter, Hester tries to stir the broken man back to life. Over his objections that he is too wretched to deserve anything other than punishment from the authorities, she demands:

> "And what hast thou to do with all the iron men, and their opinions? They have kept thy better part in bondage too long already! . . . The future is yet full of trial and success. *There is happiness to be enjoyed! There is good to be done! Exchange this false life of thine for a true one . . . Preach! Write! Act! Do anything, save to lay down and die!* . . . Why shouldst thou tarry so much as one other day in the torments that have so gnawed into thy life!" (chapter 17, emphasis added)

This, perhaps, is the lesson we all ought to carry through life, whatever our soul's response to our circumstances. Sin is inevitable, but it does not need to be the centerpiece of our faith. There is a future waiting to be filled. There is joy in creation. There is love to be shared and kindness to offer. Why would we not release this guilt-riddled existence that keeps us trapped in a system we can't win? Why would we not want to escape from the clutches of a person who conceals their own desire to maintain power in the guise of healing, guiding, and caring for us? Why would we condemn ourselves for the gentle and sensitive conscience God has created within us?

Hester's advice to Dimmesdale is, ultimately, the same we can offer to ourselves as we face our own spiritual anxiety. Let us do whatever we must to free ourselves from toxic systems that seek to imprison us in circumstances that keep us from being our truest selves—the beautiful, strong, talented, worthy creations God made us to be with gifts to share with the world, voices to raise, and lives to live that sing back the glory of our Creator simply by merit of our existence.

DISCUSSION QUESTIONS

Introduction: Poisonous Piety

1. What is the connection between the "radium girls" and spiritual anxiety?
2. Has your experience with the Holy Spirit not matched up with the experience of those around you? How did that feel? In what ways have you adapted to it?
3. If you have spiritual anxiety, how does it manifest itself?
4. Why are the spiritually anxious more susceptible to spiritual abuse?

Chapter 1: Kool-Aid Man Jesus and Other Phobias

1. How does the term "ghosting" connect to those who experience spiritual anxiety?
2. Why are churches often a hard place for people to speak honestly about their spiritual struggles?
3. Moses, Jeremiah, and Peter are all people from the Bible

who may have struggled with spiritual anxiety. Can you think of others?

4. Reread the lists of spiritual anxiety markers on pages 10–12. Which ones most closely match your experience with or understanding of spiritual anxiety?

5. How has your faith environment affected your spiritual anxiety, knowing that spiritual anxiety is situational and not chronic?

6. The author wrote about her own personal experiences with spiritual anxiety growing up in 1990s culture wars. Does her experience resonate with yours? What memories might you have of your own spiritual anxiety?

7. How does naming a fear and categorizing it help to overcome it?

8. How are those who are neurodivergent and those who have spiritual anxiety connected? How are they not connected?

Chapter 2: The Mind and Christ

1. How has your faith community addressed the issue of spiritual anxiety or anything related to the symptoms of spiritual anxiety? Discuss this even if (especially if) your church has never addressed this topic.

2. How can a person's demographic labels affect their spiritual connection? (Demographic label examples: White, Black, Hispanic, male, female, non-binary, cisgender, gay, straight, middle class, working class, etc.)

3. Define deconstruction. Has your view of deconstruction of religious beliefs changed after reading this chapter?

4. What are some beliefs or practices of your faith that might heighten or magnify spiritual anxiety?

5. What's the difference between deconstructing faith traditions and deconstructing God?

6.   How was Jesus a deconstructionist? Do you agree or disagree with this premise? Why?

7.   What is shame? How is it used in spiritual abuse?

8.   If churches are made of imperfect people and imperfect systems, how can regular members speak out against practices and doctrines that promote spiritual abuse or spiritual anxiety?

Chapter 3: Involuntary Internalized Legalism

1.   For fun: Do you have any books you've intended to read but for whatever reason, haven't? What are they?

2.   How does legalism come into play in your own spiritual journey?

3.   What are some formulas that churches prescribe to their members as a way of detracting from sin? How does not adhering to those formulas then become an "unofficial sin" within the church? (For example, asking all members to disconnect their cable to prevent watching porn or having a strict dress code for youth group trips.)

4.   Read Romans 7:14–25. How does this passage connect to the internal struggle of the spiritually anxious?

5.   What has been a formula presented to you as faithful living?

6.   Have you ever heard of Ignatian discernment? What does "comparing options of moral equivalence" mean?

Chapter 4: Discipline—Control through Fear

1.   What are your experiences with *memento mori* that negatively impacted your well-being?

2.   How has fear controlled you in the past?

3.   How have you experienced end times theology or fear tactics in your spiritual life?

4.   Read the story of Nadab and Abihu in Leviticus 10:1–2. How

does it come across differently through the lens of abuses of power and not blind obedience?

5. When reading and interpreting the Bible, how can we move from being afraid of God toward paying attention to the revelation of our own human hypocrisy?

6. Have you encountered the stories of Jephthah or Achan in the Old Testament? How have you interpreted them (or had them interpreted for you) in the past? How do you see them now?

7. What do we do when the Bible gets weird?

8. How do you see parental discipline of a child after reading different interpretations of popular scriptures that "promote" corporal punishment?

9. What do you think of the statement "Fear is not a sin"?

Chapter 5: Dogma—Control through Indoctrination

1. What is the difference between doctrine and indoctrination?

2. Have you experienced or witnessed a church "kicking out" or abandoning a member because of that member's beliefs? What do you remember?

3. Have you experienced fear based on your denomination's particular belief on an issue?

4. Read the parable in Luke 14. What are your reactions to it after reading this chapter?

5. How do you view the ideas of sin, grace, and forgiveness? Do sins carry different weights to you?

6. Have you ever experienced relationships that prioritized institutional doctrine over the relationship? How did you deal with that?

7. What is the difference between devotion to God and obedience to an institution—especially when that institution is a church?

8. Discuss the ideas of orthodoxy, orthopraxy, and orthopathy.
9. Can you think of any problematic or toxic attitudes or beliefs you once held? How have you changed?

Chapter 6: Decoration—Control through Praise

1. How can praise be used as manipulation or control?
2. How does the parable of the talents change in meaning when the focus shifts to the master's misuse of power and not the servants' abilities to gain more money in the master's absence?
3. What can churches do to fight against exploitation of people?
4. Have you ever experienced burnout in service to a church or ministry? How can the story of the good Samaritan leave room for taking care of your own needs or obligations while still serving God by loving your neighbor?
5. How do you feel about the word "enough"?
6. Do you struggle with spiritual perfectionism? If so, how do you deal with it?
7. How does knowing the Holy Spirit (or "Comforter") is present within you help with your thoughts of perfectionism?

Chapter 7: Denial—Control through Rejection

1. Anne Hutchinson's tragic story shows what sometimes happens to dissenters of church authority. When have you seen or experienced similar treatment?
2. How can examining your own motives help to separate threats to your faith from challenges to your faith?
3. What have been your experiences with church and gossip? How has that experience affected your spiritual anxiety?
4. What can churches do to balance a healthy accountability be-

tween calling out abusive behavior and keeping gossip from tearing up relationships?

5. Where do churches find their authority to deny membership or revoke the Christianity of others?

6. What is your current state of feeling the Holy Spirit at work in your church or spiritual community?

7. Reflect on Anne Hutchinson's quote: "Better to be cast out of the church than to deny Christ."

Chapter 8: Degradation—Control through Shame

1. After reading this chapter, can you distinguish the difference between guilt and shame? How is this harder to distinguish in religious settings?

2. Can you think of a time when you were made to feel shame in your past, but looking back on it you see that what you did wasn't worth the shame you felt?

3. Why is shame such an effective tool of control?

4. What are some practical ways in which those who struggle with spiritual anxiety can fight off feelings of shame?

5. What are morally neutral issues that often get turned into shame-based accusations?

6. Have you encountered the story of the Samaritan woman at the well from John 4 before? How did you initially perceive the woman? How do you see this story differently after reading this chapter?

7. What has been your experience with doubt and faith? What encouraging words or stories have you found that help you with doubt?

8. "It is a blessing of provision, not a sin." How might this story of accidentally tasting food in the middle of fasting help you with feelings of shame?

Chapter 9: Diminishment—Control through Dehumanizing

1. Read chapter 1 of the book of Esther. How does spending some time reading about Vashti as a "woman of the Bible" change your perspective of her?

2. How have you seen the church connect disabilities with matters of faith?

3. When have you felt that someone has created a narrative for you that they then expected you to fill?

4. Where might you be setting expectations on others that they do not want?

5. Why should we seek to look beyond empathy? Do you agree with this idea?

6. This chapter is all about spiritual anxiety in connection to dehumanization. Where might you be dehumanizing others unintentionally? How can you take steps toward changing that?

Chapter 10: Domination—Control through Power Imbalance

1. How have power imbalances in the church affected your faith?

2. Have you heard of Junia (Romans 16:7) before? What does the story of "Junia" being changed to "Junias" make you think about?

3. What emotions do you notice in yourself when reading about the Slave Bible and other agenda-driven translations of the Bible?

4. Do you have stories from the theology of Purity Culture you would like to share?

5. Why do you think the author chose to discuss Purity Culture in the chapter on power imbalances rather than the chapter on shame?

6. What is compulsory forgiveness, and how can it be dangerous?

7. In light of power imbalances, how can Christians see God as a God of forgiveness and a God of justice? How do justice and forgiveness work together?

8. Dietrich Bonhoeffer urged Christians who were reading the Bible to align themselves with the audience receiving the word of the Lord, not the voice of God presenting it. How might this posture change the way you read Scripture?

9. With so many church and faith communities abusing power, what can Christians do to continue practicing their faith in community in a safe way?

Conclusion: Preach, Write, Act

1. Spiritual anxiety is a natural result of abuse. How could your spiritual anxiety be pointing out wrong within your community and not within yourself?

2. How can your questioning of God be an indication of closeness to rather than separation from God?

3. How will you carry on the work of walking with God and forgiving yourself as you deal with your own spiritual anxiety?

ACKNOWLEDGMENTS

It is impossible to capture the scope of appreciation I have for the countless people who have supported this book and encouraged me in the process of writing it.

First and foremost, I need to thank the individuals whose stories influenced and impacted this book in significant ways. My sincerest thanks to all of you for your honesty and vulnerability in sharing experiences and memories that, in many cases, are still painful, distressing, or raw. I believe that your bravery will help readers find healing and hope and will show hurting people that they are not alone.

To the superlative team at Eerdmans, including William Hearn, Caroline Jansen, Jason Pearson, Shane White, Kristine Nelson, and especially the infinitely patient and accommodating Jenny Hoffman—I cannot thank you all enough for your combined time and talents that made this book what it is. To James Ernest, thank you for your vision and leadership in tackling these kinds of issues in modern Christianity. And, of course, to Trevor Thompson, who championed this book from the start: thank you from the bottom of my heart for recognizing the need for these conversations and for working to bring them to a broader audience.

To publicist extraordinaire Michelle Kafka and the entire team at Kafka Media Group who worked so hard to get the book in the right hands: you are amazing.

To the many wonderful church leaders and religious mentors in my life, both now and as I was growing up, who cared about people's health alongside their souls: thank you. You are the reason I knew there was something more to faith than anxiety.

To the scholars, critics, and reviewers who read the manuscript early on and offered their endorsements, opinions, and blurbs for the book: thank you for your time and interest in this project.

To Kelly Wiggains, a maven of curriculum design: thank you so much for your help with developing the discussion questions at the end. And to you and Kristen Chapman both, my TBTs—even when I was incapable of carrying on any conversation that did not revolve around this topic, you two listened, encouraged, asked questions, and didn't mute our text thread, which pretty much makes y'all the best friends any writer could ever ask for, ever.

To Beth Moore and the late, great Rachel Held Evans: in many ways, you gave the rest of the "good church girls" permission to finally speak honestly and frankly about the questions, concerns, and challenges on our minds.

To my cheerleaders/great cloud of witnesses, including but not limited to my amazing friends, beta readers, and encouragers in Arkansas, California, Colorado, Florida, Illinois, Minnesota, North Carolina, New Jersey, New York, Oklahoma, Oregon, Tennessee, Texas, Virginia, Washington, the UK, and Rwanda, and all the family, friends, pastors, ministers, and others who prayed for me during this process: words will never be able to fully convey the depth of my gratitude. To my diversity and sensitivity readers, including Lee Williams and Amy Thomas, thank you for your perspectives and guidance. Debbie Smith and Cassie Hanjian, you both deserve medals for your encouragement, wisdom, and direction. And to the entire Portland Seminary '22 Cohort and faculty, I feel so blessed to have shared my journey with you. You all are *truly* good eggs.

And, finally, all my love and thanks to my family. To my sister, who was a sounding board for so much of this, thank you for reading drafts, finding typos, and listening to me work out some of these ideas in real time. To my parents, grandparents, and in-laws who have been tremendously supportive even when the subject matter skewed into uncomfortable topics, thank you so much for trusting me to engage in prayer and fasting while writing this. To Aaron, who listened, discussed, and gave me time and space to make this manuscript what it needed to be, thank you for the belief that this project mattered deeply both for readers and for my own spiritual healing. And to Bridget, who is my reason for everything, my sincerest prayer is that you grow up in a faith tradition that sees you, hears you, and values you as a full and equal member of God's family. May you never need a book like this, but thank you for giving me the courage and resolve to write it.

NOTES

Introduction

1. Kate Moore, *The Radium Girls: The Dark Story of America's Shining Women* (Naperville, IL: Sourcebooks, 2017), 42.

2. M. Szamatolski, "Report to New Jersey Department of Labour," January 30, 1923.

Chapter 1

1. For more information about the Enneagram and especially its application in spiritual formation, a good place to start is Christopher Heuertz, *The Sacred Enneagram: Finding Your Unique Path to Spiritual Growth* (Grand Rapids: Zondervan, 2017).

2. I recognize that there is quite a bit of debate within the autism community as to whether it is more respectful to say someone "has autism" or "is autistic"; some of these conversations extend to other types of neurodivergence as well. After speaking with several individuals directly affected, I have decided throughout this book to use "people-first language" that gives primacy to the individual rather than the condition unless there is a clearly defined preference within

NOTES TO PAGES 19–46

the community for different terminology. I do recognize, however, that opinions and preferences vary.

3. This was just one of many, many metaphors used by *Brio* magazine to discuss Purity Culture in the 1990s.

Chapter 2

1. Eugenie Samuel, "Water Torture," in *New Scientist*, February 24, 2001, https://www.newscientist.com/article/mg16922795-000-water-torture/.

2. C. Ryan, R. B. Toomey, R. M. Diaz, S. T. Russell, "Parent-Initiated Sexual Orientation Change Efforts with LGBT Adolescents: Implications for Young Adult Mental Health and Adjustment," *Journal of Homosexuality* 67, no. 2 (2020): 159–73. https://pubmed.ncbi.nlm.nih.gov/30403564/.

Chapter 3

1. I have three.

2. No judgment. I've been trying to finish the final sixty pages of the *Lord of the Rings* trilogy since 1994. Do I appreciate that it's awesome? Totally. Does that mean I have ever picked up the book with all the best intentions and still not gotten distracted by something else? Nope.

3. This is different from the theorem you probably learned in high school geometry that "*If A equals B and B equals C, then A must equal C*," because that theorem is rooted in a state of being that is already in existence; the values are objective, immutable values. Five will always and only ever equal five. If something changes that, it ceases to be five anymore; it is now something different entirely. The quantities being compared are fixed; if they change, the equation changes.

In a slippery slope, you are either measuring cause and effect, which are not fixed or inevitable and can be impacted by any number of internal or external factors, or else you are making false equivalencies where you take as fact that one thing is the same as or can be judged by the same standard as another. This is a logical fallacy. *A* does not automatically (or even logically) lead to *Z*, nor is it established fact that *A* equals *Z*. Legalism, however, takes the stance that *Z* is not only the result but the equal of *A*. Another way to think of it is in terms of *reductio ad absurdum*, or "reduction to the absurd," which is a rhetorical technique in which an argument or stance is taken to its most extreme or absurd conclusion. Legalism can function in much the same way; it takes a polarized outcome played out to the absolute limit of possibility and applies it as the reasonable standard for a belief or behavior.

4. Tiffany Yecke Brooks, *Gaslighted by God: Reconstructing a Disillusioned Faith* (Grand Rapids: Eerdmans, 2022), 135–36.

5. I can neither confirm nor deny that this goat reference is directly tied to the preceding allusion to *Let's Make a Deal*.

Chapter 4

1. Names have been changed or omitted.

2. There are thirty-eight.

3. "Jesus Is Coming Soon" by R. E. Winsett, 1942.

4. Once, when I was visiting a church in a new town where I had just moved, a deacon pulled the communion tray out of my grasp because he did not know me and therefore did not know if I had been baptized and was worthy to partake.

5. There are actually some rabbinic traditions that maintain that this story is not about priestly misconduct at all but is rather about Nadab and Abihu making deliberate efforts to enter into ecstatic union with God. The result is that God "eats" (*akal*) them—that is, God consumes them into the very being of the divine because of their genuine desire to be nearer to it. This interpretation takes the possible interpretations of the story even farther afield from one of slavish obedience.

6. Megan Schmidt, "8 Richest Pastors in America," Beliefnet article, https://www.beliefnet.com/faiths/christianity/8-richest-pastors-in-america.aspx.

7. Aram Rosten and Joshua Schneyer, "How Jerry Falwell Jr. Mixed His Personal Finances with His University's," Reuters article shared by Yahoo News on September 4, 2020, https://news.yahoo.com/jerry-falwell-jr-mixed-personal-153308601.html; and Chris Gayomali, "Jerry and Becki Falwell's Illicit Years-Long Affair with a Miami Pool Boy, Explained," GQ article, August 25, 2020, https://www.gq.com/story/jerry-falwell-jr-love-triangle.

8. John P. Bartkowsoki and Christopher G. Ellison, "Divergent Models of Childrearing in Popular Manuals: Conservative Protestants vs. the Mainstream Experts," *Sociology of Religion* (Oxford University Press) 56, no. 1 (Spring 1995): 23.

9. Bartkowsoki and Ellison, "Divergent Models of Childrearing," 30–31.

10. Verse 21 notes "But if the slave survives a day or two, there is no punishment, for the slave is the owner's property," so let's acknowledge the qualms *that* ought to raise.

Chapter 5

1. Emphasis original. All excerpts from chapter 9 of Zora Neale Hurston, *Their Eyes Were Watching God* (Philadelphia: Lippincott, 1937).

2. "A Very Old Man with Enormous Wings," in *Leaf Storm, and Other Stories*, trans. Gregory Rabassa (New York: Harper, 1972).

3. Emily Strohm, "Jinger Duggar Vuolo on Growing Up under 'Cult-Like' Religious Beliefs: 'I Was Terrified of the Outside World,'" *People* online, 18 January 2023.

4. The best resource I know of that explores this topic is the outstanding book by Thomas A. Santa, CSsR, *Understanding Scrupulosity: Questions, Helps, and Encouragement* (Liguori, MO: Liguori, 2007).

5. This translation of the *Didache* appears in *Lost Scriptures: Books That Did Not Make It into the New Testament*, ed. Bart D. Ehrman (New York: Oxford University Press, 2005).

Chapter 6

1. I have to once again extend my sincerest apologies to Ms. Tan for accidentally sitting on her dog when I was a first-year doctoral student and she visited the English Department at Florida State University in 2005.

2. Amy Tan, *The Joy Luck Club* (New York: Putnam's, 1989), 155–56.

3. While it is important to acknowledge that the concept of *phār-makon* is central to Derridian deconstruction in philosophy, we will not be parsing its significance here.

4. Desmond Tutu, *No Future without Forgiveness* (New York: Doubleday, 2000), 84.

5. Just a few examples of recent studies that explore the link are as follows: Chang Chen et al., "Adverse Childhood Experiences and Multidimensional Perfectionism in Young Adults," *Personality and Individual Differences* 146 (2019): 53–57, https://doi.org/10.1016/j.paid.2019.03.042; Bianka Dobos et al., "What Makes University Students Perfectionists? The Role of Childhood Trauma, Emotional Dysregulation, Academic Anxiety, and Social Support," *Scandinavian Journal of Psychology* 62, no. 3 (2021): 443–47, https://doi.org/10.1111/sjop.12718; Danielle S. Molnar et al., "Perfectionism and Perceived Control in Posttraumatic Stress Disorder Symptoms," *International Journal of Mental Health and Addiction* 19, no. 6 (2021): 2204–18, https://doi.org/10.1007/s11469-020-00315-y.

Chapter 7

1. Portions of Anne Hutchinson's story in this chapter first appeared as "The Woman Who Told Puritan Boston to Go Pound Sand"

as part of The Lēros Project (https://www.substack.com/Tiffany YeckeBrooks), 19 January 2023.

2. Roger Williams, "The Bloody Tenant of Persecution," 1644.

3. Winthrop also found time to help author the Massachusetts Body of Liberties which, among other things, was the first legal document endorsing the enslavement of indigenous peoples in North America. So, you know, he was . . . *quite a guy.*

Chapter 8

1. Kate McCord (a "protective pseudonym") includes a brief but heart-wrenching look at the way Afghan women responded to the Samaritan woman's shame in her memoir *In the Land of Blue Burqas* (Chicago: Moody Publishers, 2012), 305.

2. Solomon Schechter and Joseph Jacobs, "Levirate Marriage," entry in the *Jewish Encyclopedia*, https://jewishencyclopedia.com /articles/9859-levirate-marriage.

3. Suetonius, *Life of Tiberius* 43.1–2; 44.1–2.45.

Chapter 9

1. Rachel Held Evans, "All Right, Then, I'll Go to Hell," May 23, 2012, https://rachelheldevans.com/blog/huck-finn-hell.

Chapter 10

1. The quotes and summary included here are taken from chapters 45–56 of *Tess of the D'Urbervilles*, by Thomas Hardy.

2. Ingrid Clayton, "What Is Trauma Bonding?," *Psychology Today*, September 16, 2021; emphasis original.

3. A lot like a Bit-O-Honey.

4. It must be pointed out that some translators insist the grammar implies simply that Junia was "known to the apostles" rather than being counted as one of them. But this rendering is by no

means universal or even the most widely accepted theory, nor does it change the fact that the gender of her name was altered. For more information on this topic, visit The Junia Project (https://www.Junia Project.org).

5. For more information, please see Brigit Katz, "Heavily Abridged 'Slave Bible' Removed Passages That Might Encourage Uprisings," January 4, 2019, *Smithsonian Magazine*, https://www.smithsonian mag.com/smart-news/heavily-abridged-slave-bible-removed-passa ges-might-encourage-uprisings-180970989/.

6. It should be noted that there have been other selectively edited, agenda-driven versions of the Bible to be published in history, including *The Women's Bible*, by suffragist Elizabeth Cady Stanton. Unlike the insidious goals of the Slave Bible, however, which was designed to keep enslaved people enslaved, *The Women's Bible* was designed to help a marginalized group attain a level of social justice. *The Women's Bible* was a "critical study of biblical texts that are used to degrade and subject women in order to demonstrate that it is not divine will that humiliates women, but human desire for domination." https://library.hds.harvard.edu/exhibits/incompara ble-treasure/woman%27s-bible.

7. Daniel Silliman, "Inside RZIM, Staff Push Leaders to Take Responsibility for Scandal," in *Christianity Today*, January 5, 2021, https://www.christianitytoday.com/news/2021/january/rzim-ravi -zacharias-turmoil-spa-allegations-investigation.html.

8. Tara Isabella Burton, "A Megachurch Pastor Resigns after Misconduct Allegations: The Larger Problem Remains," in *Vox*, https:// www.vox.com/identities/2018/4/13/17234606/bill-hybels-willow -creek-resignation-megachurch-pastor-scandal.

9. https://www.facebook.com/VinceRVitale, February 23, 2021.

10. Dietrich Bonhoeffer, *Life Together*, trans. John W. Doberstein (New York: HarperSanFrancisco, 1954), 56.

INDEX OF SCRIPTURE AND OTHER EARLY CHRISTIAN WRITINGS

OLD TESTAMENT

Genesis

1:16	100
1:20	149
2:25	206
3	247
3:10	84
3:16	246
4	98
7:15	149
49:10	92

Exodus

2	9
17:5-6	80
20:13	86
21:20	92
24:1-2	81
24:9-11	81
28:1	80-81

Leviticus

10:1-2	81

Numbers

4	82
20:2-13	79
20:12	78
24:17	92

Deuteronomy

3:23-27	80
3:26	80
6:4-5	39
23:19-20	134
25:56	189

Joshua

6-7	85
7:24-25	85

Judges

3	185

11-12	86
11:30-31	86
11:32	86
11:36-39	86-87

1 Samuel

6:3-9	82
7:1-2	82
7:7	84
19:11-17	255
19:15-17	257
25:44	255

2 Samuel

3:13-16	255
6:6-7	82
6:21-23	255
12	256
21:8	256

1 Chronicles

13:7-11	82

Esther

1:11	216
1:17–18	216

Job

38:36	57

Psalms

27:14	61
63:1	93
101:3	16
106:32–33	80

Proverbs

3:3–7	56
8:17	92
11:27	92–93
13:24	92, 93
31	226, 228, 229
31:10	227
31:31	227

Ecclesiastes

12:13	83–84
12:13–14	84

Isaiah

5:20	264
5:23	264
58	263
64	149
64:6	147–48

Jeremiah

7:31	87
17:9	56
20	9
22:13	245
23	9

Daniel

1:15	185

Micah

4:1–2	94
4:3	94
4:4–5	94
6:8	259

NEW TESTAMENT

Matthew

4	259
5	36, 111
5:21–22	110
5:29	230
5:29–30	249
5:48	146
6:3–4	48
6:27	21
6:27–33	174
7:20	180
10:35–36	173
10:39	173
11:28–30	268–69
12:18	141
12:18–22	140
12:30	162
12:31	74
18	93
18:6	199
18:9	230
19:29	173
25	133
25:1–13	136
25:37–40	136–37
26:15	141

Mark

1	259
9:40	162
11:12	141

11:12–14	140
11:13	140
11:20–24	140
12:18–27	38
12:28–34	39
12:34	40
14:13–15	235–36
25:24–28	134

Luke

4	259
4:18	38
5:8	9
6	36
6:43–45	180
7	9
7:41–43	111
10	141–42, 234, 244
10:27	234
10:29	234
10:33	234–35
10:33–37	142
11:42–43	37
11:46	37
14:8–11	158–59
14:12–14	107, 160
14:15	159
14:16	108
14:18–24	107–9
19	133
19:6	138
19:6–11	137–38
19:12	138
19:14	135
19:26	133
19:27	135
19:45–46	138
22:7–13	235–36
24:5	175

John

1:1	43

1:4	43–44	8:7–12	249	**Titus**		
1:5	44	11	76	1	47, 228–29	
1:9	43–44	11:22	47–48	3:5	124	
2	159	11:27–29	76			
2:1–11	119	12:8–10	194	**Hebrews**		
4:10	187	12:10	52	10	150	
4:11–29	187–88	13:5	48	10:22	150	
7:14–25	51			10:24	150	
8:32	268			10:25	150–51	
12:4–6	141	**Galatians**		13:17	48, 240	
12:44	259	3:26–28	246			
14:16	150	5:6	122–23	**James**		
14:26	150	5:22–23	34	1:5	57–58	
15:26	150			1:27	233	
16:7	150	**Ephesians**		3:9	214–15	
19:11	112	1:16–19	57			
20:28	192	3:4–5	243	**1 Peter**		
		4:12	45	3:7	250	
Acts		5:18	120			
2:38	104	5:21	263	**1 John**		
15:22	243			4:8	28, 86, 94	
15:39	150	**Philippians**				
16:16–19	140	2:12	268	**Revelation**		
17:11	161	4:6	21	12:7–9	109	
Romans		**1 Thessalonians**		**EARLY CHRISTIAN**		
1:16	43	5:17	16, 50	**TEXTS**		
5	246	5:22	20			
7:14–25	51			*Apostolic Tradition*		
8:26	271	**1 Timothy**		20:1–2	123	
12	209	3	47, 228–29			
12:2	124	3:1–11	125–26	*Didache*	123	
12:4	209	3:3	125	2:2	199	
12:21	209	3:5	125			
13:1–5	257	3:8	172	*Homily on Romans* by		
13:5	258	3:9	125	**John Chrysostom** 31		
16:7	242–43	3:10	126			
		3:11	172, 228			
1 Corinthians		5:23	119			
6:19	271					